SHAPING THE FUTURE

SHAPING THE FUTURE

~

ADVANCING THE UNDERSTANDING OF LEADERSHIP

PETER HERNON, EDITOR

LIBRARIES UNLIMITED

AN IMPRINT OF ABC-CLIO, LLC
Santa Barbara, California • Denver, Colorado • Oxford, England

Library of Congress Cataloging-in-Publication Data

Shaping the future : advancing the understanding of leadership / Peter Hernon, editor.
   p. cm.
  Includes bibliographical references and index.
   ISBN 978-1-59884-615-7 (pbk. : acid-free paper) — ISBN 978-1-59884-616-4 (ebook)
1. Library administration—United States. 2. Leadership—United States. 3. Library administration—Study and teaching (Graduate)—United States. 4. Leadership—Study and teaching (Graduate)—United States. 5. Library administrators—Training of—United States. I. Hernon, Peter.
Z678.S495 2010
025.10973—dc22   2010028696

ISBN: 978-1-59884-615-7
EISBN: 978-1-59884-616-4

14 13 12 11 10   1 2 3 4 5

This book is also available on the World Wide Web as an eBook.
Visit www.abc-clio.com for details.

Libraries Unlimited
An Imprint of ABC-CLIO, LLC

ABC-CLIO, LLC
130 Cremona Drive, P.O. Box 1911
Santa Barbara, California 93116-1911

This book is printed on acid-free paper ∞
Manufactured in the United States of America

CONTENTS

1
Leadership and a Research Perspective

2
The MLIP Program

3
Conclusion

ILLUSTRATIONS

FIGURES

TABLES

FOREWORD

Its time has come—the program and this book. When the Graduate School of Library and Information Science (GLIS), Simmons College, announced its intention to create a PhD program in managerial leadership (MLIP) designed for library and information practitioners, my first thought was, "It's about time!" Not only is the program in its fifth year at the time of publication of this book, but it is also successfully meeting its goals, namely being a doctoral program in managerial leadership that involves students in learning—through coursework, research, and interaction with many leaders in the profession—about leadership and in contributing to the body of research and scholarship on managerial leadership. The students become better prepared to lead their libraries in meeting their organization's and institution's mission and vision and to face the leadership challenges that lie ahead.

I have had the opportunity and pleasure of serving as a Simmons College Professor of Practice for this PhD program and have been a strong proponent of a doctoral program in leadership for library and information science *practitioners*. The program provides a venue for bright managerial leaders not only to enhance their leadership skills through the rigors of research and other scholarly activities but also to apply what they have learned to their home institutions.

Shaping the Future is unique in that it combines the philosophical, scholarly, and research aspects of managerial leadership with the Simmons MLIP program itself. It shows examples of the scholarly work of the doctoral students in the program. Some of the student research papers have been published in well-known, peer-reviewed journals in the profession, and soon a number of the dissertations will be finalized and the students will have graduated.

Camila A. Alire, EdD
President, American Library Association
Professor of Practice, MLIP, Simmons College
Dean Emeritus, University Libraries, the University of
New Mexico and Colorado State University

PREFACE

In the summer of 2008, the Graduate School of Library and Information Science, Simmons College, Boston, received an additional grant from the Institute of Museum and Library Services (IMLS), supplementing the original 2005 multiyear grant that enabled the development of the successful concentration in the school's PhD program focused specifically on managerial leadership in the information professions (MLIP). This program contributes to the successful future of leadership in library and information settings by creating a flexible, innovative doctoral program that nurtures and strengthens the intellectual and interpersonal assets of students as working managers, actively involves leading practitioners in shaping the educational experience, and generates rigorous research to improve the knowledge base and the practice of managerial leadership.

The MLIP program differs from leadership institutes and other doctoral programs in a number of ways. First, as compared to leadership institutes, it is intensely research focused. Program delivery is designed for working managers, but it is a PhD degree—by definition a research-focused course of study. Second, the MLIP program has a longer timeline, allowing for fuller investigation and exploration of leadership theories through comprehensive research studies. Third, the MLIP program results in the achievement of a recognized degree demonstrating exceptional proficiency in integrating theory and practice.

As we prepare to admit the fifth cohort, we find that some of the students' written work can be widely shared and that there is a need to call for more research on leadership in the profession than this program can ever provide. The purpose of this book therefore is twofold: (1) to share some of the case studies and scenario plans that the students have written and that program faculty recommend for inclusion in this book, and (2) to be that advocate for research in library and information science (LIS). As the amount of research on leadership proliferates, little of that literature is published in LIS. Undoubtedly, many in the profession are unaware of much of this literature, but they might suspect—incorrectly—that it has no relevance to them.

Libraries are complex organizations that require both managers and leaders. There is much to learn about transformational leadership, situational leadership, emotional intelligence, resonant leadership, and other theories and their application in settings associated with the information professions. Leadership is directed internally to libraries as well as externally to the communities and stakeholders that libraries touch. As a result, it is critical that LIS researchers add to the base of leadership research and encourage LIS practitioners to investigate and apply research findings, whether they come internally or externally to LIS. Such research should better connect libraries to an organizational culture of assessment and evaluation and to using the evidence gathered for accountability and service improvement as the nation recovers from the recent severe economic downturn.

This book should be of interest to everyone wanting a general overview of leadership and how others in the profession view it and seeking an opportunity to discuss leadership and contribute to the research literature. Other audiences include instructors of leadership institutes, librarians leading professional associations, faculty teaching management and leadership courses in LIS schools, and the students enrolled in those courses. In 2006 Donald E. Riggs made a point that is worth reiterating:

Schools of LIS were teaching administration courses, whereas business schools were teaching management courses. Now business schools are teaching leadership courses and LIS schools are teaching management. Only a few LIS schools now offer a course on leadership. In some schools, the management course is taught by a person who has not served as a library manager, or has little interest in the topic. We all need to take the responsibility of preparing future library leaders more seriously.[1]

Today, those management courses may contain a unit on leadership.

It is my hope that the focus on research, the case studies, and selected scenario plans presented here will help all of us take seriously that responsibility of preparing future leaders. These are clearly times that require leadership and a service vision as libraries declare their commitment to service to their communities as their highest priority. Jennifer Howard captured the environment of today nicely when she wrote: "At many university libraries, the toxic economy has eaten away at staffing levels and collections-and-acquisitions budgets. It has deflated endowments and disrupted plans to build new facilities and upgrade equipment." On a positive note she added: "But in response, librarians are doing more than tightening their belts. Some see the crisis as a chance to change the way they do business. . . . [The crisis] has spurred efforts to dream up ambitious solutions to big problems."[2] Following through on those dreams requires leadership and often the types of evidence that only research can produce.

Peter Hernon

NOTES

1. Donald E. Riggs, "Ineffective [Bad!] Leadership," in *Making a Difference: Leadership and Academic Libraries: Leadership and Academic Libraries*, ed. Peter Hernon and Nancy Rossiter, 181 (Westport, CT: Libraries Unlimited, 2007).

2. Jennifer Howard, "Libraries Innovate to Counter Cuts," *The Chronicle of Higher Education* LVI, no. 14 (November 27, 2009): A1.

ACKNOWLEDGMENTS

I would like to thank the Institute of Museum and Libraries Services for its support of the program. Their support far exceeds the two grants they provided. Their staff attend our programming and actively participate in the discussions. I would also like to thank Michèle Cloonan, Candy Schwartz, Jennifer Andrews, Caryn Anderson, Deanna Beattie, James Matarazzo, members of the Advisory Board (past and present), the professors of practice, members of the external program review committees, and all of the guest speakers who have directed stimulating conversations on leadership since the founding of the program.

1

∼

LEADERSHIP AND A RESEARCH PERSPECTIVE

1

~

MANAGERIAL LEADERSHIP IN ACADEMIC AND PUBLIC LIBRARIES: AN INTRODUCTION

Peter Hernon

At bottom, becoming a leader is synonymous with becoming yourself.[1]

As numerous writers have exclaimed, there are many definitions of leadership, and everyone has a favorite. Leadership is basically an activity that individuals—leaders—perform. Most likely, individuals are not born as leaders with a fully developed set of qualities, abilities, experiences, and knowledge. In fact, leaders do not all possess the same qualities, abilities, experiences, and knowledge. Although any definition of leadership must be sufficiently broad to encompass different leadership theories and styles, nobody practices a generic view of leadership that applies to every situation. Other general observations are that not all managers are leaders, leaders require followers, and leadership is not always a positive activity; leadership might be negative (destructive or ineffective).

In essence, leadership relates to establishing direction (a guiding vision) and influencing others to not only follow that direction but also strive to achieve that vision. Managerial leadership refers to that activity in which mangers help an organization establish and achieve its purpose and direction (as reflected in mission and vision statements and strategic plans). Effective managerial leadership depends on individuals who continue to develop their talents as managers and leaders. Development refers to engaging in rigorous self-assessment, offsetting critical weaknesses that inhibit the accomplishment of the stated direction, enhancing organizational efficacy, and understanding how to move organizations forward in challenging times as well as how to motivate others to follow. Given the stress and the complex nature of the work that librarians in key managerial positions perform on a daily basis, leadership development also requires an ability to recognize and cope with resonance—engaging effectively "in a conscious process of renewal on both a daily basis and over time."[2]

Leaders need not be managers, but leadership does involve setting a guiding vision that others will follow and then ensuring follow-through to accomplish that vision. Leadership then has two components: vision and action (defined as follow-through or influencing—motivating—others to realize that vision). When librarians work in teams or in other capacities, they might be involved in the action component but not the setting of the vision; they might set goals of productivity for the team.

Library directors, who in fact are leaders, might be both leaders and followers; in conjunction with others they might lead at the institutional or broader organizational level (e.g., with other deans, provosts, department heads, and city managers or mayors). In some situations they take direction from the mayor, provost, and so forth, but do not sacrifice their vision. A question becomes, "To what extent do they compromise their vision, especially in times of severe fiscal retrenchment?" The answer is most likely that if they fail to influence others to maintain the vision or find the vision is sufficiently compromised, they have no recourse but to resign. Compromising the vision may result in angry followers, who will no longer follow. Such compromise might result in the loss of trust.

Stakeholders in academic institutions demand transparency and accountability, for instance, as explained in the Higher Education Opportunity Act of 2008 (P.L. 110-315). Compliance with such requirements calls for both management and leadership, that is, leadership willing to nurture transparency and demonstrate the extent to which institutions meet their missions and stakeholder expectations. Leadership will also be required to move academic institutions to use the data collected for improving learning and meeting declared outcomes. After all, it appears that much of the data that institutions, including their libraries, collect do not lead to improvement in learning at the program level and in service improvement. Data therefore may be generated but not used effectively or be ineffectively used.

If the director is not a leader, others in the organization might fill the leadership vacuum. However, they might lack the resources to motivate staff to accept their vision—a vision that might or might not apply to the entire library. Ideally, the director should be a leader and involve others in achieving a vision. If others lead, they likely influence followers to achieve a goal. Should definitions of leadership at other levels of the organization replace the word *motivation* with *influence*? When directors are leaders, they likely have resources to motivate others.

Leadership involves doing the following:

- Develop or establish a vision.

- Take or see that action is taken to meet the vision.

- Have followers.

- Have an ability to motivate or influence others.

- Engage in managed change.

A vision, which provides a clear sense of where the organization is going, may not originate with a particular leader. That person might borrow, adapt, or draw on the vision of others, or develop the vision in collaboration with others.

IMAGE OF A LEADER

A number of writings aimed at a general readership identify individuals as effective leaders. Abraham Lincoln, the sixteenth president of the United States, is often included on such lists. As Doris Kearns Goodwin, in *Team of Rivals*, notes, for later generations, he "has unequalled power to captivate the imagination and to inspire emotion."[3] Furthermore, he had "a tough-minded appreciation of the need to protect his presidential prerogatives . . . and a masterful sense of timing." He also exhibited compassion, honesty, humility, and empathy.[4]

Although he does not appear on any similar list, Cesar Millan, known as the dog whisperer, encourages "a strong, stable, and organized pack where every member knows its place and follows the rules established by the pack leader. The pack instinct is perhaps the strongest natural motivat[ion] for a dog."[5] A logical question is, "But what has this to do with human leadership?" As an avid viewer of his television show, I constantly watch people walk their dogs, or, to be precise, watch their dogs walk them. The animals are in control of the walk; they lead the human and go in whatever direction they want. Clearly these people are followers and not pack leaders. Perhaps many people are more comfortable as followers and view their dogs in human terms; they do not want to hurt their animal's feelings or create the impression of being a disciplinarian. It is essential that pack leaders treat everyone the same and act in a consistent, balanced manner. Perhaps the biggest lesson is that people need to move from a state of followership to leadership. Millan discusses the transformation of humans into leaders as they, for instance, control their emotions (remain calm and avoid negative emotions), express a willingness to learn and change their behaviors, and gain new experiences.

From examples such as these, it is clear that leaders have a purpose and a sense of self. They are also self-confident and trustworthy, and they have integrity. In *On Becoming a Leader*, Warren Bennis characterizes these qualities as displaying "a distinctive voice," which is "the ability to relate to others," but he adds another quality: "adaptive capacity," which refers to "the ability to respond quickly and intelligently to relentless change."[6]

SITUATIONAL CONTEXT

Leadership has been characterized as situational in that a situation may call for the application of a particular leadership theory or style. As Donald E. Riggs observes: "It is not uncommon to think that a leader in one environment will be successful in another environment. In some cases, nothing could be further from the truth." He continues: "One should not assume that an effective leader in one library would transfer that success to another library. This is not true. The situation determines, along with the characteristics of the library leader, whether the new leader will be effective or ineffective."[7]

Those situations may occur within an organization or the community being served. Perhaps the most important part of situational leadership for researchers studying academic and public libraries is to identify and ultimately study the actual occurrence of leadership as opposed to perceptions about leadership.

LEADERSHIP QUESTIONS

Managerial leaders working in libraries address seven questions:

1. Where is the organization (library) going?

2. What do the library, its parent organizations, and customers truly value?

3. How will the library reach its goals as it strives to realize its vision?

4. Where are we now?

5. Do we know where we are?

6. Who cares about what?

7. Who decides what?

The first two questions involve setting a vision and strategic directions that challenge the organization to be forward-thinking and seek to improve. The vision and strategic directions for libraries relate to the improvement of services, the development of new ones that address shifting customer expectations and information-seeking behavior, and the service directions in which the library will invest its resources.

The third question deals with the action plan and the resulting strategic plan. That plan addresses the other questions. The action plan has an evaluation, and perhaps an assessment, component, with a feedback loop to the stated goals and objectives and their accomplishment.

ONE VIEW OF LEADERSHIP: MLIP IN THE INFORMATION PROFESSIONS

In *Making a Difference*, Peter Hernon, Candy Schwartz, and Caryn Anderson introduce a new PhD Program in Managerial Leadership in the Information Professions that the Institute of Museum and Library Services (IMLS), together with Simmons College, funded for more than $1.5 million (a multiyear grant), which tended to focus on academic libraries.[8] That program began in 2005. Three years later, the same two parties provided an additional $1.8 million for the development of a component aimed at public and state libraries (another a multiyear grant). The purpose of this nonresidential program for full-time practitioners is to create successful future leaders in library and information settings and generate rigorous research to improve the knowledge base and practice of managerial leadership.

A leadership model (http://www.simmons.edu/gslis/docs/phdmlip_models_new_ permission.pdf), which was adapted from a model developed by the National Center for Healthcare Leadership, guides the curriculum and assessment activities. The model consists of twenty-five distinct leadership competencies arrayed in three broad areas (transformation, accomplishment, and people): examples of the competencies include achievement orientation (surpassing a standard of excellence), analytical thinking, problem solving, good communication skills, organizational awareness, professionalism, and team leadership. (Chapter 7 elaborates on the doctoral program that serves as the foundation for this book.)

LEADERSHIP QUALITIES

As the Strategic Leadership Group of the Public Library Association (Chicago, July 10, 2009) concluded after a day-long discussion, leadership qualities might be cast in three perspectives:

1. **Navigate self:** Act with integrity and self-awareness, make communities better through service to all/acting for the common good, have respect and understanding for individuals, and align what I think with what I say and do.

2. **Navigate communities:** Work with and through others, build and leverage relationships, understand and communicate from the customer's perspective, and deliver impact and results based on a vision.

3. **Navigate organizations:** Discover, take risks, seize opportunities, cross-cut abilities (become competent to handle change and able to anticipate and lead), and recognize and grow potential in others.

As already noted, discussions of leadership often include a set of qualities (abilities and traits) that leaders should possess. For instance, they should demonstrate a passion (for libraries), have integrity, convey a sense of trust, have curiosity and a guiding vision (appropriate to the organization), accept responsibility, be comfortable with change, and learn from mistakes.

The qualities identified by the Strategic Leadership Group are associated with emotional intelligence, which "involves the ability to perceive accurately, appraise, and express emotion; the ability to access and/or generate feelings when they facilitate thought; the ability to understand emotion and emotional knowledge; and the ability to regulate emotions to provide emotional and intellectual growth."[9] Peter Hernon, Ronald R. Powell, and Arthur P. Young have identified the relevant qualities that library directors prize.[10] As they note, however, librarians need not possess all of the qualities; the critical qualities might be shared among the senior management team.

Gary N. Fitsimmons recast the qualities that Hernon, Powell, and Young explored and asked approximately 4,000 administrators of academic institutions who hire library directors to rate the relative importance of those qualities and to add any they believed should be there. Those administrators were listed in the *Higher Education Directory* of 2005,[11] and the response rate was minimal (less than 10 percent overall). Nonetheless, the study adds to the list of emerging qualities. These might be recast in terms of management and leadership. Fitsimmons reminds us to include others (e.g., higher education administrators) in reviewing a generic set of qualities; to this, we might add other stakeholders and other managers working in the libraries.

Additional qualities for managerial leaders include

- a service focus,

- confidence,

- good communication and listening skills,

- treating people with respect,

- enjoying what they are doing,

- setting a positive example—being a role model,

- making good hiring decisions, and

- rising to the occasion as the situation demands.

It is especially important that, during the current economic downturn, managerial leaders learn to do more with less (continually striving to achieve the vision) and demand greater efficiency. Most likely in the near future, a number of libraries will have a smaller workforce and have to find new ways to motivate or influence the staff.

ISSUES REQUIRING EFFECTIVE LEADERS

Libraries have evolved from being collection focused to blending services and roles that help the parent institution or organization accomplish its mission and strive to achieve its vision. Through collaboration academic libraries become facilitators and dedicate space and resources to involving different units on campus and beyond. The goal is to support the learning process and the mission of the institution in new and exciting ways, some of which may involve entrepreneurial activities. Collaboration can enrich the perspective of a library while at the same time reinforcing the view of the library as a place—"a place for students and faculty to read and study, to gather and deliberate, and to question, challenge and support one another."[12]

Within such an environment, there is an "expectation" that academic librarians will provide articulate, effective leadership; such leadership "too often creates stresses in both . . . [the] personal and professional lives" of librarians.[13] Effective leadership provides the follow-through for achieving a strategic plan and a way to guide how the economic recession impacts the library's infrastructure (collections, staff, technology, and facilities) and other academic units.

Table 1.1 (p. 8) identifies the areas that will challenge leaders in public and state libraries for the foreseeable future. Such challenges deal with changes in community building and customer demographics, the rate of assimilating technology, and finances,

Table 1.1
Critical Issues Facing Public and State Libraries*

Issues	Components
Operating in the political environment	• Governing structures, governing bodies, and relationships • Politics • Statutory and legal issues
Fiscal/financial management and leadership	• Enterprise creation and management • Revenue enhancement • Resource allocation • Resource reallocation (what to stop and start in tough times) • Collaborations for financial efficiency
Planning for leading	• Strategic planning • Tactical implementation • Demographics: who is served—aging, generations, ethnicity, and language
Accountability and assessment	• Outcomes and evidence-based research and decision making • Performance standards and metrics • Transparency as an organizational value
Ethical issues and values	• State and local ethics statutes/rules • Contracting issues
Interaction with stakeholders	• Building effective relationships • Education (primary school up) • Government agencies and officials • Small business • Other constituencies and collaborators • Library Friends organizations • Library foundations and support organizations
Crisis management	• Media relations • Disaster management • Election/funding loss • Financial crisis • Intellectual freedom challenges • Library closings/hours reductions • Crime • Homelessness
Staff development	• Collective bargaining • Succession planning • Turnover and training
Service development	• Evaluating/embracing trends and fads • Marketing and public relations • Literacy (early childhood, adult, computer/technology)

*This table previously appeared in Peter Hernon and Ellen Altman, "Embracing Change—Continuous Improvement," *American Libraries* 41, no. 1 (January 2010): 53; and Peter Hernon and Ellen Altman, *Assessing Service Quality: Satisfying the Expectations of Library Customers* (Chicago: American Library Association, 2010), 178.

while simultaneously identifying, recruiting, preparing, and retaining a diverse, talented, and energetic workforce. At the same time, librarians seek out new partnerships while retaining successful ones. In essence, during the economic downturn, managerial leaders must cope with resource reductions and reallocations while repurposing and rethinking collections, services, and staff roles.[14]

The Council on Library and Information Resources has produced a series of case studies that show how some libraries have created innovative services that use new technologies or have been influential in addressing public policy within the communities they serve.[15] The goal is for leadership training programs to use these case studies as well as the brief ones contained in this book.

Academic Libraries of the Future

Once there was no doubt what comprised a library. It was recognized for its book collection and perhaps reading rooms. Today, there is more disagreement among librarians and between central administration and librarians. Everyone agrees that libraries are changing but disagrees about what they will become. Those in central administration see libraries as cost centers; they see the expenses, not the possible revenues or nonmonetary value such as the role of the library in attracting and retaining faculty. Libraries may participate in entrepreneurial and other activities that enhance the reputation and prestige of the institution.

Scott Carlson sees the merger of libraries, student centers, and sports centers as a way to develop a new center that will "invigorate the campus as a social and academic hub."[16] That center may also have an art center and radio station. A vice provost for academic planning and programs at the University of California System sees the future library as "sparsely staffed, highly decentralized, and . . . [having] a physical plant consisting of little more than special collections and study areas." He envisions most services as virtually outsourced as universities, in response to the economic downturn, dramatically restructure library operations.[17]

Whatever future emerges, leadership vision becomes critical, as does establishing buy-in to achieve that vision. At the same time, the vision varies among libraries, directors, and stakeholders. Libraries are taking on new roles and services, not all of which will be outsourced. Clearly, the future will focus on a shared leadership, namely how others (including stakeholders) buy into that vision.

Public Libraries of the Future

In *Assessing Service Quality*, Ellen Altman and I explore alternate visions that apply to public libraries as well. The current economic downturn has led to substantial budgetary cuts, or cycles of such cuts, and reconsideration of the services that public libraries will offer.[18] In *The Customer-Focused Library*, Joseph R. Matthews recognizes that, as public libraries continue to change, they are increasingly offering a wide range of services. In the process they can redefine themselves. It is imperative, he argues, that librarians be innovative, provide superior customer services, and recruit and retain a talented staff comprising "people persons," work well together, and embrace change. He asks, "Is the library becoming more valuable in the lives of our customers so that they have a compelling reason to visit, physically and virtually, again and again?"[19]

SUCCESSION PLANNING

One of the directors interviewed in chapter 3 speculates that, within the next five years, most (if not all) directors of libraries whose institutions are Association of Research Libraries (ARL) members will retire or assume positions elsewhere. Others speculate that once the economic recession of 2008/2009 and its aftermath conclude, many library directors—well beyond ARL—will retire. At the same time, other members of the senior management team might do the same.

The workforce will likely change, as will the nature of the work performed. The workforce will become younger as many students go directly from undergraduate to master's programs in schools of library and information science. At Simmons College, for instance, 29 percent of the student body entering the master's program since 2007 has never worked in libraries or at all! Furthermore, the master's degree is not the only way to enter the profession. As university libraries engage in entrepreneurial activities and cooperate with institutional and noninstitutional partners, there will be increased opportunities for individuals with backgrounds in information technology, marketing, business, development, and other specialties to join the library workforce.

Despite all the changes librarians are discussing, libraries infrequently engage in succession planning, a term that implies more than replacement planning. It involves the identification, development, and long-term retention of talented individuals at the upper level of management in libraries. Another aspect is to plan for staff retirements or departures and to determine the replacement qualities and positions. Among the new positions that some libraries are creating, on either a temporary or permanent basis, is an assessment officer. For instance:

- Training & Assessment Librarian, "who will be responsible for designing, implementing and delivering training for library employees that will provide the skills and knowledge critical to the excellent delivery of a benchmark level of service to patrons. The successful candidate will work with departmental managers to implement changes indicated by assessment findings. Assessment activities will focus on the comprehensive user experience in the library, including face-to-face and virtual interaction. The Training & Assessment Librarian will be part of the new Learning Commons, now in the design phase, which focuses on the role of libraries and library technology in the teaching and learning process, and integrates reference assistance with technology, writing, and ESL assistance. This position reports to Associate University Librarian for Learning and Technology Initiatives."

  "*Responsibilities:* The Training & Assessment Librarian takes the lead on identifying a benchmark level of service expected at all public service locations, and designs and delivers training programs to staff who work at those locations, likely to include customer service, campus information, and the most basic reference service. Assists with designing and delivering training to public-service librarians and support-staff who provide mid-level reference service. Assesses service at all public service desks, and collaborates with supervisors to determine how to improve service. Works with existing committees and departments and instruments . . . to develop a regular process for usability and assessment activities. Participates in the provision of reference and research support in the Learning Commons. Candidates should have a commitment to library service and scholarly excellence."[20]

- Electronic Collections & Assessment Librarian, Collection Development, who should be "an energetic and motivated librarian to participate in the building, assessment, and management of the Libraries' collection with particular emphasis on electronic resources. . . . Working in collaboration with colleagues, bibliographers, and relevant committees, this position identifies and analyzes collection metrics to broadly inform collection management and purchase decisions. This position also facilitates the licensing, management, evaluation, and promotion of the Libraries' growing collection of electronic resources and open access content. In addition, this position participates in special projects and scholarly communication initiatives. The successful candidate may also assume bibliographer duties in an area of the candidate's expertise. Significant parts of the responsibilities of this position are research and creative work and service in keeping with the tenure standards."[21, 22]

- Assessment Librarian, who will report to the director and "will co-ordinate and implement assessment activities and create a knowledge base documenting user preferences and behaviours. Responsibilities may also include provision of reference services or collection management/liaison services."[23]

As these examples illustrate, the work life of librarians will continue to change. With the focus today on evaluation and assessment, there is a need for librarians at all levels of the organization to understand evaluation and assessment research and the role that quantitative and qualitative data collection plays.

MEMBER LIBRARIES: ASSOCIATION OF RESEARCH LIBRARIES

Writing in 1973, Arthur McAnally and Robert Downs noted that the directorship of a major university library could no longer be considered a lifetime post. The average span for a director was five to six years, and in 1972 half of the ARL university libraries had changed directorships within the preceding three years; four of them had changed twice.[24] At that time it was unsettling to associate university libraries with so much change in directorships.

Using the *ARL Membership List* for May 2009, the author checked each library home page to see if there has been a recent change in director or plans for an upcoming change. One library announced that its director would be leaving in January 2010 to assume a position at Oxford University. The *Membership List* indicates the year in which the individual assumed the directorship and identifies the gender for the entire population and the birth date for some. The author found errors in the gender classification, which he fixed as he visited each Web site; tracked down more birth dates; reviewed the graduate degrees that the directors have; and determined the race and ethnicity of the directors.

Figures 1.1 through 1.6 (pp. 12–14) depict the ninety-three directors of university libraries in the United States; omitted are interim and Canadian directors as well as those of nonuniversity libraries.

As Figure 1.1 indicates, the largest percentage of directors is female; clearly, over time, there has been a gender shift, with women now in the majority (fifty-six women and thirty-seven males) and in some very prestigious institutions. The ARL can no longer be characterized as a "good old boys' club."[25] Figure 1.2 shows that five directors were born in the 1930s: 1936 to 1938. Of those born in the 1940s, thirteen were born between 1942 and 1944. From 1945 to 1949, most were born in 1947 (eleven), followed by 1949 (six) and 1946 (five). Of those born in the 1950s, seven were born in 1950, followed by four in 1952; three were born later in the decade: 1958 (one) and 1959 (two). Only one director was born in 1961, and data were unavailable for twenty-seven directors.

Of the ninety-three directors, two are African American. Apparently some directors are from South Africa, Asia, the Middle East, and Romania; most likely they are all American citizens.

Eighteen directors have a doctoral degree, two of whom have an EdD. Three of those with a PhD do not have a master's in library science (MLS); their doctorates are in history (two) and economics (one). For thirty-two directors, the MLS is their highest degree; two of them received their degrees outside the United States, and some have completed postgraduate coursework. Twenty-eight directors have master's degrees in addition to the MLS. (e.g., in business administration, music, and public administration). The highest degree for thirteen directors was undetermined (see figure 1.3).

The length of their tenure as director varies widely (see figure 1.4). One became director in 1978 and three in 2009. A total of fifty-seven (61.3 percent) became director in 2000 or later; figure 1.5, which focuses on the years 2005–2009, shows that the largest number of directors assumed that position in 2005 and 2007. For the directors represented in this figure, the birth years for half (fourteen, 50 percent) were unavailable. Nine of these directors (32.1 percent) were born between 1947 and 1953 (see figure 1.6).

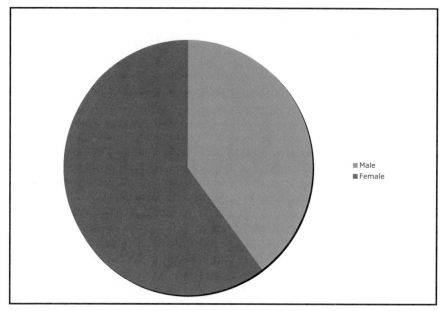

Figure 1.1 Gender of ARL University Library Directors

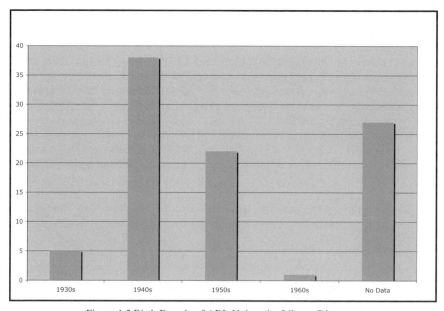

Figure 1.2 Birth Decade of ARL University Library Directors

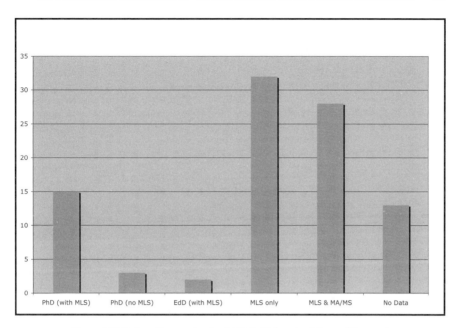

Figure 1.3 Highest Degree Attained (ARL University Library Directors)

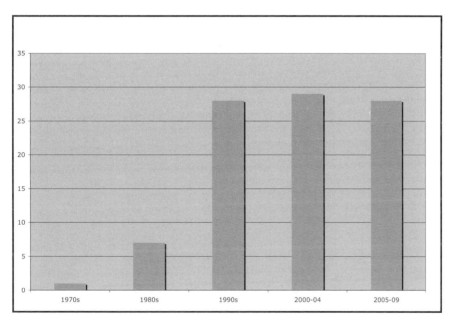

Figure 1.4 Year Became Director

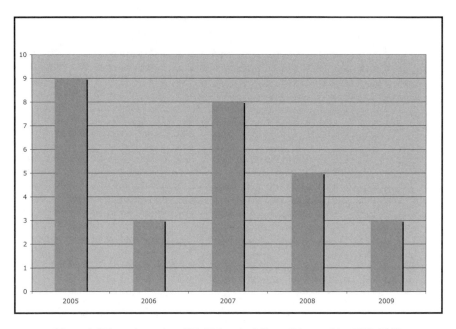

Figure 1.5 Those Assuming ARL University Library Directorship, 2005–2009

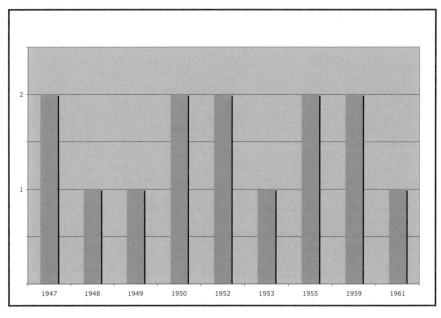

Figure 1.6 Birth Years for Those Assuming ARL University Library Directorship, 2005-2009

For those who became directors in 2005 or later, data on prior position were available for half. Of this group, seven were assistant university librarians (AULs) at other ARL university libraries; three were internal candidates, either interim directors or department heads; three were directors of another ARL university library; and one was the director of a non-ARL university library.

Complementary insights emerge from *The ARL Annual Salary Survey* for 2008–2009 (see http://www.arl.org/stats/annualsurveys/salary/sal0809.shtml), which, among other things, shows that the ARL directors who are women now earn more than their male counterparts, and that there is a difference in salary between directors in public and private institutions.

There has been a dramatic change in directorships since 2000, and the pace of change is likely to remain high given the age of a number of directors. If data were gathered for other types of academic institutions and for public libraries, what patterns, especially at the larger organizations, would emerge? What impact, if any, will changes at the director level have on libraries—their guiding visions and service roles—as the information-gathering practices of faculty and students continue to change? Further, once the current economic recession is over, will the number of retirements of both directors and their senior management teams increase as predicted?

READINGS

As librarians familiarize themselves with various leadership theories, styles, and practices, they might consult the appendix to this chapter as well as the writings of Barbara Kellerman, James MacGregor Burns Lecturer in Public Leadership at the Kennedy School of Government, Harvard University. In *Bad Leadership*, she contends that bad (ineffective and unethical) leadership is not an aberration, but a ubiquitous and insidious part of everyday life that must be carefully examined and better understood. She highlights seven types of bad leadership.[26] In another work, she focuses on followership and characterizes different types of followers, reminding us that it is a mistake to focus solely on leaders; rather, both leadership and followership merit attention.[27]

One final author merits mention. Organizational psychologist J. Richard Hackman, who has studied teams in various organizations, outlines an approach for applying his concepts to different organizations and for identifying effective teams. With teams playing a central role in many libraries, his work merits study and more application to libraries.[28]

CONCLUDING THOUGHTS

Writing in 1997, Riggs reflected on the future of academic libraries. He maintained that

[a]s academic libraries are becoming more complex and confusing, reshaping and renewing themselves, and undergoing unparalleled changes, transformational leadership is in great demand. Excellent managers and transactional leaders are certainly needed too, but there has to be that "something extra" ingredient in leading the libraries into the new century [and beyond].[29]

Transformational leadership, which unites leaders and followers in the pursuit of common goals, "is a process of evoking and managing the emotions of followers—very consistent with concepts of emotional intelligence."[30] As Joan R. Giesecke points out, the key behaviors of transformational leadership are individualized consideration, intellectual stimulation, inspirational motivation, and idealized influence:

Individualized consideration describes the compassionate leader who genuinely cares about followers, is encouraging, and makes personal contact with followers. Intellectual stimulation behavior leads to creative thinking, encouraging imagination by followers, challenging the status quo, and encouraging risk taking. Inspirational motivation behavior includes clarifying vision and mission, and inspiring others to achieve more than they thought they could do. Idealized influence behavior is seen in the cliché "walk the talk" where actions match the vision. Leaders develop trust among followers and exhibit great commitment. Using these four behaviors, leaders are able to motivate followers to transcend self-interest, [and] promote higher achievement, higher morale, and greater change possibilities.[31]

As this chapter indicates, other leadership theories apply to libraries. Among these are situational leadership, emotional intelligence, authentic leadership, transformational and transaction leadership, and resonant leadership. Chapter 2 discusses relevant theories. Still, it is most likely that, with the fast pace of today, library staff most likely want effective management and, in some instances, they do not receive it.

Leaders not only manage change, they must be comfortable with it in their own lives.[32]

NOTES

1. Warren Bennis, *On Becoming a Leader* (Reading, MA: Addison-Wesley, 1989), 9.

2. Richard Boyatzis and Annie McKee, *Resonant Leadership: Renewing Yourself and Connecting with Others through Mindfulness, Hope, and Compassion* (Boston: Harvard Business School Press), 9. See also Annie McKee, Frances Johnston, and Richard Massimilian, "Mindfulness, Hope, and Compassion: A Leader's Road Map to Renewal," *Ivey Business Journal* 70, no. 5 (May/June 2006): 1–5.

3. Doris Kearns Goodwin, *Team of Rivals: The Political Genius of Abraham Lincoln* (New York: Simon & Schuster, 2005), xix.

4. Ibid., xvii.

5. "Cesar's Way: Cesar's Tips." Available at http://www.cesarsway.com/articles/Cesar%27s%20Tips/649?page=1&cat=2 (accessed May 14, 2009).

6. Warren Bennis, *On Becoming a Leader* (Cambridge, MA: Perseus Book Group, 2005), xxi, xxii.

7. Donald E. Riggs, "Ineffective [Bad!] Leadership," in *Making a Difference: Leadership and Academic Libraries*, ed. Peter Hernon and Nancy Rossiter, 186 (Westport, CT: Libraries Unlimited, 2007).

8. Peter Hernon, Candy Schwartz, and Caryn Anderson, "Managerial Leadership as an Area of Doctoral Study," in *Making a Difference*, 229–50.

9. John D. Mayer and Peter Salovey, "What Is Emotional Intelligence," in *Emotional Development and Emotional Intelligence: Educational Implications*, ed. Peter Salovey and Davie J. Sluyter, 10 (New York: Basic Books, 1997).

10. See Peter Hernon, Ronald R. Powell, and Arthur P. Young, *The Next Library Leadership: Attributes of Academic and Public Library Directors* (Westport, CT: Libraries Unlimited, 2003); Peter Hernon, Ronald R. Powell, and Arthur P. Young, "University Library Directors in the Association of Research Libraries: The Next Generation, Part One," *College & Research Libraries* 62, no. 2 (March 2001), 116–45; Peter Hernon, Ronald R. Powell, and Arthur P. Young, "University Library Directors in the Association of Research Libraries: The Next Generation, Part Two," *College & Research Libraries* 63, no. 1 (January 2002): 73–90. See also Peter Hernon and Nancy Rossiter, "Emotional Intelligence: Which Traits Are Most Prized," *College & Research Libraries* 67, no. 3 (May 2006): 260–75; Peter Hernon, Camila A. Alire, and Joan R. Giesecke, *Academic Librarians as Emotionally Intelligent Leaders* (Westport, CT: Libraries Unlimited, 2008).

11.   Gary N. Fitsimmons, "Academic Library Directors in the Eyes of Hiring Administrators: A Comparison of the Attributes, Qualifications, and Competencies Desired by Chief Academic Officers with Those Recommended by Academic Library Directors," in *Advances in Library Administration and Organization*, vol. 26, ed. Edward D. Garten, Delmus E. Williams, James M. Nyce, and Janine Golden, 265–315. (Bingley, UK: Emerald Group Publishing Limited, 2008). See also Jennifer Arns, "Challenges in Governance: The Leadership Characteristics and Behaviors Valued by Public Library Trustees in Times of Conflict and Contention," *The Library Quarterly* 77, no. 3 (2007): 287–310.

12.   Suffolk University, Sawyer Library, "Mildred F. Sawyer Library: Long-Range Plan: Strategic Directions, July 1, 2005–June 30, 2010" (Boston, MA: Sawyer Library). Available at http://www.suffolk.edu/files/SawLib/2005-2010-strat-plan.pdf (accessed September 23, 2009).

13.   "ACRL/Harvard Leadership Institute for Academic Librarians." Available at http://www.ala.org/ala/mgrps/divs/acrl/events/leadershipinstitute.cfm (accessed September 23, 2009).

14.   See Anne Goulding, *Public Libraries in the 21st Century: Defining Services and Debating the Future* (Surrey, UK: Ashgate Publishing, 2006).

15.   Council on Library and Information Resources, "Public Library Case Studies" (Washington, DC: The Council). Available at http://www.clir.org/pubs/reports/case/case.html (accessed September 23, 2009).

16.   Scott Carlson, "Is It a Library? A Student Center? The Athenaeum Opens at Goucher College," *The Chronicle of Higher Education* LVI, no. 4 (September 18, 2009): A16–17.

17.   "Libraries of the Future," *Inside Higher Ed* (September 24, 2009). Available at http://www.insidehighered.com/layout/set/print/news/2009/09/24/libraries (accessed September 24, 2009).

18.   Peter Hernon and Ellen Altman, *Assessing Service Quality: Meeting the Expectations of Library Users*, 2nd ed. (Chicago: American Library Association, 2010).

19.   Joseph R. Matthews, *The Customer-Focused Library: Reinventing the Public Library from the Outside-in* (Westport, CT: ABC-CLIO, 2009), 87.

20.   Georgia State University, University Library, "Training & Assessment Librarian." Available at http://www.library.gsu.edu/jobs/pages.asp?ldID=70&ID=2744&typeID=0 (accessed October 7, 2009).

21.   University of Colorado at Boulder, University Libraries, "Job Opportunities: Electronic Collections & Assessment Librarian." (No longer available.)

22.   See also John Fudrow, "Extensible Librarian: Libraries, Assessment, and Technology" (Pittsburgh, PA: University of Pittsburgh, December 25, 2009). Available at http://johnfudrow.wordpress.com/ (accessed December 28, 2009); Library Assessment Conference, "Assessment Plans: Four Case Studies" (Seattle, WA, 2008). Available at http://www.lib.uchicago.edu/e/atatarka/aplans.html (accessed September 11, 2009).

23.   University of Alberta Libraries, "Assessment Librarian." Available at http://libraryassessment.info/?p=116 (accessed October 7, 2009).

24.   Arthur M. McAnally and Robert B. Downs, "The Changing Role of Directors of University Libraries," *College & Research Libraries* 34, no. 2 (1973): 103–35.

25.   In 1933 fifteen women directed ARL libraries. For the next thirty-five years, only two women were appointed to directorships. From 1970 to 1973, four women were appointed. From these data, William L. Cohn concludes that, as ARL member libraries grew in budgets and collection size, fewer women became directors. See William L.

Cohn, "An Overview of ARL directors, 1933–1973," *College & Research Libraries* 37, no. 2 (March 1976): 137–44.

26. Barbara Kellerman, *Bad Leadership: What It Is, How It Happens, Why It Matters* (Boston: Harvard Business School Press, 2004).

27. Barbara Kellerman, *Followership: How Followers Are Creating Change and Changing Leaders* (Boston: Harvard Business School Press, 2008).

28. J. Richard Hackman, *Leading Teams: Setting the Stage for Great Performance* (Boston: Harvard Business School Press, 2002). See also Elaine Martin, "Team Effectiveness and Members as Leaders," in *Making a Difference*, 125–42.

29. Donald E. Riggs, "What's in Store for Academic Libraries' Leadership and Management Issues," *The Journal of Academic Librarianship* 23, no. 1 (January 1997): 8.

30. Bernard M. Bass and Ronald E. Riggio, *Transformational Leadership*, 2nd ed. (Mahwah, NJ: Lawrence Erlbaum Associates, 2006), 173.

31. Joan R. Giesecke, "Modeling Leadership Theories," in *Making a Difference*, 55.

32. Bennis, *On Becoming a Leader* (1989), 171.

APPENDIX: A SELECTIVE READING LIST*

General

Bass, Bernard M., and Ronald E. Riggio. *Transformational Leadership.* Mahwah, NJ: L. Erlbaum Associates, 2006.

Bennis, Warren G. *On Becoming a Leader.* Reading, MA: Addison-Wesley, 1989; Cambridge, MA: Perseus Publishing, 2003.

Boyatzis, Richard E., and Annie McKee. *Resonant Leadership: Renewing Yourself and Connecting with Others through Mindfulness, Hope, and Compassion.* Boston: Harvard Business School Press, 2005.

Goleman, Daniel. "What Makes a Leader? *Harvard Business Review* 76, no. 6 (1998): 93–102.

Hernon, Peter, Joan Giesecke, and Camila A. Alire. *Academic Librarians as Emotionally Intelligent Leaders.* Westport, CT: Libraries Unlimited, 2008.

Hernon, Peter, and Nancy Rossiter. *Making a Difference: Leadership and Academic Libraries.* Westport, CT: Libraries Unlimited, 2006.

Kouzes, James M., and Barry Z. Posner. *The Leadership Challenge.* San Francisco: Jossey-Bass, 2002.

Northouse, Peter G. Leadership: *Theory and Practice.* 5th ed. Thousand Oaks, CA: Sage, 2009.

Scenario Planning

Giesecke, Joan. "Scenario Planning and Collection Development." *Journal of Library Administration* 28, no. 1 (1999): 81–92.

Giesecke, Joan, ed. *Scenario Planning for Libraries.* Chicago: American Library Association, 1998.

*Source: The various courses in the PhD Program in Managerial Leadership in the Information Professions (Boston: Simmons College, Graduate School in Library and Information Science).

Lindgren, Matts, and Hans Bandhold. *Scenario Planning: The Link between Future and Strategy*. New York: Palgrave Macmillan, 2003.

Robbins, Gordon C. "Scenario Planning: A Strategic Alternative Challenging Managers to Look Ahead." *Public Management* 77, no. 3 (1995): 4–9.

Metrics

Dugan, Robert E., Peter Hernon, and Danuta Nitecki. *Viewing Library Metrics from Different Perspectives*. Santa Barbara, CA: ABC-CLIO (Libraries Unlimited), 2009.

Research Methods

Klenke, Karin. *Qualitative Research in the Study of Leadership*. Bingley, UK: Emerald Group Publishing Ltd., 2008.

Powell, Ronald R., and Lynn S. Connaway. *Basic Research Methods for Librarians*. Westport, CT: Libraries Unlimited, 2004.

Diversity

Alire, Camila A. "Diversity and Leadership: The Color of Leadership." *Journal of Library Administration* 32, nos. 3/4 (2001): 95–109.

Warner, Linda S., and Keith Grint. "American Indian Ways of Leading and Knowing." *Leadership* 2, no. 2 (May 2006): 225–44.

Financial Management and Leadership

Abraham, Anne. "Financial Management in the Nonprofit Sector: A Mission-based Approach to Ratio Analysis in Membership Organizations." *Journal of American Academy of Business* 10, no. 1 (2006): 212–17.

Birdsall, Douglas G. "The Micropolitics of Budgeting in Universities: Lessons for Library Administrators." *The Journal of Academic Librarianship* 21, no. 6 (November 1995): 427–37.

Blosh, Marie. "Changing the Way We Do Business." *American Libraries* 34, no. 1 (January 2003): 48, 50.

Coffman, Steve. "What If You Ran Your Library Like a Bookstore?" *American Libraries* 29, no. 3 (March 1998): 40–46.

Durrance, Joan C., and Karen E. Fisher-Pettigrew. "Toward Developing Measures of the Impact of Library and Information Services." *Reference & User Services Quarterly* 42, no. 1 (Fall 2002): 43–53.

Elliott, Donald S., Glen E. Holt, Sterling W. Hayden, and Leslie E. Holt. *Measuring Your Library's Value: How to Do a Cost-benefit Analysis for Your Library*. Chicago: American Library Association, 2007.

Hoff, Kathryn S. "Leaders and Managers: Essential Skills Required within Higher Education." *Higher Education* 38, no. 3 (October 1999): 311–31.

Holt, Glen E., Donald Elliott, and Christopher Dussold. "A Framework for Evaluating Public Investment in Urban Libraries." *The Bottom Line: Managing Library Finances* 9, no. 4 (1996): 4–13.

Kaplan, Robert S. *Balanced Scorecard and Nonprofit Organizations*. Cambridge, MA: Harvard Business Publishing, 2002.

Kaplan, Robert S. "Strategic Performance Measurement and Management in Nonprofit Organizations." *Nonprofit Management & Leadership* 11 (2001): 353–70.

Kusack, James M. "Understanding and Controlling the Costs of Library Services." *Library Administration & Management* 16, no. 3 (Summer 2002): 151–55.

Matthews, Joseph R. *Scorecard for Results: A Guide for Developing a Library Balanced Scorecard*. Westport, CT: Libraries Unlimited, 2008.

Snyder, Herbert W. "It Was the Best of Practices and the Worst of Practices: Case Study of Public Library Financial Management." *Library Administration & Management* 16, no. 2 (Spring 2002): 95–96.

Weiner, Sharon. "The Contribution of the Library to the Reputation of a University." *The Journal of Academic Librarianship* 35, no. 1 (2009): 3–17.

Weiner, Sharon. "Library Quality and Impact: Is There a Relationship between New Measures and Traditional Measures?" *The Journal of Academic Librarianship* 31, no. 5 (2005): 432–37.

Human Resource Management

Losey, Michael R., Susan Meisinger, and David Ulrich, eds. *The Future of Human Resource Management: 64 Thought Leaders, Explore the Critical HR Issues of Today and Tomorrow*. Hoboken, NJ: Wiley, 2005.

Noe, Raymond, John R. Hollenbeck, and Barry Gerhart. *Human Resource Management: Gaining a Competitive Advantage*. New York: McGraw-Hill/Irwin, 2006.

O'Toole, James, Edward E. Lawler, and Susan R. Meisinger. *The New American Workplace*. New York: Palgrave McMillan, 2006.

Ulrich, Dave, and Wayne Brockbank. The *HR Value Proposition*. Boston: Harvard Business School Press, 2005.

Managing and Leading in a Political Environment

Bolman, Lee G., and Terrence E. Deal. *Reframing Organizations: Artistry, Choice, and Leadership*. San Francisco: Jossey-Bass, 2003, 2008.

Bolman, Lee G., and Terrence E. Deal. *The Wizard and the Warrior*. San Francisco: Jossey-Bass, 2006.

Ciampa, Dan. "Almost Ready: How Leaders Move Up." *Harvard Business Review* 83, no. 1 (2005): 46–53.

Collins, Jim. *Good to Great and the Social Sectors*. Boulder, CO: Jim Collins, 2005.

Nielson, Gary L., Bruce A. Pasternack, and Karen E. Van Nuys. "The Passive-Aggressive Organization." *Harvard Business Review* 83, no. 10 (2005): 82–92.

Peebles, M. Ellen. "Into the Fray." *Harvard Business Review* 83, no. 1 (2005): 15–18.

Pfeffer, Jeffrey. Managing *with Power: Politics and Influence in Organizations*. Boston: Harvard Business School Press, 1992.

Schein, Edgar H. *Organizational Culture and Leadership: A Dynamic View*. San Francisco: Jossey-Bass, 1998.

Todaro, Julie. *The Power of Personal Persuasion: Advancing the Academic Library Agenda from the Front Lines.* Chicago: Association of College and Research Libraries, 2006 (ACRL toolkit).

Managerial Leadership in Public Settings

See also publications by the Urban Libraries Council. Available at http://www.urbanlibraries.org/displaycommon.cfm?an=5 (accessed September 22, 2009).

Harriman, Joy H.P. *Creating Your Library's Business Plan.* New York: Neal-Schuman, 2008.

Koontz, Christie M., Dean K. Jue, and Bradley W. Bishop. "Why Public Libraries Close?" Tallahassee: Florida State University, 2008. Retrieved from WEBJUNCTION (Library Management): http://www.webjunction.org/c/document_library/get_file?folderId=11041537&name=DLFE-2600002.pdf (accessed September 22, 2009).

McClure, Charles R., and Paul T. Jaeger. *Public Libraries and Internet Service Roles.* Chicago: American Library Association, 2009.

Issues in Information Policy

American Library Association, Association of College & Research Libraries. Web Site on Scholarly Communication. Available at http://www.ala.org/ala/mgrps/divs/acrl/issues/scholcomm/scholarlycommunication.cfm (accessed September 22, 2009).

American Library Association, Washington Office. Web Site on Copyright. Available at http://www.ala.org/ala/aboutala/offices/wo/woissues/copyrightb/copyright.cfm (accessed September 22, 2009).

Association of Research Libraries. Web Site on Public Policies. Available at http://www.arl.org/pp/ (accessed September 22, 2009).

Association of Research Libraries. Web Site on Scholarly Communication. Available at http://www.arl.org/sc/ (accessed September 22, 2009).

Band, Jonathan. *A Guide for the Perplexed: Libraries and the Google Library Project Settlement.* Chicago: American Library Association, 2008.

Borgman, Christine. *Scholarship in the Digital Age: Information, Infrastructure, and the Internet.* Cambridge, MA: MIT Press, 2007.

Boyle, James. *The Public Domain: Enclosing the Commons of the Mind.* New Haven, CT: Yale University Press, 2008.

Brown, Laura, Rebecca Griffiths, and Matthew Rascoff. *University Publishing in a Digital Age.* New York: Ithaka Report, 2007.

Committee for Economic Development. *Promoting Innovation and Economic Growth: The Special Problem of Digital Intellectual Property.* Prepared by Paul Horn, Elliot Maxwell, and Susan Crawford. Washington, DC: Committee for Economic Development, 2004. Available at http://www.scrawford.net/display/report_dcc_new.pdf (accessed September 22, 2009).

Computer and Communications Industry Association. *Fair Use in the U.S. Economy: Economic Contribution of Industries Relying on Fair Use.* Washington, DC: Computer and Communications Industry Association, 2007. Available at http://www.ccianet.org/CCIA/files/ccLibraryFiles/Filename/000000000085/Fair UseStudy-Sep12.pdf (accessed September 22, 2009).

Crews, Kenneth D. *Copyright Law for Librarians and Educators; Creative Strategies and Practical Solutions*. Chicago: American Library Association, 2006.

Hall, Gary. *Digitize This Book: The Politics of New Media and Why We Need Open Access Now*. Minneapolis: University of Minnesota Press, 2008.

Hernon, Peter, Rowena Cullen, and Harold C. Relyea. *Comparative Perspectives on E-government*. Lanham, MD: Scarecrow Press, 2006.

Hernon, Peter, and Harold C. Relyea. "Information Policy." In *Encyclopedia of Library and Information Science,* 1300–15. New York: Marcel Dekker, 2003.

Hernon, Peter, and Laura Saunders. "The Federal Depository Library Program in 2023: One Perspective on the Transition to the Future." *College & Research Libraries* 70, no. 4 (July 2009): 51–70.

International Federation of Library Associations (IFLA), Committee on Copyright and Other Legal Matters. Available at http://www.ifla.org/en/clm (accessed September 22, 2009).

Maron, Nancy. *Current Models of Digital Scholarly Communication*. Washington, DC: Association of Research Libraries, 2008.

McClure, Charles R., and Paul T. Jaeger. "Government Information Policy Research: Importance, Approaches, and Realities." *Library & Information Science Research* 30, no. 4 (2008): 257–64.

Neal, James G. "Copyright Is Dead . . . Long Live Copyright." *American Libraries* 33, no. 11 (2002): 48–51.

Neal, James G. "A Lay Perspective on the Copyright Wars: A Report from the Trenches of the Section 108 Study Group." *The Columbia Journal of Law and the Arts* 32 (Winter 2009): 193–205.

Relyea, Harold C. "Federal Government Information Policy and Public Policy Analysis: A Brief Overview." *Library & Information Science Research* 30, no. 1 (2008): 2–21.

Scholarly Publishing and Academic Resources Coalition (SPARC) Web Site. Available at http://www.arl.org/sparc/ (accessed September 22, 2009).

Solove, Daniel J. *The Future of Reputation*. New Haven, CT: Yale University Press, 2007.

Suber, Peter. "Creating an Intellectual Commons through Open Access." In *Understanding Knowledge as Commons*, edited by Charlotte Hess and Elinor Ostrom, 171–208. Cambridge: MIT Press. 2006.

University of California, Office of Scholarly Communication. "Reshaping Scholarly Communication." 2009. Available at http://osc.universityofcalifornia.edu/ (accessed September 22, 2009).

Vaidhyanathan, Siva. *Copyrights and Copywrongs: The Rise of Intellectual Property and How It Threatens Creativity*. New York: NYU Press. 2003.

Wilkinson, Margaret, and Gerolami, Natasha. "The Author as Agent of Information Policy: The Relationship between Economic and Moral Rights in Copyright." *Government Information Quarterly* 26, no. 2 (April 2009): 321–32.

Willinsky, John. *The Access Principle: The Case for Open Access to Research and Scholarship*. Cambridge: MIT Press, 2006.

Privacy and Civil Liberties

Bennett, Colin J. *The Privacy Advocates: Resisting the Spread of Surveillance.* Cambridge: MIT Press, 2008.

Buschman, John. "Who Defends Intellectual Freedom for Librarians?" *Academe* 95, no. 5 (September–October 2009): 15–17.

Solove, Daniel J. *The Digital Person: Technology and Privacy in the Information Age.* New York: New York University Press, 2004. See also http://papers.ssrn.com/ sol3/papers.cfm?abstract_id=667622; http://docs.law.gwu.edu/facweb/dsolove/ (accessed September 22, 2009).

There is relevant material at the following Web sites:

World Privacy Forum, http://www.worldprivacyforum.org/ (accessed September 22, 2009)

Robert E. Gellman's Web site, http://bobgellman.com/rg-files/rg-biblio.html (accessed September 22, 2009)

Center for Democracy and Technology, http://www.cdt.org

Electronic Privacy Information Center, http://www.epic.org/

Fund-Raising and Entrepreneurial Strategies

Burlingame, Dwight F., ed. *Critical Issues in Fund Raising.* New York: John Wiley & Sons, 1997.

Butler, Meredith, ed. *Successful Fundraising: Case Studies of Academic Libraries.* Washington, DC: Association of Research Libraries, 2001. (ERIC ED 471956).

Clay, Edwin S., and Patricia C. Bangs. "Entrepreneurs in the Public Library: Reinventing an Institution." *Library Trends* 48, no. 3 (2000): 606–18.

Corson-Finnerty, Adam, and Laura Blanchard. *Fundraising and Friend-Raising on the Web.* Chicago: American Library Association, 1998.

Dewey, Barbara I. "Fund-Raising for Large Public University Libraries: Margin for Excellence" *Library Administration and Management* 20, no. 1 (Winter 2006): 5–12.

Dove, Kent E. *Conducting a Successful Fundraising Program: A Comprehensive Guide and Resource*, 9–24, 42–83, 134–268, 369–476. San Francisco: Jossey Bass, 2001.

Franklin, Brinley. "The Privatization of Public University Research Libraries." *portal: Libraries and the Academy* 7, no. 4 (2007): 407–14.

Hart, Theodore R. "ePhilanthropy: Using the Internet to Build Support." *International Journal of Nonprofit and Voluntary Sector Marketing* 7, no. 4 (2002): 353–60.

Hazard, Brenda L. "Online Fundraising at ARL Libraries." *The Journal of Academic Librarianship* 29, no. 1 (2003): 8–15.

Jennings, Karlene Noel, and Jos Wanschers. *Library Development.* SPEC Kit 297. Washington, DC: Association of Research Libraries, 2006.

Klein, Kim. "Philanthropy in America." In *Fundraising for Social Change*, 5th ed., 5–18. San Francisco: Jossey-Bass, 2007.

Martin, Susan K. "Academic Library Fund-Raising: Organization, Process, and Politics." *Library Trends* 48 no. 3 (2000): 560–78.

Martin, Susan K. "Achieving a Vision in Downsizing Times: A Series of Questions." *The Journal of Academic Librarianship* 24, no. 4 (1998): 318–19.

Martin, Susan K. "The Changing Role of the Library Director: Fund-Raising and the Academic Library." *The Journal of Academic Librarianship* 24, no. 1 (1998): 3–10.

Neal, James G. "The Entrepreneurial Imperative: Advancing from Incremental to Radical Change in the Academic Library." *portal: Libraries and the Academy* 1, no. 1 (2001): 1–13.

Ruggiero, Anne, and Julia Zimmerman. "Grateful Recipients: Library Staff as Active Participants in Fund-Raising." *Library Administration & Management* 18, no. 3 (2004): 140–45.

Smith, Jono. "How to Build Relationships & Achieve Fundraising Success in a Web 2.0 World." Presented at the Technology in the Arts 2008 Annual Conference. Available at http://www.fundraising123.org/article/how-build-relationships-and-achieve-fundraising-success-web-20-world (accessed September 23, 2009).

Steele, Victoria, and Stephen D. Elder. *Becoming a Fundraiser: The Principles and Practice of Library Development.* 2nd ed. Chicago: American Library Association, 2000.

Taylor, Merrily E. "It's Hard to Make Friends: What to Think about in Creating a Friends of the Library Group." *Library Trends* 48, no. 3 (2000): 597–605.

Webber, Daniel. "Understanding Charity Fundraising Events." *International Journal of Nonprofit and Voluntary Sector Marketing* 9, no. 2 (2004): 122–34.

Wedgeworth, Robert. "Donor Relations as Public Relations: Toward a Philosophy of Fund-Raising." *Library Trends* 48, no. 3 (2000): 530–39.

Welch, Jeanie M. "The Electronic Welcome Mat: The Academic Library Web Site as a Marketing and Public Relations Tool." *The Journal of Academic Librarianship* 31 no. 3 (2005): 225–28.

Winston, Mark D., and Lisa Dunkley. "Leadership Competencies for Academic Librarians: The Importance of Development and Fund-raising." *College & Research Libraries* 63, no. 2 (2002): 171–82.

Futurism

Campbell, Jerry. "Changing a Cultural Icon: The Academic Library as a Virtual Destination." *Educause Review* 41, no. 1 (January–February 2006): 16–31.

Dupuis, John. "Twenty-nine Reports about the Future of Academic Libraries." Available at http://jdupuis.blogspot.com/2009/02/twenty-nine-reports-about-future-of.html (accessed September 23, 2009).

Lewis, David L. "A Strategy for Academic Libraries in the First Quarter of the 21st Century." *College & Research Libraries* 68, no. 5 (2007): 418–34.

2

~

LEADERSHIP THEORIES THAT LEAD TO EFFECTIVE PRACTICE

Maureen Sullivan

A leader is best when people barely know he exists, when his work is done,
his aim fulfilled, they will say: we did it ourselves.[1]

Lao-Tzu, who lived from 604 to 531 BC, understood the very nature of effective leadership, as the above quotation indicates. Leadership is a process of influence, and effective leaders inspire others to accomplish results. Centuries later those who study and write about leadership have returned to an understanding that leadership occurs when followers are motivated to achieve results by leaders who facilitate and support their work. Recent theories and models offer a variety of practices for effective leadership. Although each has its distinctive characteristics, there is a set of common themes among them.

First and foremost, effective leaders develop relationships with followers based on trust, honest and open communication, authenticity, and flexibility. They bring emotional intelligence to their work and create resonance in these relationships. They understand that the organization is a dynamic system, subject to continuous change in today's complex world. They know and practice behaviors that lead to productive results. These leaders know themselves, are committed to their own development and that of their followers, and remain attuned to continuous learning.

Discussion of leadership theories revolves around works of such individuals as John Kotter; Warren Bennis; Burt Nanus and Joan Goldsmith; James Kouzes and Barry Posner; Lee Bolman and Terrence Deal; Daniel Goleman, Richard Boyatzis, and Annie McKee; and Ronald Heifetz. Each of these individuals has studied leadership in practice and has developed a theoretical framework for understanding effective leadership in practice.

SOME THEORISTS AND THEORIES RELEVANT TO MANAGERIAL LEADERSHIP

In his classic article, "What Leaders Really Do,"[2] John Kotter addresses the fundamental differences between management and leadership. He states that "leadership and management are two distinctive and complementary systems of action." The function of management is to "produce order and consistency" through the key activities of planning, budgeting, organizing, staffing, controlling, and problem solving. The function of leadership is to "produce change and movement" by establishing direction through creation of vision and setting priorities, aligning followers to the vision and priorities through communication and building commitment, and motivating and inspiring them by empowering them and creating conditions under which they can satisfy their needs through the work they perform.

Kotter makes the case for organizations to develop leadership competence in their managers. He acknowledges that not all managers are effective leaders. He also argues that managers can develop leadership competence and that organizations have an obligation to develop the leadership capacity of their managers. He essentially calls for organizations to develop a cadre of managerial leaders. "The real challenge is to combine strong leadership and strong management and use each to balance the other."[3]

Strategies for Effective Leadership and Transformation

Warren Bennis and Burt Nanus identified four key leadership strategies essential to ensuring organizational effectiveness and efficiency.[4] These four arose from a two-year study in which they asked a group of leaders to respond to a set of questions about their own experiences and capabilities with leadership. The four leadership strategies follow:

1. *Attention through vision.* Effective leaders engage the attention of followers by communicating a compelling picture of a desired future for the organization. Leaders clarify the expectations they have of followers and are explicit about what is required to accomplish the vision. By inspiring followers to focus on the vision, leaders elicit their commitment to achieve the results necessary to meet the vision.

2. *Meaning through communication.* Bennis and Nanus discovered that effective leaders are very good communicators and are skilled in making and managing meaning in the work of the organization. They refer to effective leaders as social architects, individuals who are successful at shaping and transforming the culture or social architecture of the organization. Wilfred H. Drath and Charles J. Palus offer this description: "Leadership is the process of making sense of what people are doing together so that people will understand and be committed. Or one might say that leadership is the social sense-making process that creates interpersonal influence—in other words, one person does what some other person influences him or her to do because doing it makes sense to both people."[5]

   Leaders communicate meaning by creating a compelling vision that will take the organization forward, by developing commitment to the vision, and by making the vision and the process to achieve it a part of the day-to-day experience.

3. *Trust through positioning.* Trust is the foundation of effective interpersonal relationships. Positioning is the work that leaders do to accomplish the vision. The vision is a set of ideas, and positions are the actions leaders take to implement the vision. Effective leaders are trustworthy. They are consistently honest, open, and direct in their communication with followers. Their actions are consistent with their words. They have integrity and consistently demonstrate their trustworthiness. Warren Bennis recently collaborated with Daniel Goleman and Patricia Ward Biederman on the essay, "Creating a Culture of Candor,"[6] in which they describe

what it means to be a transparent leader and offer strategies for creating an organizational culture in which leaders and followers will say what they think and thereby build relationships of trust and openness.

4. *Deployment of self.* Effective leaders know themselves and are attuned to how they behave and how their behavior is seen and perceived by others. They remain open to learning about themselves from their followers and from their experiences. Bennis and Nanus identified the following as characteristic of effective leaders: recognition and acceptance of uncertainty; knowledge that mistakes lead to learning, development, and improvement; an orientation toward the future and possibility; interpersonal competence; and self-knowledge.

   Leaders have positive self-regard and a high degree of emotional maturity. They accept others for who they are, not who they would like them to be. They approach problems and relationships with an orientation to the present and future, not the past. They treat others with courtesy and respect. They trust others, even in situations of great risk. They are confident and do not seek or need validation or approval from others.

Based on his earlier work with Nanus, in 1997 Bennis collaborated with Joan Goldsmith to describe the nature of leadership required in organizations and offer this definition of successful leadership:

Truly successful leadership today requires "teams, collaboration, diversity, innovation, and cooperation." Leadership has begun to take on a new dimension. The leadership we are seeking is one that is empowering, supportive, visionary, problem-solving, creative, and shared. We are calling for a *continuum* of leadership that includes indirect leadership exerted through support and networking or scholarly studies or symbolic communication; and that extends to direct leadership of the sort that is exercised by world leaders through speeches and similar means. On that continuum, each of us can find a place and a means of expressing ourselves.[7]

Bennis and Goldsmith describe four general expectations that constituents have of their leaders: (1) purpose, direction, and meaning in the work of the organization; (2) trust and integrity; (3) optimism about the future; and (4) a bias for action and results. They also identify three organizational requirements for the "effective, creative, and productive workplaces where, rather than suppressing ourselves, we are able to use our talents to express our contributions": (1) alignment with a common vision; (2) empowerment of all involved; and (3) a learning, inquiry-based, and reflective culture.

Five Practices for Exemplary Leadership

In their research to understand effective leadership through the perspective of followers, James Kouzes and Barry Posner also found a common set of behaviors. They defined them as the Five Practices of Exemplary Leadership:

1. *Challenge the process.* Exemplary leaders seek challenging opportunities to innovate, improve, and bring about change. They question the status quo and seek improvement in work processes and organizational systems. They experiment and take risks. They actively learn from experience and see mistakes as opportunities to learn and improve.

2. *Inspire shared vision.* Exemplary leaders pay attention to trends and developments, especially those that are likely to affect their organizations. They clarify their own personal vision of the preferred future and invite others to contribute to the creation of a common vision. They have a positive and optimistic view of the future. They engage others and focus attention on areas of mutual interest.

3. *Enable others to act.* Exemplary leaders foster collaboration and develop trust in their relationships with others. They actively involve followers in planning, problem solving, and decision making. They delegate meaningful work to foster learning and development. They empower by delegating the responsibility, authority, and accountability for the accomplishment of meaningful work. They help followers develop competence and encourage them to reach their potential. These leaders are skilled in coaching and mentoring.

4. *Model the way.* Exemplary leaders know their own values and beliefs. They act in accordance with these values and beliefs. They set an example by ensuring that actions follow words and values. They model the behavior they expect from others. They set a path to achieve consistent progress by planning and by segmenting work activities and projects into achievable steps. They build commitment in followers by clearly communicating the vision for change and engaging them in the work to achieve the vision.

5. *Encourage the heart.* Exemplary leaders encourage followers to achieve their goals. These leaders recognize and express appreciation for the contributions of followers. In doing so, they personalize the recognition to individual needs and interests. They celebrate accomplishments and are creative in coming up with ways to do this. They have fun and encourage others to enjoy what they are doing.[8]

Reframing Leadership: The Four Leadership Frames

Lee Bolman and Terrence Deal describe leadership as "a subtle, holistic process of mutual influence fusing thought, feeling, and action to produce cooperative effort in the service of purposes and values embraced by both the leader and the led."[9] They developed the four frames model to better understand organizational behavior. These frames are structural leadership, human resource leadership, political leadership, and symbolic leadership. Bolman and Deal assert that each leader has his or her own, preferred frame or lens through which he or she takes in information, interprets this information to give meaning to experience, and decides what actions to take. Bolman and Deal advocate knowing one's preferred leadership frame and developing the ability to reframe a situation through the other three to expand the understanding of the situation and enable action that will be most effective.

1. *The structural frame of leadership.* This frame emphasizes the importance of formal roles, rules, and responsibilities. The organization is a complex machine that functions best when policies, rules, and the chain of command are designed to enable effective coordination of a wide range of work activities. The leader's work is logical thinking, careful analysis, ensuring an effective organizational structure and well-designed management systems, and making the right decisions.

2. *The human resource frame of leadership.* People are primary in this frame. The organization is an extended family comprised of individuals with their own needs, feelings, styles, and preferences. The leader's work is to listen, coach, motivate, develop strong interpersonal relationships, and empower people. The leader facilitates, guides, and supports.

3. *The political frame of leadership.* In this frame, organizations are places where various individuals and interest groups compete for power and scarce resources. This competition leads to conflict and the formation of coalitions based on special interests. The organization is a jungle. The leader's work is to advocate, negotiate, network, build alliances, defuse opposition, and influence important individuals and constituencies.

4. *The symbolic frame of leadership.* The metaphor for the organization in this frame is the theater. The organization is seen through the lens of its culture. Rituals, symbols, ceremonies, and stories convey meaning and purpose. The work of the leader is to inspire, communicate a compelling vision, and frame experiences to shape meaning, encourage belief in possibilities, and give followers hope for the future.

The key to effective leadership is the capacity to reframe a situation in order to view it from more than one perspective. Reframing enables a leader to expand her or his understanding of the situation, better manage complexity, and choose a more informed and better course of action.[10]

Emotional Intelligence and Resonant Leadership

In *Primal Leadership*, Daniel Goleman, Richard Boyatzis, and Annie McKee describe how the competencies of emotional intelligence contribute to effective leadership.[11] Emotional intelligence is the ability to manage relationships and oneself effectively. This scheme originally consisted of five domains, but the authors recast them as four domains, each of which has associated traits: self-awareness, self-management, social awareness, and relationship management.[12]

Goleman, Boyatzis, and McKee postulate that a leader's mood and tone affect how he or she behaves and that this behavior has a direct impact on others. The leader's emotional state affects the emotional state of followers and this, in turn, influences their behavior and performance. The authors' research led them to formulate a model of six leadership styles (see table 2.1, p. 30). Each springs from different components of emotional intelligence. Two of the styles, commanding and coercive, have an overall negative impact on organizational climate and performance results. Three of the remaining styles—affiliative, democratic, and pacesetting—have a positive effect. The visionary style is the most strongly positive style. None of the styles, they note, works in every situation, and in practice, most leaders use some combination of styles.

Goleman, Boyatzis, and McKee also introduced the concepts of dissonance and resonance in the relationships that leaders have with followers. When dissonance occurs followers are demoralized, have difficulty managing their own emotions and the effects of stress, and experience burnout. In contrast, "when a leader triggers resonance, you can read it in people's eyes: They're engaged and they light up."[13]

Boyatzis and McKee explain this kind of leadership thus:

Resonant leaders are in tune with those around them. This results in people working in sync with each other, in tune with each others' thoughts (what to do) and emotions (why to do it). Leaders who can create resonance are people who either intuitively understand or have worked hard to develop emotional intelligence—namely, the competencies of self-awareness, self-management, social awareness, and relationship management. They act with mental clarity, not simply following a whim or an impulse.[14]

Boyatzis and McKee propose three key components of resonant leadership:

1. *Mindfulness:* The capacity to be fully aware of all that one experiences *inside the self*—body, mind, and spirit—and to pay full attention to what is happening around us—people, the natural world, our surroundings, and events. A deep level of self-knowledge and paying consistent attention to what is happening in one's experience lead to confidence and authentic behavior.

Table 2.1
The Six Leadership Styles

The Commanding Style	Leaders in this style expect immediate compliance. They tell what needs to be done and demand compliance. The underlying emotional intelligence competencies of this style are a strong achievement drive, initiative, and self-control.
The Pacesetting Style	This style emphasizes high standards for performance. The leader sets the pace and very high standards for performance. He or she expects others to keep up and do things better and more quickly. The underlying emotional intelligence competencies of this style are conscientiousness, drive to achieve, and initiative.
The Affiliative Style	Creating harmony, keeping followers happy, and building strong relationships are the key activities in this style. Affiliative leaders focus on motivating through positive feedback and developing a sense of belonging among followers. The underlying competencies for this style are empathy, building relationships, and communication.
The Democratic Style	When leaders use this style they work with followers to reach consensus through participation in discussion. They engage followers by inviting them to share their ideas, building trust and facilitating the group conversation until the group reaches a conclusion to which there is shared commitment. The underlying competencies for this style are collaboration, team leadership, and communication.
The Coaching Style	In this style the leader develops individuals for future work and performance. The leader spends time with individuals in one-on-one sessions that are focused on performance improvement over time, delegating for learning and development, and preparing the individual to grow and increase his or her competence. The underlying competencies of this style are developing others, empathy, and self-awareness.
The Visionary Style	This "most strongly positive" style motivates followers to pursue a vision by focusing on how their work contributes to the organization's goals and strategic directions. Visionary leaders engage followers by focusing on their individual performance; clearly communicating performance standards; providing regular, specific feedback targeted to improving performance; and empowering followers to decide how they will act. The underlying emotional intelligence competencies for this style are self-confidence, empathy, and change catalyst.

2. *Hope:* An emotional state accompanied by clear thoughts about what the future can be and how to get there. With hope, we look forward to a future that is exciting and full of possibility. This positive view of the future provides a sense of purpose and direction. It inspires others to have the commitment to pursue the possibilities. Hope includes optimism, excitement, dreams, aspirations, and a consistent focus on the positive.

3. *Compassion:* "Empathy and caring in action."[15] In compassion, leaders are attuned to the emotional states of others. "Compassion is a combination of deep understanding, concern, *and a willingness to act* on that concern for the benefit of oneself and others."[16]

Adaptive Leadership

In *Leadership without Easy Answers*, Ron Heifetz introduced the concept of "viewing leadership in terms of adaptive work." He defined this adaptive work as "the learning required to address the conflicts in the values people hold, or to diminish the gap between the values people stand for and the reality they face." Adaptive leadership is "the practice of mobilizing people to tackle tough challenges and thrive."[17]

This theory of leadership calls for the following practices of effective leadership:

- Embrace the challenges and focus on change that leads to survival and the capacity to thrive.

- Identify what exists in the current situation that will be of use or essential in the future and carry this forward.

- Learn to live in the disequilibrium that accompanies large-scale organizational change. Learn to tolerate the discomfort and help others to do so.

- Be prepared to experiment, take smart risks, and improvise.

- Create a work environment in which diverse perspectives, ideas, and approaches are expected. Value diversity in individuals and include these individuals in the change process.

- Design new work processes and organizational systems.

- Anticipate that change will be disruptive and be prepared to help individuals deal with the losses they experience. Expect followers to adapt and refocus their energy and develop the capacity to meet the new challenges.[18]

Adaptive leadership is based on the premise that people have the capacity to change and adapt to meet the challenges of an increasingly complex world. It calls for leaders to design systems and structures to enable adaptation and provide guidance and support for people as they let go of what no longer serves a purpose and embrace the need to develop new approaches that will lead an organization and its staff to thrive in the future.

CONCLUDING THOUGHTS

The theories of leadership that inform and guide effective practice call for the engagement of followers; building relationships based on trust and authentic behavior; diagnosing the situation and choosing a response that will result in the best approach for the organization, its staff, and its future; and paying continuous attention to the development of self and others. The work of leadership is to listen, learn, empower, respect, inspire, motivate, and engage followers in the accomplishment of meaningful results for the organization. This work is necessarily done in a context of uncertainty, ambiguity, and challenge. Managerial leaders today face unprecedented challenges but have significant opportunities to innovate and make a difference in the lives of others.

—————

An executive team on its own can't find the best solutions. But leadership can generate more leadership deep in the organization.[19]

NOTES

1. "Brainy Quotes: Lao Tzu Quotes." Available at http://www.brainyquote.com/quotes/authors/l/lao_tzu.html (accessed February 1, 2010).

2. John Kotter, "What Leaders Really Do," *Harvard Business Review* 68, no. 11 (May–June 1990): 103–11.

3. Ibid., 103.

4. Warren Bennis and Burt Nanus, *Leaders* (New York: Harper & Row, 1985).

5. Wilfred H. Drath and Charles J. Palus, *Making Common Sense: Leadership as Meaning-making in a Community of Practice* (Greensboro, NC: Center for Creative Leadership, 1994), 4.

6. Warren Bennis, Daniel Goleman, and Patricia Ward Biederman, "Creating a Culture of Candor," in *Transparency: How Leaders Create a Culture of Candor* (San Francisco: Jossey-Bass, 2008).

7. Warren Bennis and Joan Goldsmith, *Learning to Lead: A Workbook on Becoming a Leader*, 2nd ed. (Reading, MA: Addison-Wesley, 1997), xv. (Also available in a third edition [Cambridge, MA: Basic Books, 2003].)

8. James Kouzes and Barry Posner, *The Leadership Challenge*, 3rd ed. (San Francisco: Jossey-Bass, 2002).

9. Lee Bolman and Terrence Deal, *Reframing Organizations: Artistry, Choice, and Leadership*, 2nd ed. (San Francisco: Jossey-Bass, 1997), 296. (Also available in a fourth edition [San Francisco: Jossey-Bass, 2008].)

10. Ibid.

11. Daniel Goleman, Richard Boyatzis, and Annie McKee, *Primal Leadership: Learning to Lead with Emotional Intelligence* (Boston: Harvard Business School Press, 2002).

12. For a discussion of those domains and their application to library and information science, see Patricia A. Kreitz, "Leadership and Emotional Intelligence: A Study of University Library Directors and Their Senior Management Teams," *College & Research Libraries* 70, no. 6 (November 2009): 531–54; and Peter Hernon, Joan Giesecke, and Camila A. Alire, *Academic Librarians as Emotionally Intelligent Leaders* (Westport, CT: Libraries Unlimited, 2007).

13. Goleman, Boyatzis, and McKee, *Primal Leadership,* 20.

14. Richard Boyatzis and Annie McKee, *Resonant Leadership* (Boston: Harvard Business School Press, 2005), 4.

15. Ibid., 178.

16. Ibid., 77.

17. Ron Heifetz, *Leadership without Easy Answers* (Cambridge, MA: Belknap Press of Harvard University Press, 1994), 22.

18.   Ron Heifetz, Alexander Grashow, and Marty Linsky, *The Practice of Adaptive Leadership: Tools and Tactics for Changing Your Organization and the World* (Boston: Harvard Business Press, 2009).

19.   Ron Heifetz, Alexander Grashow, and Marty Linsky, "Leadership in a (Permanent) Crisis," *Harvard Business Review,* 87, no. 7 (July–August 2009), 68.

3

~

THE PERSPECTIVES OF SOME ACADEMIC LIBRARY LEADERS

Peter Hernon

Public higher education is under siege. Immense cuts are occurring because of state budget shortfalls.[1]

For years, there have been numerous discussions about the profound changes that technology brings to libraries. In the economic downturn of 2008 and 2009, discussions shifted to the soft economy and numerous problems such as the fact that every state has a severe budget deficit that will not be eliminated in the near future. Many academic institutions have seen a sharp decline in their endowments, increased pressure on their operating budgets, a rise in tuition and other fees, declining or expanding enrollments, consolidations of academic programs, and in some instances, staff layoffs and/or the inability to replace staff who retire or depart. Librarians, faculty, and staff face greater stress in their work lives, and such a bleak picture, among other things, calls for leadership. Coping with the recession clearly represents a test of institutional and organizational leadership.

Leadership becomes important for those institutions and organizations unwilling to accept the status quo and, perhaps because of the impact of the economic recession, forced to engage in retrenchment of the services they offer. Managerial leadership ensures that the institutional mission and vision continue to guide service roles and responsibilities, and it helps to identify and overcome structural and other problems. Leadership is essential for ensuring a commitment to outcomes assessment at the program and institutional levels (advancing student learning outcomes) and challenging the workforce not to lose sight of its role in making a positive and significant commitment to achieving academic excellence and providing the institution with the services most needed.

There are probably as many different definitions of leadership as there are people who try to define it. As Peter G. Northouse points out, leadership "is much like the words *democracy*, *love*, and *peace*. Although each of us intuitively knows what he or she means by such words, the words can have different meanings for different people. As soon as we try to define leadership, we immediately discover that leadership has many different meanings."[2]

Leadership can be viewed from different levels of the library and the institution in which it resides. At the director's level, that person may be in a position to offer rewards to motivate staff to accomplish the vision. At other levels, especially within teams, there may not be incentives for motivation, but there may be other ways to influence others to accomplish goals. Leadership, in brief, is a process of social influence: it is purposeful and goal directed.

PROBLEM STATEMENT

During the presidential debates of 2008, David Gergen and Andy Zelleke wrote a column in the *Boston Globe* complaining about the poor quality of questions asked of the candidates in the debates.[3] They proposed a set of categories and related questions to ascertain a candidate's vision and leadership. No study has recast those categories for a general examination of leadership. The purpose of this chapter is to adapt that column into a study that probes leadership among academic library directors during the economic downturn. What qualities and categories do they rate as most important?

Instead of focusing on a particular theory or style, this research returns to a general perspective on leadership, and it identifies areas that future researchers can probe in greater detail. The findings should be of value to researchers studying leadership and those working in libraries coping with the impact of the economic recession and wanting to see what some leaders actually say. The downturn provides an excellent opportunity to probe leadership and provide findings that have broad utility. (This chapter also sets up the study of public library leadership reported in the next chapter.)

LITERATURE REVIEW

An examination of comments about the Gergen and Zelleke column in blogs and letters to the editor shows that the categories are regarded as important, and the respondents offer some additional questions that complement those categories. Almost no commentaries, however, suggested the list might be adapted to study nonpresidential leadership. The only exception is a column by Jack Welch and Suzy Welch, in which they identify the most important characteristics for choosing a chief executive officer for a company or a U.S. president. They believe "there is more overlap than not between running a company and running the country."[4]

One of the categories suggested by Gergen and Zelleck, but not by Welch and Welch, is trust. C. Shawn Burke, Dana E. Sims, Elizabeth H. Lazzara, and Eduardo Salas provide a detailed examination of that quality. As they note, "a key component in a leader's ability to be effective within . . . [organizations] is the degree to which subordinates and co-workers trust . . . [leaders]." They regard transformational leadership and shared values as "the building blocks of trust."[5] Their article illustrates that a study might delve more into trust than the present chapter does.

A special issue of *Leadership*, a quarterly journal published by Sage, is devoted to leadership in higher education. That issue provides a context for this study as it examines leadership during a time of economic recession, environmental change, and social fragmentation. The conclusion of this special issue is that higher education is at a crossroads. Institutions of higher education are expected to meet an ever-expanding range of often conflicting goals and priorities. These institutions contribute to the national economy and are accountable for achieving their mission and economic efficiency, the mass education of students, a close engagement with employers, and the delivery of work-based learning for mature students, as well as producing cutting-edge research.[6]

Carla J. Stoffle, Barbara Allen, David Morden, and Krisellen Maloney argue that libraries must advance the fundamental values of the profession "even if it means basic changes in library and librarian activities."[7] They maintain that "each library and librarian needs a values statement and regular values discussions among staff to guide actions before problems arise or decisions have to be made."[8] They point to the statement of principles on a library's home page, which can now be found at http://www. library.arizona.edu/about/organization/principles.html. One such principle is "We honor our commitments by doing what we say."

Finally, in "The Entrepreneurial Imperative," James G. Neal addresses one of the categories of the study presented here. He proposes that libraries reposition themselves to pursue new opportunities by becoming entrepreneurial organizations. New income streams, he argues, can enhance the activities, programs, services, and collections that libraries maintain.[9] The question is, "To what extent will libraries embrace his perspective as they cope with the cutbacks brought about by the economic downturn?" The following study provides some preliminary insights.

PROCEDURES

The author collapsed the fifteen categories that Gergen and Zelleke developed into twelve, eliminating redundancy and clarifying the content. He added the six categories that Welch and Welch proposed. When a set of questions appeared in a category, those questions were rewritten to make them applicable to libraries. Both Maureen Sullivan and Robert E. Dugan commented on the draft survey form and called for additional changes. Due to the length of the form (see the chapter appendix), the author only conducted interviews with eight library directors—seven directors of libraries whose institutions are members of the Association of Research Libraries (ARL) and one director of a prominent university library that is not an ARL member. The author knows these directors and regards them as leaders in the profession. One of the directors gained his position in 2009.

This chapter reviews the full set of categories and the corresponding questions and, based on the findings, reduces the length of the form. It took forty to sixty minutes to administer the entire survey during in-person or telephone interviews. This time frame is too long for widespread use.

FINDINGS

As discussed in chapter 1, a number of directorships within ARL have changed since 2000 and particularly since 2005. Presumably a number of directorships within non-ARL settings have or will change in the next five years. As more than one of the directors interviewed notes, today's leaders are faced with a situation that they have not encountered in years, namely coping with the impact of a severe economic recession on higher education. In the past, leaders have motivated followers in part through rewards such as financial ones. Today, if there are rewards, they have likely changed significantly as there may not be pay raises and travel funds.

Values

For the eight directors the mean score for this category is 6.5 (on a scale ranging from 1 being *very unimportant* to 7 being *very important*). The core qualities associated with this category deal with the working relationships of these directors with others and how they organize their time. Their vision guides what they try to accomplish. The participants highlighted the following core qualities:

- Having integrity
- Being responsible

- Working collaboratively

- Making a commitment to the parent institution and the library's vision

- Delivering high-quality services that meet customer expectations. Service values require a high level of transparency and accountability, and they might consist of librarians being innovative with the services offered, understanding that each customer has different needs and that the label "one size fits all" does not apply, and supporting an empowered staff who shape the future

- Being flexible yet decisive

- Being honest

- Listening to what others say

- Having passion

- Having vision

One director adds three other qualities: (1) intellectual freedom in a digital environment; (2) access ("refers to what the library should be doing, while moving away from tasks to perform. The focus is on philosophy and values. It is our philosophy and set of values that should be uppermost in guiding what we do."); and (3) social responsibility. Another director suggests "bringing the right people to my organization. Recruitment is my number one job: my ability to continue to appoint the right people who want to work in this environment and who understand higher education and the mission of a public institution."

Qualities Possessed

This category affords the directors an opportunity to identify additional core values or qualities related to how people perceive them and their leadership and to motivating people to follow. The mean score is 6.375. Key qualities include

- being able to analyze problems, including an ability to find solutions;

- being approachable and demonstrating openness;

- being strategic and accountable;

- having confidence in one's abilities and projecting that confidence to others;

- being dependable;

- demonstrating effective communication and interpersonal skills;

- showing enthusiasm;

- having relevant experience;[10]

- having good self-awareness of how others perceive you;

- having high expectations of oneself and others;

- being optimistic ("I believe I can make things happen") and being positive (having a sense of accomplishment);

- "taking my work seriously but not me—able to laugh at myself";

- being trustworthy; and

- being willing to accept challenges.

One director emphasizes that he "wants people to speak honestly with him," and

tries to nurture an environment [in which] they feel they can share their thoughts without judgment or a negative reaction—[such] as the appearance of anger. One AUL has pointed out [to me] that at times I appear angry, and we have worked out a code so that if I am creating that impression we can table the issue and take a break. Other traits I find invaluable are collaboration, listening, being flexible yet decisive, and having expectations.

Furthermore, he notes that he is willing to change and learn from experiences, but "this is not always easy."

Complementary Qualities (Senior Management Team)

The mean score for this category is 4.875. For this team, the directors suggest, the qualities include

- effective communication skills,

- working hard,

- an analytical ability,

- a "real sense of rigor in what they do—doing it well,"

- having patience,

- having a good knowledge of librarianship,

- recognition in some aspect of librarianship (where they make an outstanding contribution or others turn to them as recognized experts),

- a willingness to be entrepreneurial,

- a spirit of innovation,

- political engagement in the university and in the library,

- being knowledgeable about accountability and being accountable,

- a willingness to accept challenges and gain new experiences, and

- an ability to set new directions and to offer alternatives (how to attack and solve problems). Problem solving is a key ability.

One director refers to the literature on motivational theory that emphasizes three qualities: authority, affiliation, and achievement. Recently, his senior management team completed a leadership exercise. The goal was to help them better understand themselves and to be sensitive to staff feelings, return authority to the staff, and maintain staff commitment to the organizational mission and goals. During the exercise, the team read some of the work of Daniel Burnham and Frederick Herzberg.

There was great caution in accepting the word "weaknesses." As was pointed out, "weaknesses emerge from inattention to the core mission of the library and the institution." Weakness might also apply to mismanagement, mostly financial mismanagement, or misdirected management, doing something inappropriate for the situation. A director declares, "mistakes do occur, more often than we might think. It is important to learn from them. However, mistakes might cost a person his or her job—forcing a person to a new situation."

One director thinks that weaknesses may in fact comprise areas of lack of interest. For him, the budget is one example. He hired someone to oversee the budget. "You prepare to deal with weaknesses, for instance, by hiring people who complement you—offset your weaknesses or areas of disinterest." Another director prefers not to think in terms of weaknesses, and she believes the word is inappropriate here; she "looks for strengths she does not possess."

In summary, directors may look for fit, flexibility, and a "can-do attitude." They want team members who can work with each other, middle managers, and staff, and to get their direct reports engaged in embracing change and empowering others. It is critical that the senior management team truly function as a team. It needs to avoid tension and friction and to engage in honest debate that moves a discussion forward. This director wants team players who have a cooperative spirit, listen, take risks, and possess a strong work ethic. "You do not want a situation in which some individuals are stronger and more forceful than others—you lose balance and functioning as a team."

Building a Good Senior Management Team

This category is complementary to some of the previous ones, but it achieves a higher mean score (6.875). Obviously directors of complex organizations cannot "do everything alone." One director whose library relies heavily on teams emphasizes that throughout the organization and its teams there is a need for good management and team skills. She wants people to be involved in making decisions and setting priorities for the organization that will result in new services. In her opinion, "everyone should be a situational leader. Leadership is an organizational value. It is something for everyone to develop as team members, but we must recognize that developing effective leadership comprises a 'work in progress'."

Ability to Hire a Good Senior Management Team

This category, which complements or duplicates part of the previous two categories, has a mean score of 6.125. One director changes the category to include both hiring and retaining good workers. He notes that institutions that are better off financially "may cherry-pick [library] faculty," and he is not in a competitive position to counter with financial incentives.

Members of the senior management team guide middle managers and the staff. One director expects the senior management team to nurture middle managers. He wants them to accept his vision and the staff to be empowered to follow through on that vision and the organization's goals. He does not want micro-managers who are not interested in leading others.

Another director does not view this category solely within the context of the senior management team. She conducts national searches for all library positions as she seeks "the very best people." She tries to attract junior librarians and wants to see them rise to membership on the senior management team, believing those already in the organization best understand the values she prizes. She may have to rely on her senior management team to identify capable junior librarians, but she assists in their growth. In brief, "we try to get the best out of junior level staff." An exception might be a technical position for which nobody in the library already has the skill set. In such an instance a national search might be conducted.

Employing a Diverse Workforce

The mean score for this category is 5.5. Some of the directors interviewed have a long history of supporting diversity. As they comment, it is critical to develop effective mentoring programs at three levels (the library, the institution, and the profession) and to support the recruitment, retention, and advancement of capable people, regardless of race, ethnicity, sexual orientation, and so forth. Furthermore, as one director comments, "an organization is stronger the more diverse its workforce." Nonetheless, as several directors note, organizations may be "strong" without diversity. The distinction is "one of degrees—stronger vs. strong. It is important to foster tolerance."

The ability to employ a diverse workforce, it was mentioned, varies from institution to institution, and the ability to attract such a workforce favors libraries in urban settings. People, this director notes, want a social life and a community that includes others in their race or ethnic group. African Americans, he mentions, tend to want to work in public libraries in urban settings. Native Americans, on the other hand, do not like to be far away from their families. Despite such issues he is committed to diversity and advancing it within the profession. A number of staff members live in a nearby city and commute back and forth. Without this situation, he suspects the organization would have far less diversity.

One of the directors asks, "How can we have a commitment to intellectual freedom and access, if we do not advance it in what we do and how our users see us?" Another director notes that "diversity is more than just providing a politically correct answer." Overall, this survey category is important, but it "plays differently" in different geographical areas and "is hard to realize." This director stresses that some search committees filling management and other positions might make a recommendation to a dean. The dean may not feel bound by the recommendation and might opt to hire someone else. However, this interviewee does not favor this approach: he prefers to follow the recommendation of a search committee. As he notes, it is "very important" to adhere to the law and ensure an open process.

Judgment

As reflected in the mean score of 6.625, judgment is a true test of leadership. Judgment is more than having relevant experiences and good intuition. One needs to factor in evidence-based decision making. As one director emphasizes,

we need to make decisions based on good data. We must connect evidence-based decision-making with our guiding values, analyze the situation, and make a good decision. We need to give people experiences to learn about making good decision. But those decisions must be connected to our guiding principles such as a focus on customers and what they need. It is important to be flexible and adaptable given the changing environment in which libraries function.

Another director points out that judgment "does not define the strength of a leader on a day-to-day basis." It involves an opportunity or a response to a crisis. There may not be time to reflect and consult a range of people. For instance, there may be a fire or other disaster to cope with, or a donor is willing to give a substantial amount of money. Judgment relates to both management and leadership, and it may require speedy action.

Another type of crisis, one director suggests, relates to dealing with unacceptable student behavior and demands. The administration, he finds, may not always favor the approach he takes and may go against his decisions. "It is important that the leader understand power and where it resides in the institution." He notes that "you expect leaders to have power and authority, but power may not reside with them."

Finally, one director points out that one university had to cut $4 million from its budget and did so by cutting in half the library's material budget. He concludes that this is a type of judgment in which the library is merely informed of the decision. The director, in turn, informs the staff and carries out that decision, unless the individual feels so strongly about it that he or she resigns. In other instances the library director may have input into the decision. "The pain is shared, and the library copes with the decision."

Willingness to Learn

This category produces a mean score of 6.625. Called "people from whom I have learned" in the pretest, the title was changed in recognition that learning occurs in a variety of ways (e.g., reading, listening to others, and observing people, including some for whom they never worked), and the focus is on one's willingness to learn and embrace lifelong learning. "The goal," as one director explains, "is to see what to do and conversely what not to do." She draws a distinction between positive and negative (ineffective) leadership. Additional qualities mentioned in participant responses are a sense of humor and political engagement. "Such engagement is a fundamental aspect of leadership."

Coalition Building/Advocacy

The mean score here is 6.375. This category relates to values, the library's role, and campuswide initiatives that are often interdisciplinary in nature (e.g., the creation of a learning commons). However, a larger perspective recognizes that coalition building applies to the profession and national information policies (e.g., copyright and scholarly communication). "In the past research libraries," one director points out, "built great collections. Now, we only do so with special collections. We engage in activities that transcend individual libraries and are good for the profession." Her example is SPARC (http://www.arl.org/sparc/).

One director sums up his approach to coalition building this way: "Instead of telling others what to do, we need to build an understanding of what the organization is trying to accomplish, be supportive, address how to get people to embrace new directions, and go beyond the sense of we are doing this because the director said to do it."

Advocacy consists of the following parts: identify the partners with whom you want and need to work; find common needs; agree on a common agenda; and be an advocate as well as letting the library be a subject of advocacy (for library collections, services, role within the institution, and physical space). Libraries, it was noted, "help people who may not always end up helping us. For instance, in a budget battle relating to the allocation of community resources, there may not be support for the library."

Decision-Making Style

The mean score for this category is 5.375. Only one director rates the category "7." He wants others to have a chance to be involved in shaping the decision (e.g., restructuring the organization in times of severe budget cuts). He sees trust as a core value and as a central component of decision-making style. There is a need to maintain trust by being transparent. "I tell what I am able to say. If I do not I might lose the trust of others. You cannot regain trust. . . . [I]t is better to involve people in shaping decisions." He sees the role of directors as gathering input (opinions, suggestions, and so forth), seeking help in setting priorities, and being responsible for making a decision.

Gergen and Zelleke, who adopt a for-profit perspective, equate decision-making style with decisiveness.[11] Because there are many decision-making styles, it is critical that "people know your style and what they can expect from you. They want consistency in application so they can see how to 'read you' and how to proceed." One director, who is newly hired, stresses the importance of "getting the right people in the room who can make the decisions." He is learning how decisions are made in the university, and when he has something to say he tries to influence a decision. Adopting a boxing metaphor, he is "willing to step in the ring, take some swings, get hit, and keep moving forward." He sees timing, fit, and readiness of the organization as critical to achieving change in the institution and organization, and to his ability to influence the decisions and change.

The directors view a good management team as working together to carry out its responsibilities and, in that context, some maintain that the director may be unimportant to decision-making style. Further, if a director is indecisive in identifying and accepting responsibility for a service issue, that person will not accept ownership of the problem, and another department might step in and claim ownership. The domain of that other department expands, and that department might receive funds to resolve the problem.

Increasing Participation

The mean score for this category is 6.125. The focus here is on moving the organization forward and getting staff engaged and responsible for identifying and solving problems. As a leader, one director wants to put in place the tools to accomplish participation and carry out an action plan. Another director believes this category involves some qualification. She sees increased participation as critical to management and making for an effective organization, and as linked to shared leadership.

Leading Change

The mean score for this category is 6.75. The directors comment on the changes occurring within higher education and their university, the weak economy, and the need to meet new challenges and move the organization forward. One director points out that, over the years, he has implemented numerous pilot studies (e.g., the use of Kindle 2, wireless network, and laptop loans) to meet changing student expectations. Furthermore, "if you look at an institution, it is the library that has dealt with budget cuts; academic units have not. Libraries are used to change, as is evident from their shifting from print to digital collections and resources."

Innovative Thinking/Innovation

The mean score is 5.75. Innovation is not about developing great ideas (that is creativity). Instead, it is about implementing organizational processes that allow the library to do things better, cheaper, and faster; embrace new priorities as the library fulfills existing ones; and adapt to environmental shifts.

The eight directors comment on this category thus:

- "You cannot be a leader without innovation and cannot be innovative without being a leader. Innovative leadership leads to positive change." The director places leadership and change as higher than innovation—but regards all three as important.

- Innovative thinking/innovation "is an organizational value, one that the entire organization must embrace."

- One director sees this category as occurring more at the institutional level and less at her level. Nonetheless, she expects the organization to think about the category and to develop strategies to achieve it.

- "It is more than engaging in innovative thinking. It is also critical to get others on board and make things happen. Such thinking must be transmitted throughout the library and ensure that the organization benefits from what decisions are made."

- This category "is important today due to technological changes and budget cuts. These challenges require greater innovation. Good solid performance means that you fall behind. Innovation is critical."

- This director sees innovation as essential so people do not think of what they do as "work." He wants them empowered, looking forward, trying new things. By "enjoying themselves," they "buy-in to the vision."

- "Building innovation into the organization is important. We can have innovative people, but the key is to implement that innovation and involve others. . . . [Innovation] must be associated with action and execution—the goal is to make a difference on campus."

- The category is "especially important in times of a recession and its impact on libraries. For public institutions there is a concern about the cost of tuition, and the fact that more students may go to community college. As well, the state legislature may reduce its financial support to public institutions. Innovation thus becomes very important."

Building the Confidence of Others

The mean score here is 6.375. Building confidence is linked to trust: "What you do is important; not just what you say." "Organizational success," another director points out, "means that people invest in you, follow you—take their chances with you. Related qualities include having the good of the organization at heart and commitment." It is also important to develop the abilities of others as "you try to ensure that the organization moves forward." A director finds that delegating responsibility helps to develop confidence. Furthermore, he talks with those who cause problems or make matters worse. They understand that if he calls them into his office, they will not be fired and that he is trying to solve a problem. The goal is to maintain people as productive members of the team. Another director sees this category as the responsibility of others, namely assistant and associate university librarians.

Trust

The mean score here is 6.625. Trust, a core value, complements confidence and, as one director points out, has three components: (1) "trust those with whom you work," (2) "instill the trust of the workforce in you" ("others believe what you say and see that you are committed to getting something accomplished"), and (3) "gain user trust of the library." Critical to achieving the third component is the need to "fix what does not work as you are trying to guard against user dissatisfaction." A different director adds, "there is a need to maintain trust by being transparent. I tell others what I am able to say. If I do not I might lose their trust. You cannot regain trust. As a result, it is best to involve people in shaping decisions." Another director notes that "trust is hard to build. People will not automatically trust you, so I show trust in them. I do what I say I'll do. Consistency is critical to achieving trust. And be sure to act out your values."

Vision

The mean score here is 6.625. One difference between leadership and management is that managers do not need to develop a vision to guide the organization. Vision, which is a sense of where the organization is heading, relates to change and innovation. The pace of change in academic libraries requires a constant revisiting of the vision with the focus on follow-through. Having a vision is insufficient; that vision must be combined with action, follow-through.

One participant points out that the vision need not be original to the director; "you can pick up other peoples' vision. Nobody has the only vision about how to move [an organization] forward. It is important to be exposed to different visions and to listen to others, as you shape your vision of the organization."

Resilience (Overcoming Setbacks)

The mean score for this category is 5.75. One director sees this category as more appropriate in a corporate setting. Still, he thinks that "we can anticipate the budget next year will be cut, and so we must plan." He distinguishes between organizational and personal (e.g., did not get a job offer or got a divorce) setbacks. Because the staff observe how the director reacts to organizational setbacks, he believes, such setbacks force a director to demonstrate leadership. Clearly, the director must be flexible and adaptable—"develop alternative plans but keep to your core values."

Another director likens this category to a game where the intention is to win: "We may win some innings and lose others. We cannot get discouraged but must focus on the entire game and the final outcome. We should not get upset by setbacks within an inning. We should avoid being jaded, angry, and distrustful of others. Instead, we must keep trying throughout the game."

With the cycle of budget cuts that some libraries face, another director adds, "Do not stop offering services; however, you may cut back some of them. Also do not take cutbacks out on users." The measures of success might be viewed in terms of any return of funding or recognition for the continued provision of service with fewer resources.

Finally, a director points out that when she came to this university, the staff viewed themselves as "victims," and the faculty tried to be supportive by saying the library is doing the best it can. She regarded this is as "a bad situation," because expectations were too low. Today, as "we cope with horrendous budget cuts, we try to focus on key areas, move our resources around, and view our decisions in terms of three-five years hence." She calls attention to recent accomplishments in introducing a course for all freshmen, making it easy for faculty to add library pages and guides to course syllabi that they place in course management software, and making it easy for students to request reference assistance or get access to the online public access catalog (OPAC) from the course management software. She reiterates that "we do not view the library as a victim during the recession. We exercise control over what we have and help the institution achieve its goals."

Anticipate (Seeing around the Corners)

The mean score here is 6.125. This category, which addresses vision and leading change, also looks at judgment, especially during a time of crisis. It may be impossible to anticipate all changes (e.g., a flood in the basement or a new administration). Some directors note that, with the cycle of budget cuts, this category is "a luxury" and is difficult to achieve. They try to anticipate and deal with problems, but expect further budget cuts. It is critical, as one director emphasizes, that libraries engage in assessment and evidence-based decision making. "These times demand that we have solid data that we can share with others and use to support and justify our decisions."

Another director adds that "successful leaders anticipate problems and try to avoid being caught by surprise. It is better to watch, listen, anticipate, and know the environment: the players, how they function, and how the environment reacts to them. Keep your eye on the goal not the puck."

Complementary qualities for this category are being observant, knowing what is occurring in the university, and reading extensively about assorted issues and how they might impact the institution. The participants mentioned two examples in which they try to anticipate events: (1) publishing mergers and how they might affect who offers what databases, and (2) the price of gas, which affects package delivery services (e.g., UPS), and related costs.

Execution

This category has a mean score of 6.25. One director rates this category low ("3"), whereas the others give it a "6" or "7". According to the director who assigned the low number, "I do not execute; others do. I bring together everyone involved in making the change. I see leaders as cheerleaders: build morale and support, and keep the organization moving forward." On the other hand, his role as an institutional leader differs when he is involved in issues such as fund-raising.

Other directors agree that execution involves the senior management team and others (getting everyone committed to what the organization considers to be important), and they link the category to vision, trust, and confidence, where others know "you'll do what you say—not promise what you cannot deliver." Execution complements vision but focuses on action—making things happen, setting priorities, creating a general understanding of what needs to be done, and following up on the action plan.

Other

When asked for any additional categories, the following were mentioned by the second interviewee: being entrepreneurial, being inspirational, and being an effective communicator. (The chapter author went back to the first director and asked him and all subsequent participants to rate these three categories.)

Being Entrepreneurial. The mean score here is 6.25. This category deals with leveraging assets and building resources to accomplish the vision. Leaders must anticipate problems and galvanize the necessary support. Doing so "requires an ability to think outside the box." One director reframes the issues thus: "Leaders are not necessarily entrepreneurial themselves, but they should set the tone for it." She sees leading change as more important and being entrepreneurial is one way to do this.[12] Two directors urge caution because being entrepreneurial depends on the institutional setting, and there is only so much that a library can do.

When the directors offered an example of being entrepreneurial, they tended to mention the creation of a café, which, in one instance, involves a partnership or resource sharing with an off-campus vendor. There was campus opposition, this director notes, but the ability of the library to generate revenue was the key factor in gaining a victory. Another example is the library's engagement in rights and reproduction for resources in "our digitized collections—we charge a rights fee."

Being Inspirational. The mean score here is 6.125. The participants sees it as important to inspire people to carry out the vision and to believe that the staff can make a difference. Despite the recession, institutions still want to maintain excellence. However, two directors caution that inspiration is only one approach to leadership or that it is less important in libraries than in the private sector. They may not see inspiration as one of the qualities they possess. Inspiration may come from other members of the senior management team.

One director believes the category relates to execution. She offers a reminder: "The campus must be inspired by what the library can become." In such a situation, there is a shift from people as leaders to showing what the library can become. The goal therefore is to focus on the institutional mission, and how the library can play a critical role. Furthermore,

[s]enior leaders must provide something for people to aspire to achieve—see what they do as meaningful. In the past research libraries built great collections, and . . . [the librarians] knew what the vision and goals were. Today, we try to inspire 20-30% of the professional staff. We realize we cannot inspire everyone.

Being an Effective Communicator. The mean score here is 6.75. The category goes back to execution and action, or follow-through on the vision. One director renames the category "effective strategist." This term "looks at how you support your arguments. You argue for a position and try to win the argument." Another director sees this category as a core value but issued a reminder: "I can always hire a speech-writer." She can sell her message in different ways.

Related qualities include listening and patience. "For staff to understand what you value, you may have to tell them more than once. Understanding is an ongoing process. Messages are not always absorbed immediately; it is necessary for others to pick them up." Explained another way, "when you communicate, it does not mean that people have been communicated to. They may fail to understand something and therefore repetition of the message is needed."

Finally, communication "begins with me but moves down the organization." Middle managers, this director believes, "hold the key to the health of the organization. You cannot take them for granted." He wants good communication up and down the organization as well as at vertical levels of management.

Definition of Leadership

The final question asks for a definition of leadership. The eight definitions are as follows:

1. "Leadership is the ability to set a vision, find people who believe in it, and shepherd the vision [to fruition]."

2. "Vision plus action." Action refers to follow-through.[13]

3. "Create an environment to move the organization forward and inspire others to meet the vision you set."

4. "Having followers."

5. "Keeping everyone moving in the same direction."

6. Lacking a "nice and neat definition," this director prefers to think of leadership as something that cannot be readily reduced to "a box" and simple definition. He views leadership as about empowerment—empowering the staff and letting them influence decisions. As director, he makes the decisions but wants to encourage a climate that embraces change; and he realizes that change is an unending process. He wants middle managers and staff to realize that they are involved in the change process and can help to shape it. He expects everyone to have time to reflect on the future and not just "do work." The hardest part, he finds as a new director, is getting the members of the senior management team to buy into the process. He sees them as tending to be micro-managers and not providing a suitable climate for change. He is working on this and trying to set a positive example.

7. "The ability to get people to perform, provide products that are at a higher level and are essential for the success of the whole institution."

8. "The ability to craft a vision for the organization and recruit and train the right group of people to help you carry through on that vision."

DISCUSSION

Altogether, the study probed twenty-two categories, and the mean scores for the categories range from 6.875 to 4.875 (see table 3.1). Coverage of the senior management team appears in different categories, in particular "building a senior management team" and "ability to hire good senior management team." The following categories produce a mean score of less than 6: (1) "innovative thinking/innovation," (2) "resilience (overcoming setbacks)," (3) "employing a diverse workforce," (4) "decision-making style," and (5) "complementary qualities."

Table 3.1
The Categories (Mean Scores Ranked in Descending Order)

Category	Mean
Building a senior management team	6.875
Leading change	6.75
Other: Effective communicator	6.625
Trust	6.625
Vision	6.625
Judgment	6.625
Willingness to learn	6.625
Values	6.5
Coalition building/advocacy	6.375
Qualities (attributes/competencies)	6.375
Building the confidence of others	6.375
Execute	6.25
Other: Being entrepreneurial	6.25
Increased participation	6.125
Ability to hire good senior management team	6.125
Anticipate (see around the corners)	6.125
Other: Inspirational	6.125
Innovative thinking/innovation	5.75
Resilience (overcoming setbacks)	5.75
Employing a diverse workforce	5.5
Decision-making style	5.375
Complementary qualities	4.875

Eleven categories have ties in their ratings. There were four ties in the ratings at a mean of 6.625 and 6.125, and three at 6.375. It is also important to note that additional qualities emerge in the discussion of individual categories. The directors, for instance, note the importance of listening to what others say. Clearly, effective leaders depend on good people on the senior management team but also, as some directors note, throughout the organization. They point to middle managers and the critical role they play in calling attention to the vision and ensuring follow-through on that vision.

Motivation

Traditionally, directors have relied on a reward structure to motivate staff. In the present fiscal environment, however, motivation may become a challenge. The director of one library where librarians have faculty status notes that there are formal promotion and tenure requirements, which do not change during a recession. The greatest challenge, he finds, is maintaining the quality of work life. There is no financial support for professional development, travel, conference attendance, and so on.

A New Element

It is interesting to note that one director distinguishes between financial management and financial leadership. He defines the latter as "creating and sustaining a culture of improvement to support financial management." That culture influences internal program development and service results, and, he believes, is

shaped by these six values:

1. accountability,
2. performance towards excellence,
3. communication,
4. partnerships,
5. stewardship, [and]
6. integrity.

Another director, when informed about the figures in chapter 1, expects the directorships of Ohio State University, the University of Michigan, and Penn State University to become open in a few years. He suspects that such positions will fall to those already in a directorship—probably to someone wanting to move up in the ranks of ARL members.

The Definitions of Leadership

There are differences among the definitions the participants gave, and the author did not return to the participants seeking to merge their comments into one, all-inclusive definition. Although not everyone mentions vision, it is explicit in some of the definitions. Vision is implicit when people point to a clear direction. Only two directors specifically use the word "followers." Presumably, if people are willing to follow, there is buy-in to the vision. Another two directors specifically refer to the mission statement, and there was mention of an environment that supports or promotes change.

Revisioning

One director mentioned revisioning, which presumably requires an adjustment of the original vision to an environment of retrenchment—"a fiscal environment in which there is shared pain"—and the major changes that the institution is making. Vision guides the organization or institution for the long term, and it represents something to strive to achieve. Vision requires leadership to set and follow-through to achieve.

Engaging in revisioning is really engaging in re-missioning. Eliminating academic programs is not about vision; it is a strategic issue. Downsizing and retrenchment are strategic. Re-missioning is a managerial activity. The redeployment of the budget alters the mission but probably not the vision. If the vision, for instance, is to become one of the top twenty academic research institutions, that vision is not likely to change (except maybe to being in the top thirty) based on the economics of today. The goal of providing 100 percent financial aid or offering 1,000 academic programs, however, may change. Layoffs are a result of eliminating a program or downsizing services. That is mission, not vision.

In summary, if a library engages in revisioning, most likely the organization is reexamining its mission, and paying greater attention to execution or action, namely what strategy to use to best achieve the mission. The best situation is one in which the institution engages in re-missioning and the library, a part of it, or another academic unit on campus does not go through this process alone. Unless the institution is fully engaged in change and making sacrifices, library staff may resist change and risk losing trust in the director.

A Brief Research Agenda

Although the data collection instrument is lengthy, it does provide insights into leadership. However, a number of directors may be unwilling to devote the amount of time necessary to answering each question and elaborating on their responses. Ideally, it would be nice to conduct the interviews on-site and examine relevant documentation. Even if the instrument is used, the redundancy among some of the categories should be removed.

For anyone probing leadership, there is an ongoing need to determine who is a leader and to probe leadership during the economic downturn. Libraries suffering the most from budgetary cuts might be the subject of research and how leaders, assuming leadership exists, motivate and influence others. That research might also examine stress in the workplace, self-renewal (resonant leadership), and the ability of libraries and institutions where the workforce is unionized to cope with leadership challenges. In addition, it is important to consider the use of case study research designs (withholding the names of the libraries and institutions probed).

CONCLUDING THOUGHTS

The next chapter continues the examination of leadership, but the setting moves to public libraries and the revised data collection instrument (see figure 3.1). That instrument includes the major categories reflected in this chapter. There is less interest in drawing comparisons among the directors in different settings than in refining the data collection instrument and studying leadership without making a major imposition on participants. This is important for any widely used instrument.

1. Critical Values (for Library Directors)

	↓Very Unimportant				Very Important↓		
Be approachable	1	2	3	4	5	6	7
Be entrepreneurial (includes being innovative)	1	2	3	4	5	6	7
Be inspirational	1	2	3	4	5	6	7
Be positive	1	2	3	4	5	6	7
Build the confidence of others	1	2	3	4	5	6	7
Be collaborative • Within the library • Outside the library	1	2	3	4	5	6	7
Effective communication skills and strategy	1	2	3	4	5	6	7
Effective interpersonal skills	1	2	3	4	5	6	7
Good (and accurate) self-awareness of how others perceive you	1	2	3	4	5	6	7
Integrity	1	2	3	4	5	6	7
Openness	1	2	3	4	5	6	7
Passion for work and change	1	2	3	4	5	6	7
Political engagement	1	2	3	4	5	6	7
Trust	1	2	3	4	5	6	7
Vision	1	2	3	4	5	6	7
Other (please specify)	1	2	3	4	5	6	7
_____	1	2	3	4	5	6	7
_____							

2. What are the critical values—management or leadership—for each level of management in the library?

Figure 3.1 The Revised Data Collection Instrument

From *Shaping the Future: Advancing the Understanding of Leadership* by Peter Hernon, Editor. Santa Barbara, CA: Libraries Unlimited. Copyright © 2010.

3. Topics for Discussion

Coalition building/advocacy	
Innovative thinking/innovation —implementing organizational processes that allow the library to do things better, cheaper, and faster; to be capable of embracing new priorities as the library fulfills existing ones; and to adapt to environmental shifts	
Judgment	
Involving others in carrying out the vision • Executing the vision • Motivating others	

4. How do you complete the sentence "Leadership is _____

_____

_____

_____

_____ ""?

5. Any concluding comments?

Figure 3.1 The Revised Data Collection Instrument (*Cont.*)

[B]ecause of the challenges of increasing revenue
[for institutions of higher education] there is going
to be a lot of budget cutting in the next few years.[14]

NOTES

1. Carla J. Stoffle, Barbara Allen, David Morden, and Krisellen Maloney, "Continuing to Build the Future: Academic Libraries and Their Challenges," *portal: Libraries and the Academy* 3, no. 3 (2003): 364.

2. Peter G. Northouse, *Leadership: Theory and Practice* (Thousand Oaks, CA: Sage, 2007), 2.

3. David Gergen and Andy Zelleke, "A Question of Presidential Leadership," *Boston Globe,* June 12, 2008, A13.

4. Jack Welch and Suzy Welch, "Chief Executive Officer-in-Chief: The President Needs the Same Skills as a Top-notch CEO—Only Sharper," *Business Week,* February 4, 2008, 88.

5. C. Shawn Burke, Dana E. Sims, Elizabeth H. Lazzara, and Eduardo Salas, "Trust in Leadership: A Multi-level Review and Integration," *The Leadership Quarterly* 18 (2007): 606.

6. See Special Issue, "Leadership in Higher Education: Facts, Fiction, and Futures," *Leadership* 5, no. 3 (August 2009): 291–394.

7. Stoffle, Allen, Morden, and Maloney, "Continuing to Build the Future," 363.

8. Ibid., 374.

9. James G. Neal, "The Entrepreneurial Imperative: Advancing from Incremental to Radical Change in the Academic Library," *portal: Libraries and the Academy* 1, no. 1 (2001): 1–13.

10. This quality is a key attribute for a library director guiding the library through the challenges of today. Most likely, one director maintains, such a person should have worked in public services at some point in his or her career.

11. Gergen and Zelleke, "A Question of Presidential Leadership."

12. Another director agrees and views being entrepreneurial as connected to innovation. He sees his role as guiding and enabling rather than as directing and managing. Thus, he defines the term as giving people the freedom to question what they are doing and to find better ways to do this and achieve the vision he sets.

13. Follow-through does involve management and the following phases: implementation, monitoring to ensure effective results, and adjustment.

14. Jeff Doyle, "The Impact of the Economic Recession on Higher Education and Approaches to Budget Cuts for Residence Life Departments." Available at http://www.reslife.net/html/hottopic_0409b.html (accessed October 27, 2009).

SURVEY INSTRUMENT

Values

On scale of 1 (very unimportant) to 7 (very important), how important: _____

- What are three of your core values?
- How do they shape how you lead?

Qualities Possessed (Attributes, Competencies, and Skills)

On scale of 1 (very unimportant) to 7 (very important), how important: _____

- What attributes and competencies have served you well in your position?
- What do you look for in direct reports?

Complementary Qualities (Senior Management Team)

On scale of 1 (very unimportant) to 7 (very important), how important: _____

- The focus is on weaknesses and offsetting any that the director has.

Building a Good Senior Management Team

On scale of 1 (very unimportant) to 7 (very important), how important: _____

Ability to Hire a Good Senior Management Team

On scale of 1 (very unimportant) to 7 (very important), how important: _____

Employing a Diverse Workforce

On scale of 1 (very unimportant) to 7 (very important), how important: _____

- Is it important to have a racially diverse workforce?
- If yes, how do you attract/develop individuals?
- What experiences have helped you understand the mindset and values of those with whom you work?

Judgment

On scale of 1 (very unimportant) to 7 (very important), how important: _____

- Tell me about a time when your judgment was tested in a crisis.

Willingness to Learn

On scale of 1 (very unimportant) to 7 (very important), how important: _____

- People
- Other ways

Coalition Building/Advocacy

On scale of 1 (very unimportant) to 7 (very important), how important: _____

- Can you share an example of when you were a catalyst who brought groups with polarized opinions together so that all voices were at the table?
- How do you apply advocacy to the library and its services?

Decision-Making Style

On scale of 1 (very unimportant) to 7 (very important), how important: _____

- A director's role requires decisiveness. Please share an example of your ability and willingness to be decisive.

Increasing Participation

On scale of 1 (very unimportant) to 7 (very important), how important: _____

Leading Change

On scale of 1 (very unimportant) to 7 (very important), how important: _____

- Can you give me an example of how you have overcome resistance to bring about needed change?

Innovative Thinking/Innovation*

On scale of 1 (very unimportant) to 7 (very important), how important: _____

- How do you encourage innovation?

Building the Confidence of Others

On scale of 1 (very unimportant) to 7 (very important), how important: _____

- How have you raised the confidence of senior staff and others in the library?

Trust

On scale of 1 (very unimportant) to 7 (very important), how important: _____

- Is trust a core value?
- How is trust gained? How does a leader manifest and communicate it?

Vision

On scale of 1 (very unimportant) to 7 (very important), how important: _____

Resilience

On scale of 1 (very unimportant) to 7 (very important), how important: _____

- When setbacks occur, how do you bounce back?
- What are the measures of success: How do you know you have bounced back?

Seeing around the Corners

On scale of 1 (very unimportant) to 7 (very important), how important: _____

- How do you anticipate potential problems?

---

*Innovation is not about developing great ideas (that is creativity). Instead, innovation is about implementing organizational processes that allow the library to do things better, cheaper, and faster; to be capable of embracing new priorities as the library fulfills existing ones; and to adapt to environmental shifts.

Execution

On scale of 1 (very unimportant) to 7 (very important), how important: _____

- Do you make promises?
- If yes, is it always possible to keep them? [What happens?]
- How do you ensure that priorities are accomplished—mission and goals met?

Other

_____ 1 2 3 4 5 6 7 Probe

_____ 1 2 3 4 5 6 7 Probe

_____ 1 2 3 4 5 6 7 Probe

_____ 1 2 3 4 5 6 7 Probe

Final Question

How do you complete the sentence "Leadership is _____

_____

_____

_____

_____

_____ "?

4

~

LEADERSHIP IN PUBLIC LIBRARIES

Peter Hernon

The recession represents an opportunity to create change in the organization such as by developing and implementing new models of service.[1]

News stories about public libraries during the economic recession show a sharp increase in their use for, among other things, job-seeking assistance, Internet access, entertainment, enjoyment, and borrowing reading material (not having to purchase it from a bookstore). The challenge is to deliver a great customer experience, one that exceeds customer expectations, when budgets are severely curtailed. This challenge is not easily resolved, as one librarian writing on a blog notes:

I'm a librarian for a rural library system in Ohio and we just received word today that the Governor's proposed budget will cut funding for Ohio public libraries by 50%. Many libraries will be forced to cut services and hours, or to close outright.[2]

At the same time, the recession offers an opportunity to gain new customers and ones who have not used library services in a long time. Leadership becomes critical in keeping the organization focused on achieving its service vision, while making a positive impact on library service roles, now referred to as service responses. "In simple terms," June Garcia and Sandra Nelson note that

a service response is what a library does for or offers to the public in an effort to meet a set of well-defined community needs. Roles are broadly defined categories of service; they describe what the library does in a very general way. Service responses, on the other hand, are very distinct ways that libraries serve the public. They represent the gathering and deployment of specific critical resources to produce a specific public benefit or result.[3]

The goal, in effect, is "to help library planners see the many possibilities that exist for matching their services to the unique needs of their communities."[4] A related goal should be to demonstrate the impact of the library on its community and stakeholders: How does the use of library services and resources improve the lives and abilities of those in the community?

Leadership applies to carrying through on priorities, responding to and shaping customer expectations, accountability, and perhaps even saving some public libraries from closing. Accountability, an important responsibility of leaders, is an often discussed expectation of stakeholders that want to know about the costs, the relationship between those costs and their investment, and the effectiveness of the organization. Accountability requires transparency and the ready availability of meaningful information presented in an understandable manner. One goal is to demonstrate the value of the library to stakeholders and to have them acknowledge that value.

One instance of accountability involves the Seattle Public Library. Its Web site states the following information:

On Sept. 25, 2009, Mayor Greg Nickels announced his proposed 2010 budget, which included cuts to address a projected $72 million revenue shortfall in the city's 2009–2010 biennial budget.

The Library was asked to identify approximately 5 percent in cuts—about $2.6 million. The Library's proposed cuts include:

- Reduce branch operating hours (see below): $1.2 million
- Sustain 2009 management and administrative reductions: $562,000
- Close the Library systemwide for one week (furlough): $649,000
- Extend staff computer replacement cycle from 4 years to 5 years: $23,000
- Absorb citywide inflation, health care and rate adjustments that don't affect services or staff: $200,000 above the Library Board's proposed cut.

That page also presents opportunities for public comment on the mayor's budget by attending city council meetings (the dates are given).[5]

PROBLEM STATEMENT

There are numerous stories of cities and towns facing budget shortages and instituting hiring freezes. As chapter 1 indicates, the trend of turnover at the director level in academic research libraries is likely to continue in the foreseeable future, and a number of public libraries probably face the prospect of similar turnover. Once the economy starts to improve, retirement from directorships may accelerate and other positions in senior management may open, as individuals in these roles may have the means to retire and the desire to no longer have to cope with stress and service reductions. This does not necessarily mean that the libraries will replace everyone who retires or departs or that the workforce will not shrink. One implication is that the challenges faced by public libraries require new leaders who can create a vision that inspires a smaller workforce. The purpose of this chapter is to probe leadership in public libraries at a time of significant declines in financial support from states and municipalities as well as other challenges. As in the previous chapter, coverage here does not examine any particular leadership theory or style. The insights gained from the research should be useful in associating leadership with more than a set of qualities and abilities.

LITERATURE REVIEW

Much of the literature on leadership in public libraries is opinion pieces and announcements (e.g., about leadership institutes) rather than research. In the United States, there are at least five exceptions. *The Next Library Leadership*, which highlights key leadership qualities that directors need to possess,[6] and a study of leadership diversity showing that a large number of public libraries with membership in the Urban Libraries Council have implemented diversity-related activities and programs. Still, retention presents a problem.[7] Jennifer Arns focused on the leadership qualities and behaviors of public library trustees. She offers suggestions for appointing future trustees.[8] Turning to dissertations, in 1989 Alice Gertzog studied emergent leadership, in which individuals acquire their leadership through other people in the library who accept that individual's beliefs, actions, and behavior.[9] She makes comparisons across library types. Mary Jo Venetis examines patterns of remote leadership in academic and public libraries. Remote leadership refers to the use of face-to-face interactions and interactive technology to guide employees located elsewhere.[10]

In a cross-national study in which thirty public library directors from Ireland, Britain, and part of the United States participated in in-person interviews, John Mullins concludes:

Many responses from the senior librarians indicated an apparent ignorance of any distinction between leadership and management. Eighty per cent of respondents tended to confuse leadership with headship, management, administration, or bureaucracy, or a combination of these. The findings argue that classic leadership is a relatively scarce quality in public libraries in Britain, Ireland, and America. Many public library leaders, instead, focus on management/administration.[11]

Furthermore, "public libraries require effective leadership in terms of developing and promoting vision, identifying priorities, and providing information services needed by a changing, diverse, and increasingly technologically-driven population."[12] Adding to the international focus on leadership in public libraries, Niels Ole Pors has discussed leadership, including its history in Danish public libraries.[13]

PROCEDURES

The author conducted six interviews with well-known and respected public library directors, some of whom are past presidents of the Public Library Association. These directors, from different parts of the United States, were interviewed either in person or by telephone. Given the impact of the recession and the budgetary cutbacks it has forced on public libraries, the author added "transparency" as one of the topics to the Leadership Survey (see figure 3.1, pp. 51–52).

FINDINGS

Key Qualities

Table 4.1 (p. 60) reports the means for the fourteen qualities probed. In addition, the respondents suggested another ten qualities. Because the author did not go back to query each director about the importance of the new qualities, no mean score for them was calculated. All of the directors, except one, gave trust a score of 7. They stress that directors must prove that others can place trust in them, it takes time to gain trust, and trust can be easily lost.

Table 4.1
Rating of Leadership Qualities

Qualities	Mean
Trust	6.8
Effective communication skills and strategy	6.8
Vision	6.7
Integrity	6.7
Passion for work and change	6.5
Building the confidence of others	6.3
Openness	6.3
Being positive	6.2
Political engagement	6.2
Collaborative	6.0
Good (and accurate) self-awareness of how others perceive you	6.0
Be approachable	5.7
Be entrepreneurial	5.5
Be inspirational	5.5
Other<ul><li>Be able to gain the respect of others</li><li>Be able to motivate others</li><li>Be a calculated risk-taker</li><li>Be a facilitator (a catalyst for dialogue and communication)</li><li>Be strategic</li><li>Create a culture of organizational engagement</li><li>Display a sense of humor</li><li>Do what needs to be done</li><li>Have humility (realize that you can be replaced)</li><li>Have the right blend of philosophy and pragmatism</li></ul>	

Effective communication skills and strategies also rate a mean of 6.8. Only one director objected to the inclusion of strategies; the others believed their inclusion better links this quality to leadership.

Both vision and integrity follow in the rating. All of the directors except one gave vision a score of 7, thinking that trust is more important. Two, however, would have scored it an 8, if possible, because vision "is the cornerstone of leadership." As one director explains, "trust and integrity are critical qualities, but these and the rest must be viewed in a context, namely the vision—the vision focuses on service and accepting change."

Passion for work and change would have rated higher if both elements had appeared as separate qualities, namely as passion for work and no fear of change. The directors tended not to see the association between passion and change; rather, leaders accept change and are comfortable with it as their environment changes. One director adds, "It is critical to try to control change through planning." He stresses the importance of planning, especially strategic planning, to leadership. Through planning, "you meet change with confidence." Another director disagrees, seeing planning as a managerial activity. Planning takes the mission (and hopefully the vision) and maps out how they will be undertaken. It involves many people, whereas vision is generated by one person, except in some instances where shared leadership implies sharing in the development of the vision.

Next on the list are building the confidence of others and openness. The directors view openness as a "cousin" of trust but did not rate it as highly. Two, however, see openness and approachability as synonymous; the others tend to disagree. One director inserts a caution: "It is not appropriate to share everything . . . [e.g., by placing some items on the home page]. Some things I may be willing to share if requested." The example he mentions is minutes of meetings that the public might attend.

Being positive and political engagement are important. One function of the director, one respondent notes, is to be "a cheerleader." Political engagement, most likely, is "learned on the job." Collaboration, two directors comment, applies to three contexts: within the community, within the library, and with other libraries. Participation, they note, generates goodwill and opportunities for the library. It is important to volunteer for collaborative efforts of strategic value to the library. Further, political engagement enables "you to understand how the library is viewed." This director wants local officials to take pride in the library and to think that the community receives a lot of service for a few dollars. "Still, there are times when leaders must stand alone. They must know when to do so."

Good (and accurate) self-awareness of how others perceive you means that "you need to understand what you are good at and what you are not good at. Further, you need to recognize your hot-button issues."

Approachability is linked to openness, which applies to "your relationship with the staff and broader community." Finally, being inspiring tied with being entrepreneurial for the lowest mean score. Being entrepreneurial generated some interesting comments:

- "It helps people outside the library pay attention to you. It is another level of credibility; if you have support from so and so, the community takes more notice of the library."

- This is an important quality "as long as it does not require additional dollars. Being entrepreneurial involves a rethinking of what we do and a desire to save money. . . . Can we do as much or more in different ways with fewer dollars?"

Expectation of Having Leadership Qualities among Different Levels of Management

The directors expect all managers to display some form of leadership, in part, because issues may involve more than one department (e.g., those dealing with technology). One director believes that there is some variation by position. The assistant director for public services should be more of a leader (have a vision, inspire others, and have a strong work ethic). The assistant director for administration is a manager and helps the organization function efficiently (e.g., by taking care of the scheduling). Moving down the organizational hierarchy, being a leader, he believes, depends on the position. The head of children's services should be a leader (be approachable, have integrity, and possess good interpersonal skills). This person should make children and their parents comfortable and willing to take advantage of the services offered.

Another director explains that, below the senior management team, "there is no big-picture focus, but . . . [these individuals] need to see how everything fits together." The qualities listed for managers below the rank of director include the following:

- Be able to develop the confidence of others.

- Be able to motivate others—"rally the troops."

- Be approachable.

- Be a self-starter.

- Be collaborative (with other departments in the library and city government).

- Be innovative.

- Be positive.

- Be a problem solver.

- Be trustworthy.

- Communicate openly.

- Have a passion for work and lack fear of change.

- Have confidence.

- Have good communication and interpersonal skills.

- Have integrity.

Topical Discussion

This section enables the directors to discuss coalition building and advocacy, innovative thinking and innovation, judgment, involving others in carrying out the vision, and transparency.

Coalition Building and Advocacy. The study participants see this topic as critical for effective leadership and for the library to maintain a relationship with other departments in city government and outside agencies. An example of such a focus relates to job issues: job training and placement. Further, one director sees "coalition-building and collaboration . . . [as] the roots of advocacy." Another participant comments:

- "Librarians need to be advocates and get their message across to the community. They do not want to be left out of a dialogue that may be relevant to what they are doing or plan to do. They have a role in policy discussions and in shaping funding decisions.

You do not want others to shape the image of the library; if they do, that image is likely outdated and does not reflect the value of the library to the community."

- "You are strategic in the coalitions you believe you need to be part of."

- "Libraries do not want to get lost in the competitive environment." To avoid this, one thing he does is to associate the police with the library by having the library play a role in violence prevention. He borrows terms from the police lexicon when he refers to the library, namely, "public safety," "a safe environment," and "a safe haven."

Several other respondents also discussed the competitive environment and competition with "police and fire departments, and formal education." As one director explains, "we cannot compete with police and fire, but the point is for the community to see us as indispensable. It is our hope that the public would be willing to forego some services such as street sweeping or not fixing pot holes on a weekly basis so that some money could be diverted to the library and keeping branches open."

A fourth director summarizes the components of coalition-building this way:

- "Who is your kindred spirit?"

- "Who brings something to the table you can benefit from?"

- "What are reasonable partnerships to form? Is the give and take that is required reasonable for you?"

- "Is it possible to create a win/win situation?"

- "How do you get informed citizens involved and supportive of the library?"

Finally, coalition building and advocacy include political awareness. "Any major initiative that costs money," one director explains, "is likely to require coalition-building to ensure the necessary funds are raised."

Innovative Thinking and Innovation. Innovation, as the directors stress, is important, especially during the recession, but it should be approached within the context of the vision. Still, one participant cautions, "it cannot require the expenditure of money. The context is one of rethinking what we do and saving money. We need to find ways to do as much or more than we currently do, but in different ways." Another director adds, "it is important to be alert to trends and the needs of the community. We need to maintain a competitive edge: What is viable for us to do? What do we keep? Which services are mandatory to retain?"

Judgment. As the directors note, judgment is subjective and must be viewed in a situational context—most likely situational leadership. Judgment means knowing when to bring others (e.g., the media or the mayor) into the fray. They also realize that judgment may require access to good information on which to base decisions; "depending on the situation you may not want to rely entirely on gut feelings." Clearly, judgment is a component of leadership.

Involving Others in Carrying out the Vision. The directors see this topic as central to their view of leadership. The goal is to "obtain a critical mass of staff who buy in to what we are trying to achieve. We want what we are doing to be sustainable and executed at all levels of the organization."

Transparency. They see transparency as important to accountability and as a critical component of leadership. One director likes to

get facts out to show what the library does and its value to the community. Key metrics include the amount of use of public computers, the number of people who visit the library on

Sundays (a day when they could be doing other things), the number of people who go to the library's homepage, and the number of people who attend library-sponsored events and programs.

Further, as another director explains, "decisions need to be transparent. When others are involved in decision-making and carrying out those decisions, you need to offer them the availability of transparency." A third director "explains the 'why' behind decisions. Others may disagree but you have a basis for having a conversation. If that conversation requires supporting evidence, you can work with others to find ways to collect that evidence." A fourth director sees the importance of transparency in terms of "the perception of how others see you as honest, credible, and not having an agenda. . . . [Transparency] involves trust and openness." He highlights the importance of transparency and the role of gathering evidence as libraries move into measuring outcomes or the impact of their services.

   Definition of Leadership. The directors offer the following definitions of leadership:

- "Passion and integrity combined with a constructive desire to improve—be forward-thinking, innovative, and do a better job. The focus is on helping people."

- "Vision combined with the qualities . . . [depicted in table 4.1] for the purpose of providing good customer service, ensuring staff enjoy working with people, and meeting . . . [customer] expectations. Going out of our way to be helpful."

- "Development of a vision and follow-through on that vision. Follow-through involves making decisions, gaining backing and support, building teams to carry through, and ensuring that the results move the organization forward."

- Noting that Warren Bennis has defined leaders as "people who do the right thing; managers are people who do things right,"[14] he offers the following definition: "Doing the right things at the right time and in the right way."

- "Modeling a certain behavior that creates a climate in which others will work to accomplish your vision" or "creating an organization that facilitates the accomplishment of your vision."

- "Doing what needs to be done in a big picture, long-term manner."

DISCUSSION

As in the previous chapter, each definition of leadership differs. As a set, however, the definitions tend to refer to vision and serving the public. There is also mention of the climate or the organizational culture. The qualities depicted in table 4.1 seem to reinforce the definitions. Although the study does not probe knowledge of leadership theories and styles, this might be a useful component to study in the future. The research question to explore is, "Must effective leaders be well-versed in the literature of leadership?" This question takes on added importance when the study of leadership extends down managerial levels. One of the directors interviewed suspects there will be resistance to leadership because many librarians, he believes, are not leaders and have little interest in the subject. "Librarians prefer to make something perfect before implementing it. Leaders would interpret this as a barrier to change."

   Although the author did not ask participants to identify individuals they consider leaders, one director volunteered a name—Charlie Robinson, "who inspired good people." His selection seems reasonable in part from a Google search showing the different awards named in Robinson's honor (e.g., from the American Library Association and the Urban Libraries Council).

Although this chapter does not focus on any particular leadership theory, some elements of transformational leadership emerged during the interviews. One of the components of such leadership is inspiring motivation among followers. As Bernard M. Bass and Ronald E. Riggio explain, this is accomplished by providing "meaning and challenge" to their work. They argue that any vision put forth must be "compelling" and able to get followers to display "enthusiasm and optimism."[15]

Another component, "intellectual stimulation," focuses on the ability of transformational leaders to "stimulate their followers' efforts to be innovative and creative by questioning assumptions, reframing problems, and approaching old situation in new ways."[16] The study did not define innovation in this way, but subsequent research might. It is also possible that, upon completion of the interview, the directors might be asked to complete the Multifactor Leadership Questionnaire (MLQ), which "measures a broad range of leadership types from passive leaders, to leaders who give contingent rewards to followers, to leaders who transform their followers into becoming leaders themselves. The MLQ identifies the characteristics of a transformational leader and helps individuals discover how they measure up in their own eyes and in the eyes of those with whom they work."[17] In addition or as an alternative, as part of case studies, leadership might be placed in an organizational context, through the use of an instrument such as the Organizational Description Questionnaire (ODQ), "a twenty-eight item questionnaire and resulting report which help members of an organization explore the relationship between leadership style and their organizational culture."[18]

Other components of transformational leadership, individualized consideration (a caring personality) and "idealized influence," which is about leaders as role models, were omitted from the study. Also excluded from the study was how idealized influence and inspirational motivation "usually combine to form a single factor of charismatic-inspirational leadership."[19]

Based on the comments of the directors, the data collection instrument was revised once more (see figure 4.1, pp. 66–67). It might be applied in different settings and include a section about the impact of the economic downturn on the library and its broader institution or organization and how the library is coping with a declining budget. Such studies might also examine the senior management team and get everyone to approach the answers from a team perspective. The goal is not to judge the director and that individual as a leader. If organizations were willing, studies might probe the perceptions of the followers who complete the instrument.

1. Critical Qualities (for Library Directors)

	↓Very Unimportant				Very Important↓		
Be able to motivate others	1	2	3	4	5	6	7
Be approachable	1	2	3	4	5	6	7
Be collaborative • Within the library • Outside the library	1	2	3	4	5	6	7
Be entrepreneurial	1	2	3	4	5	6	7
Be innovative	1	2	3	4	5	6	7
Be inspirational	1	2	3	4	5	6	7
Be open	1	2	3	4	5	6	7
Be positive	1	2	3	4	5	6	7
Be self-confident	1	2	3	4	5	6	7
Be strategic	1	2	3	4	5	6	7
Be a calculated risk-taker	1	2	3	4	5	6	7
Be politically engaged	1	2	3	4	5	6	7
Be trustworthy	1	2	3	4	5	6	7
Build the confidence of others	1	2	3	4	5	6	7
Display a sense of humor (able to laugh at yourself)	1	2	3	4	5	6	7
Do not fear change	1	2	3	4	5	6	7
Do what needs to be done	1	2	3	4	5	6	7
Gain the respect of others	1	2	3	4	5	6	7
Have effective communication skills and strategy	1	2	3	4	5	6	7
Have effective interpersonal skills	1	2	3	4	5	6	7
Have a good (and accurate) self-awareness of how others perceive you	1	2	3	4	5	6	7
Have the right blend of philosophy and pragmatism	1	2	3	4	5	6	7
Have humility (a realization that you can be replaced)	1	2	3	4	5	6	7
Have integrity	1	2	3	4	5	6	7
Have passion for work	1	2	3	4	5	6	7
Have a vision—a compelling one	1	2	3	4	5	6	7
Other (please specify)	1	2	3	4	5	6	7

Figure 4.1 Leadership Survey Form

2. Are leadership qualities important at each level of management in your organization? Why yes/no? If yes, which qualities?

3. Discuss (and provide an example) of each topic. Focus on the leadership aspect.

Coalition-building/advocacy	
Innovative thinking/innovation—implementing organizational processes that allow the library to do things better, cheaper, and faster; to be capable of embracing new priorities as the library fulfills existing ones; and to adapt to environmental shifts	
Judgment (needing good information to make good decisions; knowing when to bring in others, as the media, the provost, or the mayor)	
Empowering followers	
Transparency (as a leadership quality) • Explain the "why" behind decisions and making data available to others • Any limits to transparency?	

4. How do you complete the sentence "Leadership is _____
_____
_____
_____
_____ "?

5. Any concluding comments?

Future research might probe transparency as part of situational leadership and, in doing so, identify any limits that leaders place on it.

CONCLUDING THOUGHTS

As public libraries cope with diminished budgets that are unlikely to increase in the near future, can they in fact do more? They may have to follow the example of some of the academic libraries discussed in the previous chapter, identify their priorities, and support those priorities. As libraries engage in reengineering staff roles and responsibilities to meet their service priorities, researchers have opportunities to examine managerial leadership and assist in forecasting what future academic and public libraries will resemble. Research should also focus on the visions that guide the service roles and responses of public libraries and how their leaders generate buy-in. Research might also try to connect public library leadership with social roles—"the ways public libraries affect, intentionally or otherwise, their patrons and surrounding communities"[20]—and service responses.

I view leaders as signal generators . . . . Their behavior needs to provide employees with information about what's important in the organization . . . . If their behavior is inconsistent with those priorities, it's very confusing to people.[21]

NOTES

1. Comment from one of the directors interviewed.

2. "Ohio Libraries under Siege," *Daily Kos* [blog]. Available at http://www.dailykos.com/story/2009/6/21/745304/-Ohio-libraries-under-siege (accessed October 31, 2009).

3. June Garcia and Sandra Nelson, *2007 Public Library Service Responses* (Chicago: Public Library Association, 2007), 2.

4. Sandra Nelson, *The New Planning for Results: A Streamlined Approach* (Chicago: American Library Association, 2001), 146. For an excellent overview of service roles and responses, see Charles R. McClure and Paul T. Jaeger, *Public Libraries and Internet Service Roles: Measuring and Maximizing Internet Services* (Chicago: American Library Association, 2009).

5. Seattle Public Library, "About the Library: Budget—2010 Proposed Budget" (Seattle, WA: Seattle Public Library, 2009). Available at http://www.spl.org/default.asp?pageID=about_history (accessed October 31, 2009).

6. Peter Hernon, Ronald R. Powell, and Arthur P. Young, *The Next Library Leadership: Attributes of Academic and Public Library Directors* (Westport, CT: Libraries Unlimited, 2003).

7. Mark Winston and Haipeng Li, "Leadership Diversity: A Study of Urban Public Libraries," *Library Quarterly* 77, no. 1 (January 2007): 61–82.

8. Jennifer Arns, "Challenges in Governance: The Leadership Characteristics and Behaviors Valued by Public Library Trustees in Times of Conflict and Contention," *Library Quarterly* 77, no. 3 (July 2007): 287–319.

9. Alice Gertzog, "An Investigation into the Relationship between the Structure of Leadership and the Social Structure of the Library Profession" (PhD diss., Rutgers University, New Brunswick, 1989). Available from *Dissertations & Theses Full Text*, AAT 8923596.

10.   Mary Jo Venetis, "Identification of Remote Leadership Patterns in Academic and Public Libraries" (PhD diss., University of North Texas, 2008). Available from *Dissertations & Theses Full Text*, AAT. 3352149.

11.   John Mullins, "Are Public Libraries Led or Managed," *Library Review* 55, no.4 (April 2006): 237.

12.   Ibid., 246.

13.   See, for instance, Niels Ole Pors, "Managing Change in Danish Libraries," *The Journal of Academic Librarianship* 29, no. 6 (November 2003): 411–15; Niels Ole Pors, "Dimensions of Leadership and Service Quality: The Human Aspect in Performance Measurement," in *Proceedings of the Fourth Northumbrian International Conference on Performance Measurement in Libraries and Information Services: Meaningful Measures for Emerging Realities,* ed. Joan Stein, Martha Kyrillidou, and Denise Davis, 245–53 (Washington, DC: Association of Research Libraries, 2002).

14.   "Brainy Quotes: Warren Bennis" (BrainyMedia.com, 2009). Available at http://www.brainyquote.com/quotes/quotes/w/warrengbe385287.html (accessed December 12, 2009).

15.   Bernard M. Bass and Ronald E. Riggio, *Transformational Leadership*, 2nd ed. (Mahwah, NJ: Lawrence Erlbaum Associates, 2006), 6.

16.   Ibid., 7.

17.   "Multifactor Leadership Questionnaire" (Menlo Park, CA: Mind Garden, Inc.). Available at http://www.mindgarden.com/products/mlq.htm (accessed December 11, 2009).

18.   "Organizational Description Questionnaire" (Menlo Park, CA: Mind Garden, Inc.). Available at http://www.mindgarden.com/products/odq.htm (accessed December 11, 2009).

19.   Bass and Riggio, *Transformational Leadership*, 6.

20.   McClure and Jaeger, *Public Libraries and Internet Service Roles*, 2.

21.   Jennifer Chatman of the Haas School of Business at UC Berkeley, as quoted in Chip Johnson, "Oakland Mayor—Pompous, Not Politic," *San Francisco Chronicle,* December 11, 2009. Available at http://www.sfgate.com/cgi-bin/article.cgi?f=/c/a/2009/12/11/BAJE1B279T.DTL (accessed December 11, 2009).

5

RESEARCH SKILLS FOR MANAGERIAL LEADERSHIP

Danuta A. Nitecki

Somewhere, something incredible is waiting to be known.[1]

Managerial leadership in information professions is an evolving concept that views the merger of a leader's vision and implementation of an action plan to accomplish that vision as characteristics that shape the successful management of library organizations. These characteristics link imagination and creativity with practice in librarianship. The combination of creativity with practical project management to solve pragmatic problems may seem far from requiring research skills, yet these seemingly opposing characteristics are fundamental to the practice of applied research. Such research is essential as libraries develop a culture of evaluation and assessment that produces evidence of progress in meeting the institutional mission and using the feedback to make any necessary corrections. Within this context, this chapter explores issues of awareness about the need for research skills among administrators and provides an overview of learning the basics of systematic inquiry.

AWARENESS OF THE NEED FOR RESEARCH ON MANAGERIAL LEADERSHIP*

Contemporary management theories advocate that managers make decisions based on data; for instance, in managing services, they should emphasize the customer's perspective. To practice such data-driven management, decision makers require an understanding, if not a mastery, of ways to gather data systematically for a defined purpose, and the associated methods to analyze and interpret the results. If they do not gather the data, managers should understand how to judge the quality of data that others present to them.

*This portion of the chapter is based on the author's presentation, "Utilizing Qualitative and Quantitative Data for Managerial Decisions: A Developing Exploration," at the Qualitative and Quantitative Methods in Libraries International Conference, Chania, Crete, May 2009.

The growing emphasis on utilizing customer perspectives in decision making has introduced qualitative data to organizations previously managed with quantitative metrics. Justification of value, outcomes, and service quality requires data about opinions, perceptions, and preferences, which are new concepts to many library managers. The convergence of growing cultural expectations for service quality improvement and accountability with managerial approaches and methods to apply data to improve organizations and their performance poses a number of questions about librarians' engagement with these transformative trends. These questions center on the following:

- Are the pervasive expectations of managers to embrace the use of robust data for decision making paralleled by library managers?

- Do they place a high value on research-based management?

- Do they demand high-quality data upon which to base decision making?

- Do they understand probability and nonprobability sampling, and qualitative and quantitative methodologies, to gather and interpret data to use in decision making?

Developing a sufficient understanding of systematic data gathering for solving a problem or mastering the proper skills to undertake research, or at least to evaluate critically applied research, does not come easily to those who select librarianship as their profession. Managers and professional staff faced with pressures to change services, analyze operations, or address customer expectations and information needs benefit from gathering data or having data gathered. The data then are useful for service improvement and accountability.

The literature of library and information science (LIS) suggests that librarians are showing a modest interest in learning necessary skills to practice research-based management, but that they are not well prepared through their professional education in the fundamentals of systematic inquiry and methods for gathering, analyzing, and applying data for such practice. For example, one study indicates that 59 percent of LIS practitioners stated that their LIS master's programs did not adequately prepare them to conduct research, and 37 percent said these programs did not adequately prepare them to read and understand research-based publications.[2] Furthermore, these practitioners most likely have done little if anything to offset these weaknesses in the intervening years, and thus it is questionable to what degree they integrate data in their decision making. Yet, "without grounding in research and use of best evidence decision making becomes opinion-based policy making and follows an idiosyncratic approach that depends on the selective use of . . . evidence . . . or on the untested view of individuals or groups, often inspired by ideological standpoints, prejudices or speculative conjecture."[3]

Barriers to developing a research perspective and data-gathering skills include statistical anxiety, perceived irrelevance of research findings to practice, lack of incentives and rewards to use data or motivate change, a focus on findings without understanding of research design by which to generalize them and acceptance of bias, difficulty in understanding the language and presentation of published research, and the lack of time to conduct research before a decision needs to be made.[4]

In 2009 this author undertook an informal study to identify the extent of awareness of the importance and use of applied research among library administrators in their decision making. Her inquiry was guided by the following questions:

- What importance do library administrators place on data for making decisions?

- For what types of decisions do they seek data?

- What methodologies do they use to gather data needed for making decisions?

- What are the perceived barriers to pursuing research-based management?

Increased interest among academic librarians in seeking input from library users suggests that librarians have begun to incorporate principles of research-based management in improving the quality of services provided to their customers (e.g., faculty, students, and visiting scholars). However, to what extent is the "user perspective" identified, analyzed, and interpreted in ways that are aligned with decisions that library service managers make? An assumption was made that the library administrators most likely to have a need for such customer-focused data, particularly qualitative data, for their decision making are those with responsibilities for provision of customer services. This assumption directed selection of the focus for this study's design.

STUDY DESIGN

The American Library Association's Association of College and Research Libraries (ACRL) hosts a discussion group that meets twice a year at conventions to discuss matters of shared interest in administering library customer services. The membership consists of thirty-five library administrators, typically associate or assistant directors, of public services in the largest academic and research libraries in the United States and Canada. Any member may use the group directory list and listserv to send e-mail messages with comments or requests for specific information.

Focus Group Interview

In the first phase of the study a focus group interview was held on January 25, 2009, during the Midwinter American Library Association conference. Three broad questions framed the discussion:

- What are problems for which you have sought to gather data, and how important are such data to making decisions related to these problems?

- Who within your organization conducts assessment work, and do they have adequate skills to do so?

- What challenges do you face to gather and use data when making decisions?

The discussion was held in a hotel meeting room and as the second topic on a three-part agenda. More than twenty members of the ACRL group were in attendance, sitting at a large table, with additional observers from other libraries sitting around the periphery of the room. Only eleven members of the group, however, participated in the discussion and thus composed the default focus group of convenience.[5] A lively thirty-minute discussion resulted in responses to the questions posed.

According to the group, they seek data to demonstrate library support of student learning, consolidate service points, manage print/electronic serial and database subscriptions, meet user needs for collections, and plan space use for an information commons. They view data as important to illustrate the value of the library, reach consensus in making decisions, deliver on requests from university administrators, and communicate reasons for change to library staff.

No single staffing pattern for conducting research across libraries was described. Most participants acknowledged that there is insufficient library capacity to gather data as needed. Two mentioned hiring someone as needed (e.g., on a grant) to conduct assessments. Two noted their libraries have a specialist on staff who gathers and organizes data, analyzes trends and statistics on use from automated systems, reviews feedback received from users, and creates presentations for the director. Two mentioned relying on committees (with shared expertise among members) to gather data. Another version of this was expressed by one participant who described pushing responsibilities for data gathering to lower levels of staff without any authority to coordinate data gathered across units or reconcile conflicting reports.

Additional comments acknowledged an absence of adequate training among librarians in gathering or using data, although one believes libraries are moving toward a culture of evidenced-based decision making. The participants noted that the educational backgrounds of librarians fall mostly within the humanities, which do not give them exposure to the social science research skills seen as more relevant to data gathering for management. Specific mention was made of the need for deep analytical skills to understand data and for presentation skills to communicate results to multiple audiences within the library and elsewhere in the university.

The participants noted several challenges to gathering and utilizing data for decision making. One commented that metrics used in the library are individualized and, although the director wants to use counts, it is difficult to do so without a single-point person to help standardize measures and coordinate data gathering. Four participants maintained that there is insufficient time or staff expertise to gather data and guide their use, and one expressed explicit disappointment in the lack of preparation for such work in library school education.

The participants also identified cultural factors. One observed the tension between frontline staff, who had greater comfort with anecdotal evidence, and the director, who had a desire for quantifiable data. Fear was mentioned as a barrier to greater use, specifically noting that librarians are offended that their professional work might be expressed by numbers.

A few volunteered their attempts to overcome barriers. One library holds quarterly assessment forums to discuss surveys and otherwise help educate more staff about use of data. Another uses a wiki to display a tool box developed to support efforts to use data, and a library uses its strategic plan as an incentive to address assessment efforts. Finally, the comments made in the interview helped inform the design of the questionnaire instrument used in the second phase of the study.

Web-Based Survey

The second phase of the study involved a Web-based, pretested questionnaire administered through the online survey tool SurveyMonkey. As promised during the Midwinter meeting, an invitation to participate in this survey was e-mailed to the listserv of thirty-four members (excluding the author) of the ACRL Directors of Public Services on March 22, 2009. After seven weeks and two reminders, a total of eighteen administrators responded to the survey, producing a response rate of 52.9 percent.

The questionnaire consists of thirteen questions designed to address the study's research questions. First, the participants were asked to respond to three questions about the importance and role of data for decision making about public services. They were asked separately to rank on a 7-point scale the importance of operations data (e.g., inputs such as number of staff to shelve books or outputs such as number of questions answered) and customer perspectives (e.g., expectations or satisfaction with services) to four administrative activities. With one exception, as shown in table 5.1, all indicated that data are important for these administrative activities. Respondents rated operations data slightly more important than customer perspectives, especially when allocating resources and preparing reports.

Table 5.1

Perceived Importance of Data for Specific Purposes

Purpose for Data Use	Operations Data (mean)	Customer Perspective (mean)	n =
When making decisions to change public services	6.2	5.8	17
When seeking new resources for public services	5.8	5.9	17
When allocating available resources (budgets, staff)	6.4	4.9	17
When preparing annual or other reports about public services	6.2	4.9	16

Scale: 1 = very unimportant, 7 = very important

The author asked participants to think about the types of data they consider when making decisions about public services. A list of a dozen types of decisions was created from the literature and problems identified during the focus group interviews. The participants rated the importance they give to having each of three types of data when making decisions about each of the listed decisions. As before, the types of data were characterized as operations data and customer perspectives, and a new category, preexisting evidence (e.g., student demographic information or published research findings), was added. A 5-point scale and opportunity to note an item as nonapplicable were the response options. As summarized in table 5.2, there is little variation, although customer perspectives and operations data were considered slightly more important than preexisting evidence.

Table 5.2

Perceived Importance of Types of Data for Decision Making

Types of Data	Mean Score	Range of Means	Range of Responses n = 1–12
Operations data	4.1	3.5–4.5	11–12
Customer perspectives	4.3	3.6–4.9	11–12
Preexisting evidence	3.8	3.2–4.5	11–12

Scale: 1 = very unimportant, 5 = very important

Compiled from rating of importance for 12 decisions

The frequency of gathering data is another way to gauge the importance of data for decision making. From a list of metrics related to public services that are reported annually to ARL, augmented by two user perception data elements, the participants indicated on a nominal scale how often data are gathered in their libraries for each category. Except for the number of persons attending presentations, all respondents gather all of the metrics. Once a year or every few years are the common frequencies for two user perception metrics: user satisfaction and special inquiries such as prioritizing quality improvement opportunities. The other five metrics (numbers of circulation transactions, reference questions answered, instruction presentations, times library Web sites are accessed, and persons attending presentations) are gathered "daily" or "all the time."

Respondents were asked to indicate how often they systematically sought opinions held by library customers or data about the behavior of users and nonusers. As shown in table 5.3, customer opinions and user behavior data are frequently sought, but seldom, if ever, are data about the behavior of nonusers.

Table 5.3

Frequency of Seeking Types of Data before Making Decisions

Extent Data Are Sought	Always	Never	Mean Score	n =
Customer opinions	2 (13%)	0	2.9	16 (100%)
User behavior data	4 (24%)	0	2.5	17 (100%)
Nonuser behavior data	1 (6%)	4 (24%)	5.0	17 (100%)

Scale: 1 = always, 7 = never

The second topic explored in this survey identifies the types of decisions for which library administrators seek data. Responses to two questions—one involves ratings of importance of data for identified decisions and the other invites respondents to identify issues faced within the last year for which data were sought—offer insights into this topic. A list of decisions generated from comments made during the focus group discussion and the literature was used to ask respondents to rate the importance of each type of data for making these decisions.

Respondents were asked to indicate whether each type of data (operations data, customer perspectives, and preexisting evidence) is very important for twelve specific decisions relating to provision of public services. Decisions about the schedule for opening the library are almost uniformly ones for which operations data were identified as very important. Most respondents indicated that customer perspectives are very important for decisions determining the value of the library, providing access to specific serials, providing instruction about library research or information, and setting priorities for making improvements in services. The majority of respondents noted that preexisting evidence is not very important for any of the decisions. When asked to identify three decisions relating to public services they had made within the past year, they most frequently mentioned staffing services (e.g., reference desks); hours of operation; space planning; and expanding, consolidating, or continuing services.

The next topic, about methodologies they use to gather data for decision making, was addressed through four approaches related to specific decisions, frequency of use, personal knowledge to implement, and recorded examples. Respondents were asked to select methodologies used to gather data for the six most frequently identified decisions made during the past year. They typically mentioned multiple approaches to gathering data. Staffing decisions rely more on quantifiable data, with emphasis on operations, transaction logs, and user behavior; one respondent, however, listed the use of interviews. Decisions about hours of service rely mostly on quantifiable operations and user behavior data, but individuals also identified observations, customer views, and questionnaires. Decisions about service changes rely on data-gathering methodologies reflecting the type of change. The expansion or introduction of new services calls for customer views as well as operations data, and decisions about consolidating or continuing existing services depend on user behavior data, opinion, and use questionnaires, as well as transaction logs and preexisting evidence. Data to inform decisions about space planning are gathered through qualitative methods seeking customer views and using questionnaires and interviews.

Respondents were asked to estimate how frequently their libraries had used each methodology for gathering data in the past year. The methodologies used frequently are transaction log analysis, usability studies, interviewing, questionnaires, observations, and case/use studies. Administrators acknowledged no use or did not know if there was use in the past year in their libraries for methodologies associated with grounded theory, the Delphi method, concept mapping, and experiments.

Wondering if the administrator's level of confidence in implementing the different methodologies related to the frequency of their use, a question asks respondents to rate how knowledgeable they are in using each methodology. Table 5.4 shows the mean score for these ratings; the lower the score, the more knowledgeable the administrators perceived they are in implementing the methodology. Questionnaire surveys, observations, and interviewing are most familiar, with transaction log analysis, usability studies, and case or use studies also moderately well known. Responses suggest lower levels of knowledge about the remaining methodologies, with higher mean scores or indication that the administrators were not sure they know what the methodology is.

Table 5.4
Level of Knowledge about Implementing Methodologies

Methodology	Mean	Don't Know	n =
Questionnaire	1.90	0	10
Observations	2.30	0	10
Interviewing	2.30	0	10
Transaction log	2.60	0	10
Usability studies	2.70	0	10
Case/use study	2.70	0	10
Delphi method	3.00	3	9
Grounded theory	3.33	3	9
Critical incident	3.33	2	9
Concept mapping	3.44	0	9
Experiments	3.89	0	9

Scale: 1 = very knowledgeable 5 = not at all knowledgeable

The final topic explores barriers to gathering and utilizing data. This topic is addressed by three questions aimed at identifying perceived obstacles, the confidence of respondents in performing research steps assumed to be related to the process of gathering data for application to managerial decisions, and their personal preparation for involvement with research. Respondents were asked to indicate the extent to which they agree that a list of factors, identified through the literature and the earlier focus group discussion, are obstacles to their use of data in decision making. "Lack of time to pursue research before a decision needs to be made" is the statement with which most participants agreed. Other obstacles include lack of expertise within the library to conduct effective research for the type of data needed to make decisions and the perception that research findings are irrelevant to decisions needing to be made. There was little agreement that lack of incentives and the existence of evidence already published are barriers to gathering original data (see table 5.5, p. 78).

Table 5.5

Perceived Barriers to Gathering and Utilizing Data

Barriers	Mean Score (n = 17)
Lack of time to pursue research before decision must be made	5.12
Lack of expertise within library	3.94
Research findings are not relevant to decisions	3.06
Administrators do not read published research	2.94
Experience and intuition are more important than data when making decisions	2.76
Statistical anxiety	2.53
University leaders do not use data in actions relating to the library	2.53
Library directors do not seek research-based decision making	2.41
Research uses language that is difficult to understand	2.35
Lack of incentives to change services or operations	1.94
Existing data are good enough to make decisions	1.88

Scale: 1 = strongly disagree, 7 = strongly agree

Since the first phase of the study identifies the lack of both time and expertise among staff (including perceived lack of familiarity among administrators) as perceived obstacles, the questionnaire solicits ways that libraries seek and manage data for decision making. The participants could select as many approaches to gather and manage data for decision making as applied to their libraries. As reported in table 5.6, no one indicated that the library does very little, if any, data gathering, or that data are organized through a management information system. Nearly all selected two options: "as needed by staff who do not have data gathering responsibilities as a major part of their job" and "reports are available through automated systems that produce online data (e.g., online catalog use, Web-based surveys)." About half selected the options "responsibilities for data gathering appear among other duties in at least one staff member's job description," and they "seek assistance from other resources on campus." Only one-third indicate that "there is a library staff member with full-time responsibilities for assessment and/or evaluation duties."

Table 5.6

Approaches That Libraries Use to Manage Data Collection

Ways to Manage Data	Number Selected	Percentage (n = 12)
As needed by staff	11	91.7
Automated system reports	11	91.7
Distributed staff responsibilities	7	58.3
On campus assistance	7	58.3
By full-time library staff member	4	33.3
Students	3	25.0
Outsourced	3	25.0
Very little done	0	0.0
Organize data with management information system	0	0.0

A question gauges the level of involvement with research as another approach to identifying possible barriers to gathering and utilizing data among administrators. As shown in table 5.7, most indicate that they completed coursework in statistics; about half mention that they completed coursework in qualitative research, and half had research experience in a discipline other than LIS (Russian area studies, education and its history, higher education administration, business administration, nonprofit management, communications, and public administration).

Table 5.7
Administrators' Involvement with Research

Level of Involvement	Number	Percentage Selected (n = 11)
Completed course in statistics	9	81.6
Completed course in qualitative research	6	54.5
Preparation/research in other than LIS	6	54.5
Higher education other than LIS	4	36.4
Completed master's thesis	4	36.4
Published one report of research	4	36.4
Completed PhD dissertation	3	27.3

Unable to test competencies, the survey gauges the self-perceived levels of familiarity with performing research steps among administrators and their educational preparation to do so. Table 5.8 summarizes the findings from the request of participants to rate their level of confidence in performing each of basic steps of conducting research for gathering data for decision making. On average, high levels of confidence appeared with identifying published research, articulating a reason for conducting the research, analyzing insights from existing research that contribute to resolving the problem, and presenting results of research to others. Lower levels of confidence appeared with research design steps such as drawing samples, conducting content analysis, and using statistical analysis, particularly inferential statistics.

Table 5.8
Perceived Level of Confidence with Basic Research Steps

Research Steps	Mean Score (n = 17)
Identifying relevant research	6.35
Articulating reason	6.12
Analyzing existing research	5.94
Presenting results to others	5.88
Interpreting findings	5.41
Stating research questions	5.12
Formulating hypotheses	5.12
Selecting research methodology	4.65

Interpreting findings (qualitative & quantitative)	4.65
Using descriptive statistical analysis	4.53
Drawing sample	4.41
Conducting content analysis	4.29
Using inferential statistical analysis	3.29

Scale: 1 = not at all confident, 7 = very confident

DISCUSSION

The limitations of this exploratory study are obvious, and some reflect the limitations of the methodologies applied to the topic. The first phase built on the limited literature found about the topics relating to the extent and ways librarians gather data for application to managerial or administrative decision making. The group was limited to a small and conveniently available subset of library administrators. Participation was self-selected and motivated by some degree of interest in the topic. This qualitative approach to further defining the topic resulted in identification of initial types of problems for which data are gathered for decisions relating to public services, of staffing patterns by which data gathering is conducted, and of obstacles to gathering and utilizing data in management. There was no expectation that these findings would be generalizable to all library managers or administrators beyond those participating, and thus insights gained were limited to building further exploration among the subset of administrators responsible for public services. Further study might identify different factors relating to other professional foci, such as the administration of technical services, collection development, systems, or personnel managerial leadership.

The second phase of this study was intended to develop a quantitative approach to exploring the extent to which the factors identified in the first phase relating to the importance of data to decision making, the types of decisions for which data are sought, the methodologies for gathering data, and barriers to gathering and utilizing data applied among a population of administrators. The North American focus and small response sample, compounded by lack of response to some questions, certainly challenges the generalization of findings. A few comments on the questionnaires also suggest that there is an absence of common terminology relating to data gathering. For example, some may view evidence and data as interchangeable, while others distinguish these as preexisting findings and purposefully gathered new information. No inferences can be made from this study, and at best descriptive statistics should be interpreted with caution. The findings, however, may be useful in clarifying what issues are of interest to administrators and identifying where more attention may be needed to further cultivate environments of research-based management.

The study does support generally held perceptions that there is value in conducting systematic inquiry to identify data useful in decision making, at least for problems relating to library public services. It also highlights the need for better preparation of library managers. The study's indicated levels of understanding of research steps and of education in data-gathering methods, though relatively high, are likely confounded by the low self-selected participation in the survey. In other words, those who participated both in the focus group discussion and the survey are likely the administrators who are committed to the importance of managing libraries with data and are better prepared to do so than nonparticipants.

The combination of lack of time to gather data and the perceived lack of expertise within libraries to do so presents a challenge that might be minimized with improved knowledge of a framework of applied research within the profession, or at least among its managerial leaders. The remainder of this chapter provides a guided structure for developing applied research skills. It has been used as a framework for teaching research methods to doctoral students in the Managerial Leadership in Information Professions program (MLIP, Simmons College).

DEVELOPING APPLIED RESEARCH SKILLS

Research is a systematic quest for knowledge that involves a formal and intentional activity. There is no single approach that is universally adopted, and the details of research vary by the knowledge domain, traditions, and practices of different intellectual disciplines. The approach taken in the research courses taught in MLIP reflects an inquiry process with the following five stages: reflective inquiry, procedures, data quality, study implementation, and presentation of findings. Each of these contains key elements that appear in standard social science research outlines and are expected in the reporting of research. These stages provide an outline to address the context for gathering data that are meaningful in application to decision making and ultimately to improving library operations and services.

Reflective Inquiry

Reflective inquiry sets the stage for a meaningful exercise to obtain data useful to apply to problem solving. Novice researchers and many library practitioners lack appreciation for this important first stage and are eager to jump to procedures to gather data. It is not unusual for a manager to describe intentions to *conduct research* in terms of doing a survey or holding a focus group interview, without carefully reflecting on the purpose for gathering data or selecting the methodology most appropriate to addressing the desired inquiry.

Five factors are recommended to identify the problem to be addressed and a context of existing knowledge about it:

- problem statement

- literature review/theoretical framework

- logical structure

- objectives

- hypotheses and/or research questions

The problem statement is among the foreign concepts for beginners. It should contain four elements that together clarify the purpose of the research. These are an enticing *lead-in* that draws readers into the report of the research, an explicit statement of *uniqueness* that places what in the inquiry will add new insight and knowledge to the problem, the *direction* to be pursued in this unique inquiry, and an assertion of the *value* of the study, which justifies the research and suggests a promise of benefit to investing time in reading the research report. These factors are the creative components for undertaking research and may stimulate curiosity about a problem. Thinking about data needed for decision making in these terms offers managerial leaders a disciplined and systematic perspective for their quest for knowledge.

Conducting a literature review should be the simplest step of research for librarians, yet the output of the process is not always second nature. Information professionals typically know how to locate and identify published literature, but are not as well trained in selecting what is research as opposed to descriptions of activities or editorials. Another pitfall is the tendency to report the results of reading the literature as annotated bibliographies instead of synthesizing findings and insights specific to the purpose of the inquiry and thereby summarizing for the reader what is currently known about the topic. From the literature review, a theoretical framework—a conceptual base—may be identified that is relevant to the study and that may be used to structure the inquiry.

The logical structure is a graphic device that helps students sketch the potential components of the problem statement and make choices about which specific factors to pursue. The study objectives are statements of what broadly is sought to be answered, whereas the research questions or hypotheses are specified statements chosen to address the study objectives. The distinction between research questions and hypotheses is simple to remember when forming objectives in terms of an intention "to identify" or "to compare" factors under study; identification triggers research questions, whereas comparisons require hypotheses that quantify data in terms of probability about variations due to error.

Procedures

Procedures are the prescribed steps to take to pursue the purpose of reflective inquiry and involve choices in *research design* and *methodologies*. The research design choices include pragmatic issues such as where, when, and with whom to gather data. Challenges include, for example, identification of ways to define and locate specific populations such as customers (e.g., there may not be identification of recent immigrant users of reader services) or target staff (e.g., there is no directory of African American college or public library directors); of timing to best solicit response or observe representative activities; or of geographic scope of inquiry (e.g., whether resources are available to undertake a national study or one must select a smaller local setting for initial exploration).

Methodologies for data gathering have been well developed. Tested protocols that consider data quality issues are documented in standard textbooks and government publications. The challenge for practitioners designing a research project for the first time is to understand which methodologies will result in gathering data that are appropriate for the problem posed. Methodologies loosely fall within two types of research paradigms: quantitative and qualitative inquiry. Questions that seek to have data from which generalizations about a larger population can be made rely on quantitative methodologies, and to be answered require basic understanding of sampling and statistical analysis. Issues that call for initial exploration of an unfamiliar topic on the one hand, or deeper explanation of findings, on the other, lend themselves to qualitative methodologies for data gathering and analysis. Novice researchers and particularly managerial leaders impatient to "get data" may be surprised by the extensive array of methodologies available and continually being developed, the requirements of prescribed steps for gathering data, and the necessity to continue to follow protocols in the analysis of data gathered to formulate insights that can be effectively utilized in their decision making.

Data Quality

Data quality issues are typically addressed within the methodology protocols, but are emphasized as an important stage of research due to the tendency for novices to be unfamiliar with or ignore them. The two major issues for improving the quality of data collected are validity and reliability. Tests for validity aim to give feedback on the extent to which the data reflect what they are intended to address, whereas reliability aims to minimize misinterpretation and inconsistency in the data gathered. Pretests, replication, multiple coders, and multi-data gathering methods are among the techniques employed to improve potential for high data quality and are steps that are unfamiliar to many managers undertaking research.

Study Implementation

Study implementation is the stage that calls for basic project management skills, a strength of many library managers but perhaps not associated by them with research. Acknowledging that research takes time to undertake and that it might require prioritizing among job requirements or professional service activities is a necessary change for some managers and an opportunity for visionary influence for leaders. Drawing a plan to collect the data and analyze them requires realistic estimates of time and resources needed to do a good job. The ability to make such estimates is strengthened when students experience conducting research to understand its components, identify possible drawbacks, and generally appreciate both the simplicity of its rigor and the complexity of its unpredictability.

As managers, librarians can generally project well such budgets, and as leaders they could instill the practice of conducting research into the routines of library activities. Managerial leaders overcome the perceived barrier that there is always a lack of time to conduct systematic inquiry by introducing such habits as routinely reviewing data about customer perceptions of service quality or operations performance indicators, asking for available data prior to making decisions about library improvements, or budgeting resources for staff training and for encouraging pursuit of innovative research applications to library management.

Presentation of Findings

Presentation of findings may take the form of oral presentations, written documentation, publications, or postings to Web sites. When managerial leaders seek to have data used in decision making, the guidelines for presentation may deviate from the formal reporting elements of findings, discussion, and conclusion sections expected in research publications. Instead the emphasis is on bridging the gap between research and practice. Through conscious efforts to formulate effective communications, administrators should overcome their identified barriers that research findings are irrelevant or that the language used to present them is difficult to understand. Key factors that govern presentation for decision making include the target audience, the data selected to report, and the manner of conveying the results. The target audience consists of the potential recipients of the study findings (e.g., university administrators, library staff, funding agencies). Understanding their motivation to receive data and the quantity and format of information sought to make decisions is an important guide in preparing the report. The data selected for inclusion in the presentation should be sufficient to support the decision making, whether related to advocacy, accountability, or future planning. The manner of conveying the results of research should also reflect the nature of the application for which the data will be used. The presentation might be offered in the context of a staff meeting, a formal budget or donor request, or a monitor for a continuous quality improvement initiative. The format might be an oral summary, a written report, or an interactive Web-based dashboard. Regardless of the channel and format of the communication, the data should be presented in a manner that will be transmitted for the purpose and the audience in need of them, using charts, tables, and narrative effectively, with clarity and brevity.

Most managers starting their practice of research find the presentation stage to be deceptive because they already tend to be vocal and highly communicative in their work. The language of research, however, should be precise and requires appropriate use of words that have specific meaning in statistical reports but also are used differently in pedestrian communications; for example "significant," "prove," and "impact" are words not to be loosely used in reporting research findings. Although "difficult to understand research language" is identified as a barrier by administrators wishing to conduct research, it might be that the difficulty in communicating accurately is the actual barrier. This is a barrier that with a little training could be overcome.

CONCLUDING THOUGHTS

Exposure to research is perhaps one of the best ways to learn about it. Through formal training in research methods, students learn the details of how to identify the problem for research, design appropriate data gathering and analysis methods, plan and execute studies within resource boundaries, and effectively communicate results. Learning varies with individuals, but consistently repeated exposure to concepts and their application to familiar context are strategies that help develop understanding. Reading published research and paying attention to the guiding elements of the research framework presented here may also help develop familiarity. Experiencing the process through action is a powerful, but sometimes frustrating, learning approach. It is better to take the risk of discomfort in undertaking research in a learning setting, than to risk making expensive and misconceived decisions when working with invalid and unreliable data produced through poorly understood research methods.

The presence of a cultural expectation within an organization at least to have *educated consumers* who critically rely on existing knowledge or the results of commissioned research is likely to encourage greater engagement with research in libraries. Culture cannot be prescribed, but it can be encouraged to formulate. Emerging library managerial leaders may find that such encouragement might be a relatively simple gesture that potentially gives high returns. Through asking for data and supporting efforts to learn how to gather them effectively when seeking input to make decisions and setting strategic directions, managerial leaders envisioning the value of managing with data are well positioned to help information professionals also to be competent seekers of knowledge and contributors to continually improving the library.

Research is creating new knowledge.[6]

NOTES

1. "Dr. Carl Sagan Quotation (American Astronomer, Writer and Scientist, 1934–1996)." Available at http://thinkexist.com/quotations/research (accessed January 11, 2010).

2. Ronald R. Powell, Lynda M. Baker, and Joseph J. Mika, "Library and Information Science Practitioners and Research," *Library & Information Science Research* 24, no. 1 (2002): 49–72.

3. See Margaret Law, "The Systematic Review: A Potential Tool for Research-Grounded Library Management," in *Proceedings of the 33rd Canadian Association for Information Science Annual Conference, 2005,* 1. Available from http://cais-acsi.ca/proceedings/2005/law_2005.pdf (accessed January 11, 2009).

4. For an elaboration on these barriers, see Danuta A. Nitecki, "Preparing Librarians for Research-Based Management," in *Proceedings of Preparing Information Professionals for International Collaboration, the Asia-Pacific Conference on Library & Information Education and Practice (A-LIEP 2009), March 6-8, 2009, University of Tsukuba, Japan.* Available at http://a-liep.kc.tsukuba.ac.jp/proceedings/index.html (accessed January 1, 2010).

5. The libraries represented by these members were Duke University, New York University, Ohio State University, Stanford University, Texas A&M, and the universities of Alberta, Arizona, Chicago, Michigan, Washington, and Wisconsin.

6. "Brainy Quotes: Neil Armstrong." Available at http://www.brainyquote.com/quotes/keywords/research.html (accessed January 11, 2010).

6

~

A RESEARCH AGENDA

Peter Hernon

Over time, thinking about leadership has shifted from simplistic characterizations of personality traits to more complex frameworks for understanding what constitutes effective leadership.[1]

Leadership and management describe entirely different concepts, as leadership is more than a component of the functions of management. Management is the process of administering and coordinating resources to ensure that an organization accomplishes its mission and goals. Library and information science (LIS) has a managerial focus; librarians manage the infrastructure of a library: its collections, staff, technology, and facilities. For this reason, the interconnection between management and leadership is one of the domains of LIS theory and practice. The purpose of leadership is to challenge the status quo as libraries undergo a transition in organizational culture and climate, the services they offer, and workforce restructuring as they better fulfill the organizational and broader institutional mission. Management, on the other hand, prepares the infrastructure for that transition.

The term *managerial leadership* recognizes (or at least should) that leadership is not exclusively a top-down process between the *boss* as a leader and subordinates. Managerial leadership as an area of research encompasses an examination of leaders, followers, and the interaction between the two groups. In this context, leadership becomes a process whereby people influence others to develop, accept, and carry out a shared vision that guides future actions of the organization. As a result, that process is longitudinal and involves events (actions, impacts, and accomplishments). Because leadership is not always effective or positive,[2] it should not automatically be assumed that goals, milestones, and targets are always successfully met or that staff members are sufficiently motivated, inspired, or influenced to challenge themselves and others.

The purpose of this chapter is to build on the international research agenda that Candy Schwartz and I developed in 2008, which illustrates that LIS research needs to go beyond a preoccupation with understanding the style, personality, traits, and other characteristics of the boss and that person's influence on organizational dynamics and performance.[3]

LEADERSHIP

In addition to focusing on a shared vision, leadership is about giving people confidence to meet organizational expectations and to serve as change agents. It also encourages them to seek, be given, and benefit from team coaching and mentoring aimed at enhancing their knowledge, skills, abilities, effectiveness, and commitment to the transformation process. A library's staff might consist of both followers and leaders who are willing to collaborate with other institutional partners. As well, the director, if that person is truly a leader, might be more so within the organization than in representing the library to stakeholders.

With so many libraries organized into teams or small groups and involved in managing change; with new staff members expected to work together to plan, implement, administer, and evaluate services; and with libraries forging new partnerships at the institutional, local, and other levels, more librarians are becoming increasingly interested in knowing about and applying leadership theories, styles, traits, and roles. They are also trying to develop their leadership potential. Within this context, there is much interest in transformational leadership and emotional intelligence, which

helps leaders move beyond basic "people skills" to understanding how one's own reactions and feelings impact how one is perceived by others. Leaders and managers need to understand their own emotions and recognize and understand the feelings of those around them. Leaders are more successful when they pay attention to their social interactions with others in the workplace and the impact they as leaders have on those around them. It is also important for leaders to understand the impact that others' emotions have on them. When leaders are aware of the emotional side of the workplace, they are better able to create a working environment that encourages excellence.[4]

As librarians gain a better understanding of leadership theories, they need to understand that "we live in an era where leadership represents a motivational, emotional, and developmental part of organizational success."[5] Further, as Joseph B. Lyons and Tamera R. Schneider note,

the leaders of the future are faced with onerous challenges. They must be adept at influencing subordinates' motivational, emotional, and developmental needs in the stressful context of modern work. This shift in the focus of leadership effectiveness requires that leadership researchers follow suit and consider a wider range of outcome variables in leadership research.[6]

Lyons and Schneider see transformational leaders as essential for organizational success because it offers an arsenal of key behaviors related to inspirational motivation, idealized influence, individualized support, and intellectual stimulation to help an organization meet the challenges of today and the future.[7] Further, they find that transformational leaders cope well with stress and accomplish stressful tasks.

CONTEXT

Even though this chapter focuses on topical areas for future research and selected methodologies, it is important to remember that methodologies do not frame a research study. Research, which engages in problem solving, is shaped by a reflective inquiry (problem statement, literature review and theoretical framework, logical structure, objectives, research questions, and possibly hypotheses). These components, as well as the study procedures (research design and methodologies) and data quality, comprise a framework in which each component should be bonded to the others through what David R. Krathwohl calls a "chain-of-reasoning." That "chain," he points out, "is only as strong as its weakest link" and "all links . . . should be built to about the same strength." He further explains that, "as the work load is picked up by the first link [the problem statement] and passed to successive links, the work load—and therefore the nature of each link—is determined by the previous links." Furthermore, "where several links together join those above and below them, there may be trade-offs to compensate for weaknesses."[8]

It is beyond the scope of this chapter to present and relate the entire chain-of-reasoning. Still, I would be remiss if I did not underscore the importance of the theoretical framework. Vincent A. Anfara Jr. and Norma T. Mertz provide an excellent overview of theoretical frameworks and the impact of "good and useful" theory on the chain-of-reasoning.[9] In the case of managerial leadership, like other areas within LIS, there are numerous theories, some of which fit a given problem statement and set of objectives better than others. One such theory might be constructive-development theory, which relates directly to leadership and offers a way to view the complex problems that organizations face from multiple perspectives. This theory describes "how adults develop more complex and comprehensive ways of making sense of themselves and their experience."[10] Another multifaceted concept relates to trust, which is an essential component in motivating or inspiring others.[11]

RESEARCH DESIGNS

As a prelude to methodologies, research designs for leadership research might call for a longitudinal study and a comparison of several (comparable) organizations. Widely used research designs center on either a case study or the application of grounded theory. A case study is a means "for learning about a complex instance, based on a comprehensive understanding of that instance obtained by extensive description and analysis of that instance taken as a whole and in its context."[12] Grounded theory, on the other hand, "is a method for discovering theories, concepts, hypotheses, and propositions directly from data, rather than from a priori assumptions, other research, or existing theoretical frameworks."[13] Theory emerges from, and is grounded in, the data themselves.

DATA-GATHERING TECHNIQUES

This section focuses on some of the most prevalent methodologies used in leadership research, especially within LIS. As such, it builds from Karin Klenke's work on leadership research.[14] It is increasingly common for researchers to apply qualitative methods to the study of leadership. Table 6.1 (pp. 88–91) offers examples of some methodologies applicable to the study of leadership in LIS that will not be discussed in the body of this chapter. The sources listed in that table came from a review of the literature produced largely outside LIS.

The largest number of research studies related to leadership involves the distribution of a self-report survey or questionnaire. Such surveys are often in paper-and-pencil format, although more recently Web-based surveys have appeared with increasing frequency. The survey might involve the use of a predeveloped, behavior-based leadership assessment tool (e.g., the Mayer-Salovey-Caruso Emotional Intelligence Test (MSCEIT), which is an ability-based test; see (http:// www.eiconsortium. org/measures/msceit.html) that is distributed to those heading the organization or to subordinates who are asked to evaluate the director or their immediate supervisor as a leader. As an alternative, surveys might probe respondents' preference for a particular leadership theory or style and ask them to rate themselves or identify the most important qualities for individuals in their position.

Table 6.1
Selected Studies and Their Methodologies*

Methodological Focus	Defined	Examples
I. Communication (words: speaking or writing)	The research literature on leadership tends to ignore or slight the topic of communication, unless investigators focus on the great men or women who are recognized as leaders. Gail T. Fairhurst and Robert A. Sarr note that leaders in senior management positions spend a large percentage of their time communicating, and their most important tools are linguistic and symbolic. They explain the art of framing, which is a form of communication that forces others to accept the meaning that leaders give to events and that followers find persuasive. The most common area in which this type of research occurs is charismatic leadership.	See Gail T. Fairhurst and Robert A. Sarr, *The Art of Framing: Managing the Language of Leadership* (San Francisco: Jossey-Bass, 1996); Gail T. Fairhurst, "Reframing *The Art of Framing*: Problems and Prospects for Leadership," *Leadership* 1, no. 2 (2005): 165–85.
I(a). Metaphors (content analysis) and speech imagery (content analysis)	Metaphors make a message more vivid and increase its retention. They also have emotional meaning and an emotional impact on others. Researchers might ask participants to identify passages of text that are most inspiring. Those sections might be checked for use of any metaphors. Speech imagery deals with discourse analysis and conversation analysis.	Jeffrey S. Mio, Ronald E. Riggio, Shana Levin, and Renford Reese, "Presidential Leadership and Charisma: The Effective Metaphor," *The Leadership Quarterly* 16, no. 2 (2005): 287–94; Loren J. Naidoo and Robert G. Lord, "Speech Imagery and Perceptions of Charisma: The Mediating Role of Positive Affect," *The Leadership Quarterly* 19, no. 3 (2008): 283–96; Viviane Seyranian and Michelle C. Bligh, "Presidential Charismatic Leadership; Exploring the Rhetoric of Social Change," *The Leadership Quarterly* 19, no. 1 (2008): 54–76.

Methodological Focus	Defined	Examples
I(b). Aphorisms (also speech imagery)	As explained in the *Oxford English Dictionary*, an aphorism is "any principle or precept expressed in few words; a short pithy sentence containing a truth of general import; a maxim." Such rhetoric can be summarized and analyzed.	Kevin Morrell, "Aphorisms and Leaders' Rhetoric: A New Analytical Approach," *Leadership* 2, no. 3 (2006): 367–82.
I(c). Cartoons	Cartoons appearing in different media (or one medium) are analyzed for patterns.	Rachel M. Calogero and Brian Mullen, "About Face: Facial Prominence of George W. Bush in Political Cartoons as a Function of War," *The Leadership Quarterly* 19, no.1 (2008): 107–16.
II. Diaries	Participants compile diaries for a period of time. Those diaries adhere to a formal structure.	Peter Hernon, Ronald R. Powell, and Arthur P. Young, "Academic Library Directors: What Do They Do?" *College & Research Libraries* 65, no. 6 (November 2004): 538–63.
III. Ethnology and participant observation	The investigator becomes involved in the lives of the participants but guards against the lack of objectivity in viewing the findings, combines various methodologies such as interviewing participants, observing them as leaders, analyzing documents, and reflecting (perhaps generating memos that the investigator generates while applying various methods of data collection and uses to record thoughts that he or she might otherwise fail to capture).	See Constance A. Mellon, *Naturalistic Inquiry for Library Science: Methods and Applications for Research, Evaluation, and Teaching* (New York: Greenwood Press, 1990), 40–44; Bernadette Vine, Janet Holmes, Meredith Marra, Dale Pfeifer, and Brad Jackson, "Exploring Co-leadership Talk through Interactional Sociolinguistics," *Leadership* 4, no. 3 (2008): 339–60.

Methodological Focus	Defined	Examples
	Ethnography refers to fieldwork that describes and interprets a social group or system. The investigator examines the group's observable patterns of behavior and the way of life. "Typically, [for leadership studies] after a period of participant observation to establish how the workplace operates, a group of volunteers use mini-disk records to capture a range of their everyday work interactions over a period two to three weeks. … In addition, where possible, a series of regular workplace meetings is video-recorded" (Vine et al., 344).	
IV. Event history analysis or life narrative approach	Life narratives, or life stories, enable individuals to communicate personal understanding of their lives in reference to a current situation. Conveying meaning through life narratives may foster identification with followers, thus providing a basis for common understanding that permits more automatic, intuitive social interaction between leaders and followers. These life stories presumably explain why certain individuals are more likely to experience the event(s) of interest than others. This method captures the aggregated leadership actions across multiple people.	Gina S. Ligon, Samuel T. Hunter, and Michael D. Mumford, "Development of Outstanding Leadership: A Life Narrative Approach," *The Leadership Quarterly* 19, no. 3 (2008): 312–34; Boas Shamir, Hava Dayan-Horesh, and Dalya Adler, "Leading by Biography: Towards a Life-story Approach to the Study of Leadership," *Leadership* 1, no. 1 (2005): 12–39; Scott T. Allison, Dafna Eylon, James K. Beggan, and Jennifer Bachelder, "The Demise of Leadership: Positivity and Negativity Biases in Evaluations of Dead Leaders," *The Leadership Quarterly* 20, no. 2 (April 2009): 115–29. See also Gazi Islam, "Animating Leadership: Crisis and Renewal of Governance in 4 Mythic Narratives," *The Leadership Quarterly* 20 (2009): 828–36.

Methodological Focus	Defined	Examples
V. Phenomenological inquiry	Such inquiry describes a research perspective that differs from positivistic forms of inquiry. More precisely, it better brings out themes and their meaning through an examination of the experiences derived from the perceptions, thoughts, emotions, and so on, of people.	Debra L. Gilchrist, "Academic Libraries at the Center of Instructional Change: Faculty and Librarian Experience of Library Leadership in the Transformation of Teaching and Learning" (PhD diss., Oregon State University, 2007). Available from *Dissertations & Theses: Full-text* (AAT3268285).

*See also Karin Klenke, *Qualitative Research in the Study of Leadership* (Bingley, United Kingdom: Emerald Group Publishing Ltd., 2008).

Complementary to a questionnaire that is mailed (e-mail or other) or otherwise distributed, investigators might use personal or focus group interviews. Responses to open-ended questions might be subjected to content analysis, which "is a set of procedures for transforming nonstructured information into a format that allows analysis."[15] On occasion, biographies of people identified as leaders have been developed and their content subjected to analysis for insights into them as leaders. Available historical records, however, might focus more on their accomplishments than on the story behind those accomplishments: How did the individual co-opt and navigate different stakeholders and the staff to bring about that change? If a shared vision emerged, how was it developed, and how was buy-in achieved?

Some other means of data collection include an analysis of citation patterns of a body of works on leadership and a characterization of the most cited works (e.g., names of journals and publishers) and authors, as well as the age of the cited material. Additional insights might be gained from a consideration of the journal's impact factor and a review of download statistics for journal articles.

Assuming the availability of a body of independent studies focused on the same aspect of leadership that also describes the research design, the methodologies, and data-collection instruments used and offers information about the population and sample, and so on, meta-analysis might be appropriate. Such analyses refer to a set of statistical procedures used to summarize and integrate those studies.[16] Meta-analysis reveals sources of bias and is helpful for posing research questions for future study. Among other things, it cannot exceed the limits of what the researchers report.

Another method, known as the Delphi study or technique, relies on the use of sequential questionnaires in which experts share their perspectives on issues.[17] The Delphi technique is not necessarily designed to generate consensus, but it does involve a systematic refinement of prior responses. It might show, for instance, which leadership qualities are most critical for future managerial leaders and in what situations.

Concept Mapping

Concept mapping is both a process for representing data in the form of pictures or maps and a structured methodology for organizing the ideas of a group or organization. The goal is to bring together groups of multiple "stakeholders . . . and help them rapidly form a common framework that can be used for planning, evaluation, or both."[18] The maps represent the groups' thinking about a topic, show how their ideas are related to each other, and, in general, indicate "which ideas are more relevant, important, or appropriate."[19]

Interviews and other techniques might produce datasets that could be examined by the use of concept maps. These maps provide a graphic illustration of patterns among the findings. Jan Schilling, for instance, takes interview data about negative leadership and produces maps that show the antecedents of such leadership, negative leadership behaviors, and the consequences of negative leadership.[20]

Simulation and Scenarios

A simulation study, as Gary Yukl explains, involves a realistic task that continues for several periods of time and asks participants (e.g., team members) to assume the role of top executives in an organization and to engage in team and organizational learning. Simulation "is also relevant for understanding how collective learning occurs among people whose decisions and actions affect organizational processes and performance."[21]

Instead of doing a simulation exercise, researchers might develop scenarios that make projections for the next fifteen years; forecaster Joseph P. Martino indicates that the accuracy in predicting what will likely occur declines dramatically with a longer time frame.[22] According to Dana Mietzner and Guido Reger,

scenarios, as a prime technique of future studies, have long been used by government planners, corporate managers and military analysts as powerful tools to aid in decision making in the face of uncertainty. The idea behind them is to establish thinking about possible futures which can minimi[z]e surprises and broaden the span of managers' thinking about different possibilities.[23]

They recommend that the number of scenarios not exceed four and that any set of scenarios should meet criteria such as *plausibility* (each is capable of happening), *differentiation* (each differs from the others and together they offer multiple futures), *decision-making utility* (each offers insights into the future that help in planning and decision-making), and *challenging* (each challenges conventional wisdom about the future).[24] Once a set of scenarios have been developed, which scenarios do libraries endorse? Does the recession have an impact on which scenario a library selects, and what leadership is critical to the achievement of that scenario's content?[25] Senior management teams might also be asked to rewrite a scenario, adding new and deleting components, and present their guiding vision. When this occurs, researchers might gather and analyze the content of the revisions. They might also ask participants to explain how they plan to go about accomplishing the guiding vision and to discuss the leadership challenges they will face. If, by chance, teams accept the status quo as the favored scenario, this choice should be explored, as it represents a leadership void.

RESEARCH AGENDA

Figure 6.1 (p. 94), which complements the identification of research topics in other chapters and updates the depiction that Schwartz and I created, centers on three broad areas that relate to planning:

1. Accomplishments (translating vision into effective organizational performance);

2. People (creating an organizational climate that values staff and inspires them); and

3. Transformation abilities (focusing on the change process that brings people together to accomplish the organization's mission and goals—preparing the organization of the future).

These areas match those that guide the doctoral program in managerial leadership in the information professions (Simmons College). They cover twenty-five distinct leadership competencies.

Under each of the broad areas, numerous topics emerge. At the same time, relationships among the areas might be probed. As directors or other members of the senior management team retire or depart, their replacement might be someone who serves on an interim basis. Are such people leaders or caretakers? The answer might take into account the library but also engagement beyond the library, transformation abilities, mentoring, and talent management. Focusing solely on talent management, many businesses engage in succession management or planning, but do libraries? Succession planning and management are not synonymous with mentoring. In some countries, if there is leadership, it might be characterized as autocratic. Such leadership merits analysis. Finally, various aspects of the figure might be probed in the global recession as libraries make significant decisions about collections, services, facilities, and staffing that will likely have a long-term impact.

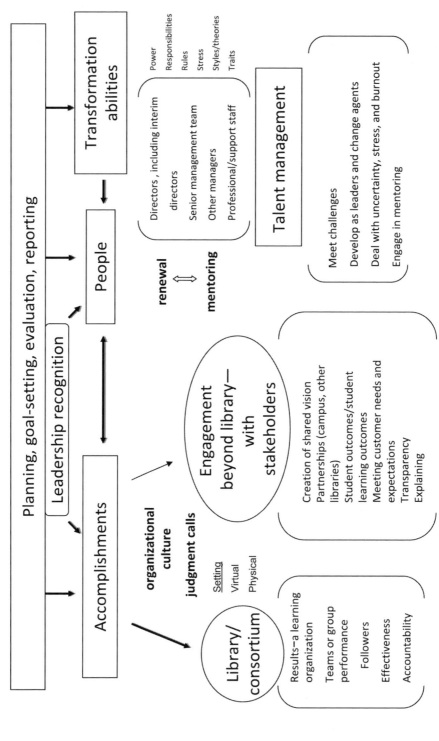

Figure 6.1 Research Agenda (Within a Country and Cross-Countries). Adapted from Peter Hernon and Candy Schwartz, "Leadership: Developing a Research Agenda for Academic Libraries," *Library & Information Science Research* 30, no. 4 (December 2008): 247.

Turning to other topics, James G. Neal discusses "feral library professionals," which refers to the hiring of more people into traditional and nontraditional library positions who do not have the credentialed degree from an accredited library school program.[26] Comparative case studies might analyze leadership in organizations that employ both feral and nonferal professionals or that include staff who represent different generations. How cohesive are staff within and across departments? Do they share a common vision—do they need to share one?

Studies might probe LIS educational programs and see whether (or how) they incorporate leadership as a student learning outcome, one that reflects what students have learned throughout their program of study and demonstrates what they can apply upon graduation. Some other possible topics include the role of power in effective leadership, the major trends in making leadership effective, the communication networks of leaders, and transformational leadership and its relationship, for instance, to the following:

- Emotional intelligence, which deals with one's ability to manage emotions and relationships and to use this ability to advance the organization's mission and goals. Emotional intelligence presumably requires *sense-giving* or shaping how people understand themselves, their work, and others engaged in that work.

- Resonant leadership, which focuses on self-awareness and self-renewal, and which enables individuals to recognize and cope with work stress.

- Distributed or shared leadership, which views leadership as more than a top-down approach. Leadership moves up the organization as well and is distributed among a number of people working in teams and groups.

- Servant leadership, which recognizes that leadership is not confined to those in formal managerial positions. The servant leader focuses on the needs and the development of followers.

Recognizing that libraries serve multicultural communities, employ diverse staff, and deal with myriad stakeholders, it is critical to evaluate different leadership theories, recognizing the strengths and weaknesses of each. Many of the prevailing theorists have not considered how multiculturalism influences what they propose. Perhaps the best illustration of this comes from Linda Sue Warner and Keith Grint, who adopt a historical perspective and compare American Indian and Western approaches and perspectives on leadership. There are differences between the practice of leadership in a tribal setting (including tribal colleges) and in other organizational settings.[27]

As researchers investigate the types of topics raised in this chapter, they should not ignore the research of Chester A. Schriesheim and Claudia C. Cogliser, who note that "the field of leadership typically employs constructs—variables that cannot be directly measured—in its research. Yet, our measures are rarely subjected to systematic assessment of their construct validity,"[28] which refers to the extent to which the theoretical construct or trait is actually measured. Schriesheim and Cogliser illustrate the importance of the construct validation process and why concerns about forgoing or short-changing that process are well founded.

The Economic Downturn

Librarians have been managing fluctuating budgets for years, but the deeper financial cuts that many libraries are currently experiencing (and will likely continue to do for the near future) require both management and leadership. A number of libraries are managing layoffs, making permanent cuts to staffing and collections, implementing collaborative and cooperative arrangements, facing significant organizational changes, and perhaps developing or revising strategic plans. This climate affords an excellent opportunity to study leadership and how leaders motivate or influence organizational change. At the same time, there is a unique opportunity to examine followership and the interaction between leaders and followers. With so many news stories about stress in the workforce, research on resonant leadership might probe how well both leaders and followers cope with stress and successfully apply resonant leadership. The goal is to promote and maintain healthy organizations.

More research might use case studies as part of their research design. For instance, research might select public libraries or academic libraries that are part of public institutions in the states facing the severest budgetary cutbacks. The purpose is to probe whether these libraries and institutions have leadership; if so, at what levels of the organization; how leaders cope with challenges; and whether the libraries engage in strategic planning and setting priorities and whether they are reviewing and resetting those priorities. Further, how do the leaders and other staff members cope with the pressures of workplace stress?

Table 6.2 illustrates choices for the selection of actual sites to study. "There are three general bases for selecting instances: convenience, purpose, and probability. Each has its function and can be used to answer certain questions. A good case study will use a basis for instance selection that is appropriate . . . [to the problem statement and the research questions]."[29] Furthermore, "only rarely will convenience be a sound basis for instance selection; only rarely will probability sampling be feasible. Thus, instance selection on the basis of the purpose of the study is the most appropriate method in many designs."[30]

Table 6.2
Instance Selection in Case Studies*

Selection basis	When to use and what questions it can answer
Convenience	Is the site selected because it was expedient for data collection purposes, what is happening, and why?
Purpose	
• Bracketing	What is happening at the extremes? What explains such differences?
• Best cases	What accounts for an effective program [or service]?
• Worst cases	Why is the program [or service] not working?
• Cluster	How do different types of programs [or services] compare with each other?
• Representative	In instances chosen to represent important variations, what is the program [or service] like and why?
• Typical	In a typical site, what is happening, and why?
• Special interest	In this particular circumstance, what is happening, and why?
Probability	What is happening in the program as a whole [or service], and why?

*Source: U.S. General Accounting Office, Program Evaluation and Methodology Division, *Case Study Evaluations*, Transfer Paper 10.1.9 (Washington, DC: GAO, 1990), 23.

CONCLUDING THOUGHTS

To gain a more complete understanding of the phenomena under investigation, it is common for studies on leadership, like research on other topical areas, to incorporate more than one method of data collection. Mixed methods, which are most prevalent with case studies, integrate quantitative and qualitative methods into one study and therefore strengthen the chain-of-reasoning presented in study findings. [31] Although it is important to expand the methodological tool chest that researchers within LIS use, it is also important to shift from studying leaders to investigating leadership events. Many aspects of leadership presented in figure 6.1 have not been addressed, and a need emerges for a fuller body of evidence-based research relevant to change management on a global basis within complex organizations such as libraries. It is also important that those within LIS contribute to the broader literature on leadership and that their works be of sufficient importance to gain recognition from scholars and researchers in other disciplines.

A thorough understanding of leadership has value to everyone working in people-centered organizations, from staff who are empowered to solve problems that library customers encounter as they seek information, to members of teams and small groups trying to improve the delivery of service to the communities that libraries service, and to middle and senior managers pursuing organizational effectiveness, while intent on changing organizational cultures and engaged in succession management or planning. [32]

NOTES

1. Nancy Rossiter, "The Research Literature on Leadership," in *Making a Difference: Leadership and Academic Libraries*, ed. Peter Hernon and Nancy Rossiter, 31 (Westport, CT: Libraries Unlimited, 2007).

2. There is an emerging literature on ineffective, bad, negative, and destructive leadership. See, for instance, Barbara Kellerman, *Bad Leadership: What Is It, How Does It Happen, and Why It Matters* (Boston: Harvard Business School Press, 2004); Special Issue on "Destructive Leadership," *The Leadership Quarterly* 18, no. 3 (2007): 171–280; and Jan Schilling, "From Ineffectiveness to Destruction: A Qualitative Study on the Meaning of Negative Leadership," *Leadership* 5, no. 1 (2009): 102–28. Also relevant is Juan M. Madera and D. Brent Smith, "The Effects of Leader Negative Emotions on Evaluations of Leadership in a Crisis Situation: The Role of Anger and Sadness," *The Leadership Quarterly* 20, no. 2 (April 2009): 103–14.

3. Peter Hernon and Candy Schwartz, "Leadership: Developing a Research Agenda for Academic Libraries," *Library & Information Science Research* 30, no. 4 (December 2008): 243–49.

4. Peter Hernon, Joan Giesecke, and Camila A. Alire, *Academic Librarians as Emotionally Intelligent Leaders* (Westport, CT: Libraries Unlimited, 2008), 8–9.

5. Peter G. Northouse, *Leadership: Theory and Practice*, 4th ed. (Thousand Oaks, CA: Sage Publications, 2007), 2.

6. Joseph B. Lyons and, Tamera R. Schneider, "The Effects of Leadership Style on Stress Outcomes," *The Leadership Quarterly* 20 (2009): 747.

7. Ibid.

8.   David R. Krathwohl, *Social and Behavioral Science Research: A New Framework for Conceptualizing, Implementing, and Evaluating Research Studies* (San Francisco: Jossey-Bass, 1985), 52. For an extended discussion of problem statements, see Peter Hernon, *Statistics: A Component of the Research Process* (Norwood, NJ: Ablex, 1994), 8–13; Peter Hernon and Candy Schwartz, "What Is a Problem Statement?," *Library & Information Science Research*, 29, no. 3 (2007): 307–9; Peter Hernon and Cheryl Metoyer-Duran, "Problem Statements: An Exploratory Study of Their Function, Significance, and Form," *Library & Information Science Research* 15, no. 1 (Winter 1993): 71–92; and Cheryl Metoyer-Duran and Peter Hernon, "Problem Statements in Research Proposals and Published Research: A Case Study of Researchers' Viewpoints," *Library & Information Science Research* 16, no. 2 (1994): 105–18.

9.   Vincent A. Anfara Jr. and Norman T. Mertz, *Theoretical Frameworks in Qualitative Research* (Thousand Oaks, CA: Sage Publications, 2006), xxvii.

10.   Cynthia D. McCauley, Wilfred H. Drath, Charles J. Palus, Patricia M. G. O'Connor, and Becca A. Baker, "The Use of Constructive-Development Theory to Advance the Understanding of Leadership," *The Leadership Quarterly* 17, no. 6 (2006): 634.

11.   C. Shawn Burke, Dana E. Sims. Elizabeth H. Lazzara, and Eduardo Salas, "Trust in Leadership: A Multi-Level Review and Integration," *The Leadership Quarterly* 18, no. 6 (2007): 606–32.

12.   U.S. General Accounting Office [now Government Accountability Office], Program Evaluation and Methodology Division, *Case Study Evaluations*, Transfer Paper 10.1.9 (Washington, DC: General Accounting Office, 1990), 14.

13.   Steven Taylor and Robert Bogdan, *Introduction to Qualitative Research Methods*, 2nd ed. (New York: Wiley, 1984), 126. See also Ken W. Perry, "Grounded Theory and Social Process: A New Direction for Leadership Research," *The Leadership Quarterly* 9, no. 1 (1998): 85–105.

14.   Karin Klenke, *Qualitative Research in the Study of Leadership* (Bingley, UK: Emerald Group Publishing Ltd., 2008).

15.   U.S. General Accounting Office [now Government Accountability Office], Program Evaluation and Methodology Division, *Content Analysis: A Methodology for Structuring and Analyzing Written Material*, Transfer Paper 10.1.3 (Washington, DC: General Accounting Office, 1989), 1. See also Tamara L. Friedrich, Christina L. Byrne, and Michael D. Mumford, "Methodological and Theoretical Considerations in Survey Research," *The Leadership Quarterly* 20, no. 2 (April 2009): 57–60.

16.   See Eric Trahan, "Applying Meta-Analysis to Library and Information Science Research," *The Library Quarterly* 63, no. 1 (1993): 73–91. See also C. Shawn Burke, Kevin C. Stagl, Cameron Klein, Gerald F. Goodwin, Eduardo Salas, and Stanley M. Halpin, "What Types of Leadership Behaviors Are Functional in Teams? A Meta-Analysis," *The Leadership Quarterly* 17, no. 3 (2006): 288–307; and Bruce J. Avolio, Rebecca J. Reichard, Sean T. Hannah, Fred O. Walumbwa, and Adrian Chan, "A Meta-Review of Leadership Impact Research: Experimental and Quasi-Experimental Studies," *The Leadership Quarterly* 20 (2009): 764–84.

17.   Robert M. Hayes, *Use of the Delphi Technique in Policy Formulation: A Case Study of the Public Sector/Private Sector Task Force* (Los Angeles: University of California, Graduate School of Library and Information Science, 1982), 1. See also John B. Harer, "Performance Measures of Quality for Academic Libraries Implementing Continuous Quality Improvement Programs: A Delphi Study" (Ph D diss., Texas A&M University, 2001). Available from *Dissertations & Theses: Full Text* (AAT 3011718).

18. Mary Kane and William M. K. Trochim, *Concept Mapping for Planning and Evaluation* (Thousand Oaks, CA: Sage Publications, 2007), 1.

19. Ibid., 7.

20. Schilling, "From Ineffectiveness to Destruction."

21. Gary Yukl, "Leading Organizational Learning: Reflections on Theory and Research," *The Leadership Quarterly* 20, no. 1 (2009): 53.

22. Joseph P. Martino, "The Precision of Delphi Estimates," *Technological Forecasting* 1, no. 3 (1970): 293–99.

23. Dana Mietzner and Guido Reger, "Advantages and Disadvantages of Scenario Approaches for Strategic Foresight," *International Journal of Technology Intelligence and Planning* 1, no. 2 (2005): 233. Available at http://www.lampsacus.com/documents/StragegicForesight.pdf (accessed December 29, 2009). They also note weaknesses associated with the development of scenarios.

24. Ibid.

25. For an example of a set of scenarios, see Peter Hernon and Laura Saunders, "The Federal Depository Library Program in 2023: One Perspective on the Transition to the Future," *College & Research Libraries* 70, no. 3 (May 2009): 351–70. The scenarios still merit further development, and the leadership necessary to achieve any of them should be probed.

26. James G. Neal, "Raised by Wolves: The New Generation of Feral Professionals in the Academic Library," *Library Journal* (February 15, 2006). Available at http://www.libraryjournal.com/article/CA6304405.html (accessed February 24, 2009).

27. Linda Sue Warner and Keith Grint, "American Indian Ways of Leading and Knowing," *Leadership* 2, no. 4 (May 2006): 225–44.

28. Chester A. Schriesheim and Claudia C. Cogliser, "Construct Validation in Leadership Research: Explication and Illustration," *The Leadership Quarterly* 20 (2009): 725.

29. U.S. General Accounting Office, *Case Study Evaluations*, 22.

30. Ibid.

31. See Raya Fidel, "Are We There Yet? Mixed Methods Research in Library and Information Science," *Library & Information Science Research* 30 (2008): 265–72.

32. Peter Hernon, "Preface," in *Academic Librarians as Emotionally Intelligent Leaders*, ed. Peter Hernon, Joan Giesecke, and Camila A. Alire, xi (Westport, CT: Libraries Unlimited, 2008).

2

~

THE MLIP PROGRAM

7

REVISITING MANAGERIAL LEADERSHIP AS AN AREA OF DOCTORAL STUDY

Peter Hernon

Managerial leadership calls for individuals to possess a set of attributes that makes them effective managers and successful leaders.[1]

Managerial leadership, a term that was apparently first used in the early 1950s, applies to the link between leadership and management, views management from the perspective of leadership, and in some instances is viewed as synonymous with leadership. For instance, it might focus on business challenges that organizations face or might face and the transformative learning experiences that individuals and corporate managers might encounter. No definition or characterization has gained general acceptance, and in fact even when used in the literature, the term is often left undefined. The implication is that everyone understands what the term means.

The Graduate School of Library and Information Science (GSLIS) at Simmons College (Boston, Massachusetts) laid the foundation for a PhD program in managerial leadership that replaced a program that culminated in a doctor of arts (DA) degree. Responding to a Carnegie Foundation call for institutions to create DA degrees as an alternative to the PhD, Simmons instituted the DA in library and information science in 1973. This was the first doctoral program at Simmons. It looked at management as an applied discipline that requires academic grounding and substantial work experience and produced graduates who were prepared to manage libraries. By the early 2000s Simmons was moving toward the creation of PhD programs, and at the same time the demand for leaders to manage changing organizations was increasing and new leadership institutes emerged. In 2005 a grant from the Institute of Museum and Library Services (IMLS) provided the impetus for moving a PhD program that prepares managers to study leadership in the information professions out of the conceptual realm and into practice. In this program, the term *managerial leadership* applies to those in significant managerial positions, initially predominantly in academic libraries. Hernon, Schwartz, and Anderson describe the first two years of the doctoral program in managerial leadership in the information professions (MLIP).[2]

The purpose of this chapter is to discuss developments in the program since receiving a second grant from IMLS in 2008. Together, with both multiyear grants IMLS and Simmons have invested more than $3 million in the program and in the education of future managerial leaders in library and information settings. The second grant focuses on leadership in the context of public and state libraries, offering state and public library managers in middle- to upper-level management the opportunity to hone their skills by working closely with academic faculty and acknowledged library leaders. Successful applicants are awarded full tuition and a travel stipend. We still admit academic libraries.

THE PROGRAM

The MLIP program nurtures and strengthens the knowledge, abilities, and skill sets of students as working managers and introduces them to rigorous research that adds to their knowledge base in library and information science (LIS) and their experience in the practice of managerial leadership.

The MLIP program differs from leadership institutes and other doctoral programs in a number of ways. First, as compared to leadership institutes, it is research focused. Second, students pursue the program continuously and over a longer time line, allowing for fuller investigation of leadership theories and exploration of these theories through comprehensive research studies. Third, program graduates achieve a recognized degree and demonstrate exceptional proficiency in integrating theory and practice.

The MLIP program differs from other doctoral programs in LIS in that the entire program is set in the context of managerial leadership, with the focus on leadership theories and their application to the workforce. Most important, there is an emphasis on advancing students' understanding of research and their ability to perform research and scholarship that contributes to the theory of organizational management and change. This is critical to assisting leaders who need to cope with accountability, effectiveness, efficiency, and service improvement.

Program Goals

The goals of the program are to

- prepare individuals for careers as change agents and leaders in managing libraries and other information-related organizations in an environment of globalization and convergence of disciplines;

- create an environment in which inquiry and critical questioning are valued, individual strengths are enhanced, and individual weaknesses are recognized and overcome;

- engender in students an ability to engage in analytical thinking and problem solving;

- establish a culture that nurtures the advancement and dissemination of new knowledge related to managing libraries as complex organizations;

- provide students with a conceptual understanding of organizations and behavior within them; and

- guide students in developing competencies in interpersonal and communication skills, leadership, and facilitation.

These goals are accomplished through a program of courses and modules that combine short, intensive, face-to-face instruction sessions, independent study, online activities, and group work. In addition to the structured coursework, program activities include presentations to diverse stakeholder groups and a variety of research and analysis projects that generate an extensive portfolio for every student, featuring publishable business cases, scenario plans, issue briefs, and research and analytical papers (see chapters 9 and 11 for examples of student work).

Cohorts of students engage with each other in some courses and through a private student listserv. Activities are designed to enhance the ability of students to work effectively in teams and to stimulate and nurture the intellectual exchange that is a fundamental characteristic of the doctoral experience. At the annual and midwinter conferences of the American Library Association and the annual program of the Public Library Association, we put on a luncheon program or reception for the board of advisors, faculty, and students with a guest speaker. Before, during, and after the program there is ample opportunity to meet and exchange ideas about leadership and research. Further, during the on-site portion of a school term, there are also guest speakers and opportunities for various cohorts to visit.

Advisory Board

The board of advisors, which consists of leaders of professional organizations and libraries, includes the following people:

- Camila A. Alire, past president of the American Library Association and dean emerita at the University of New Mexico and Colorado State University

- Joan R. Giesecke, dean of libraries, University of Nebraska-Lincoln

- Luis Herrera, city librarian of San Francisco

- Bernard A. Margolis, state librarian of New York

- James M. Matarazzo, professor at Simmons College

- Cheryl Metoyer, associate professor at the University of Washington

- James G. Neal, vice president for information services and university librarian, Columbia University

- Danuta A. Nitecki, dean of libraries, Drexel University

- Nancy Robertson, state librarian of Michigan

- Peggy Rudd, state librarian of Texas

- Jan Sanders, director of Pasadena (CA) Public Library

- Denise Stephens, vice provost for information services, the University of Kansas

- Duane Webster, executive director emeritus, Association of Research Libraries

- James F. Williams, dean of libraries, the University of Colorado, Boulder

- Anne Wolpert, director of libraries, Massachusetts Institute of Technology

- Jerome Yavarkovsky, former university librarian, Boston College

Board members offer advice in all phases of the program. For instance, they review policies, make suggestions about sources of future funding to support students, and, together with program faculty, help to recruit possible applicants to the program and support the program's strong commitment to diversity. Some of them teach in the program, and others have provided a lunchtime discussion of leadership with the students, program faculty, and other board members.

THE FACULTY

The faculty consists of Peter Hernon, a senior member of the GSLIS faculty, and the following nationally and internationally known practitioners, who serve as professors of practice:

- Camila A. Alire
- Patricia Deyton
- Robert E. Dugan
- Joan Giesecke
- Luis Herrera
- James G. Neal
- Danuta A. Nitecki
- Jan Sanders
- Maureen Sullivan

The professors of practice bring practical work experiences as leaders of complex organizations. In most cases they direct library systems or units or consult for numerous libraries and professional associations. Patricia Deyton is a member of the highly respected Simmons School of Management and oversees part of the capstone course.

Each course is taught by two professors of practice, except for the research courses and independent projects, which Peter Hernon directs with the assistance of Danuta Nitecki. These collaborations enrich the learning experience and provide students with ample mentoring, thereby reinforcing the competencies specified in the leadership model (discussed later in the chapter). The faculty emphasize the practical dilemmas encountered in libraries and integrate theory and practice. At the time of the qualifying examination, Hernon drafts the set of questions, which the professors of practice, in turn, review. For most of the students, Hernon serves as chair of the dissertation committees. Professors of practice can serve as committee members, and other members come from Simmons faculty or a student's own recommendation.

STUDENT BODY

The admission process is very competitive. Since the first cohort began the program in May 2006, there have been five cohorts totaling twenty-four students (a cohort does not exceed eight individuals). As is true of all doctoral programs, there has been some attrition.

The first grant emphasized middle- to senior level managers in academic libraries who are poised to make lasting contributions to the profession and who would benefit from the program. The students are encouraged to complete the program within three years, while working full time, but the economic downturn and career advancement might unintentionally lengthen the program for some. With the second grant, the emphasis shifted to middle- to senior-level managers in public and state libraries.

Of the twenty-four students,

- seventeen are female and seven are male;
- thirteen work in academic libraries, eight in public libraries, two in state libraries, and one is at OCLC;
- seventeen are Caucasian, four are African American, two are Asian American, and one is Native American; and
- five are working on their dissertations.

Another eight students are expected to take their qualifying examination over the next year and to begin working on their dissertations. Finally, the twenty-five students come from a wide range of states (Arizona, California, Colorado, Florida, Georgia, Illinois, Massachusetts, Maryland, Nebraska, New Hampshire, Ohio, Oregon, Virginia, and the District of Columbia), and one student, who is not covered by either grant, is from Canada.

One student has received the David A. Kronick Traveling Fellowship (May 2009). This grant awards each year one $2,000 fellowship to cover the expenses involved in traveling to three or more medical libraries in the United States or Canada, for the purpose of studying a specific aspect of health information management. Figure 7.1 shows what student papers, research and other, have appeared in the professional literature. The number will continue to increase, as the program stresses the importance of publication in well-known, peer-reviewed journals. The dissertations will also create publishing and speaking opportunities.

Casey, Anne M. "Distance Learning Librarians: Their Shared Vision." *Journal of Library & Information Services in Distance Learning* 3, no. 1 (January–March 2009): 3–22.

Cawthorne, Jon. "Leading from the Middle of the Organization: An Examination of Shared Leadership in Academic Libraries." *Journal of Academic Librarianship*, 36, no. 2 (March 2010):151–57.

DeLong, Kathleen. "The Engagement of New Library Professionals in Leadership." *Journal of Academic Librarianship* 35, no. 5 (September 2009): 445–56.

Kreitz, Patricia A. "Best Practices for Managing Organizational Diversity." *Journal of Academic Librarianship* 34, no. 2 (March 2008): 101–20.

Kreitz, Patricia A. "Leadership and Emotional Intelligence: A Study of University Library Directors and Their Senior Management Teams." *College & Research Libraries* 70, no. 6 (November 2009): 531–54.

Lim, Adriene. "The Readability of Information Literacy Content on Academic Library Web Sites." *The Journal of Academic Librarianship* 35, no. 4 (July 2010): forthcoming.

Piorun, Mary. "Evaluation of Strategic Plans in Academic Medical Libraries." *Library & Information Science Research* 33 (2011): forthcoming.

Figure 7.1 Student Publications

CURRICULUM

The curriculum model positions the program at the intersection of management, leadership, and LIS. Students are expected to understand and demonstrate their leadership competencies within the disciplinary, temporal, geospatial, and political contexts in which library and information enterprises operate. The curriculum model (http://www.simmons.edu/gslis/docs/phdmlip_models_new_permission.pdf), adapted from a model developed by the National Center for Healthcare Leadership, and a leadership model (http://web.simmons.edu/~phdml/docs/phdmlip_models.pdf) guide curriculum and assessment activities. The latter model consists of twenty-five distinct leadership competencies arrayed in three broad areas:

- Transformation: Visioning, energizing, and stimulating a change process that coalesces communities, customers, and professionals around new models of managerial leadership

- Accomplishment: Translating vision and strategy into optimal organizational performance

- People: Creating an organizational climate that values employees from all backgrounds and provides an energizing environment for them. It also includes the leader's responsibility to understand his or her impact on others and to improve his or her capabilities, as well as the capabilities of others.

Each new cohort comes to the Boston campus in late April for an orientation to the program, a discussion of expectations for doctoral students, an overview of the courses for the first semester, and a one-day discussion of student research interests. The actual school term begins in early June in Boston. All cohorts taking courses meet during the same week, so that there is opportunity for inter-cohort interaction. Courses are offered in summer, fall, and winter and begin with five days of face-to-face intensive instruction either at Simmons or an alternate location. Table 7.1 depicts the components of the curriculum—the courses and modules. Once students have completed all of the coursework and the two research projects, they may take the qualifying examinations, and upon successful completion, they begin working on the dissertation.

OUTCOMES AND THEIR ASSESSMENT

Assessment occurs at four stages of the program. During the initial orientation and the first term of the program, students are introduced to the MLIP leadership model and twenty-five leadership competencies, which include, for instance, achievement orientation, analytical thinking, problem solving, communication skills, organizational awareness, professionalism, and team leadership. Each course focuses on particular competencies and, upon completion of courses, the faculty complete an assessment form that rates each student on the extent to which he or she has mastered each competency. Each student has an annual meeting with the faculty in which the individual makes a presentation about what he or she learned and the faculty review with the student a composite of the assessment forms completed for the past year. These review meetings occur for the first two years of the program. During the program students receive extensive feedback on their research proposals and the draft papers they prepare. This experience helps them develop the dissertation proposal and gain an understanding of the research process put into practice.

Each summer the program faculty get together over lunch and review the collective set of courses and general student progress. This discussion usually results in program improvement. For example, collective discussion revealed that students do not write as well as they should. As a result, the director of the Simmons Writing Center now meets with each new cohort and reviews with them a sample of their writing. During the first term of the program she continues to meet with individual students or whole groups as needed.

Table 7.1
The Curriculum

LIS 671, Managerial Leadership	This course reviews the major contributions to contemporary managerial leadership research, theory, and practice, including such areas as strategic planning, change management, and team building. It also places emphasis on a greater awareness of one's behavior, its impact on others, and the elements needed to influence people to accomplish desired goals in information organizations.
LIS 672, Research for Managerial Leadership	Research for managerial leadership is positioned within the larger context of social science research. The course examines the research process from conceptualization of a researchable problem, through the reflective inquiry process, to completion (including review of the publication process). The need for research in library and information science is discussed, as well as trends and issues, types of research studies, problem identification, and the setup of and reporting on activities of a research study.
LIS 675, Evaluation and Statistics	The course applies the principles of evaluation research to contemporary problems related to managerial leadership in the information professions. Building on LIS 672, Research for Managerial Leadership for Library and Information Services, it covers the fundamentals of identifying and investigating problems relevant to continuous quality improvement and communicating the results to decision makers. It also provides an introduction to statistics and accountability.
LIS 676, Financial Management	This course provides an overview of financial management for libraries, information-related organizations, and projects within the context of identified leadership values. The topics of planning, implementing, and reporting on budgets, financial management measures, internal and external communications, partnering, stewardship, and integrity are all issues that are discussed relative to the desired outcomes of institutional accountability, credibility, and trust.
LIS 677, Human Resource Management	This course is a comprehensive examination of the various functions and best practices of human resources management. This course covers human resources management (HRM) as it relates to strategic planning for human resource development; work design; recruitment, selection, and retention of staff; compensation and position classification; performance planning and assessment; labor relations; motivating and leading a diverse workforce; and staff and organization development. The course also examines the interactions among managers, organizational staff, and/or specialists.

Table 7.1 The Curriculum (Continued)

LIS 678, Managing and Leading in a Political Environment	This course covers the skills necessary for interacting with the larger communities in which libraries and information centers operate (academic institutions, municipalities, corporations). It specifically addresses advocacy and cooperation within complex, multi-stakeholder power structures as encountered when working with administrators, political leaders, and community groups (e.g., citizens, faculty, and students). The effect of political contexts on planning activities is also covered.
LIS 685, Managerial Leadership in Public Settings	This course, which is taken just before the capstone course, covers critical issues that face public and state libraries as they continue to meet present and future challenges. It specifically builds on courses previously taken and addresses significant topics that have both managerial and leadership implications.
LIS 687, Issues in Information Policy	Information policy is a set of interrelated principles, laws, guidelines, rules and regulations, decisions and other renderings, and procedures that guide the oversight and management of the information life cycle. This field of public policy intersects most disciplines and professions, including law and public administration. Information policies determine what information is publicly available, and guide organizations in their information management practices.
LIS 688, Fundraising and Entrepreneurial Strategies	Resource development, that is, the identification and successful recruitment of new sources of funds to advance the library and information services program, is an essential aspect of leadership and strategic progress. This course addresses two aspects of resource development: fund-raising and entrepreneurial strategies. The conditions and trends in the environment of libraries and information services that drive resource development are identified. The cultural, organizational, and programmatic elements of successful library fund-raising programs are reviewed and debated, with a particular focus on the role of the library leader. The function of innovation, risk taking, competition, and business planning in enabling and promoting entrepreneurial thinking and action in library and information services are discussed, with an emphasis on income-generating projects.
LIS 680, Independent Inquiry	Students execute two managerial leadership research studies. Activity may begin upon completion of LIS 672 (Research for Managerial Leadership for Library and Information Services) and concurrent with or subsequent to LIS 675 (Evaluation and Statistics). The Independent Inquiry research projects are the execution of the research proposals developed in LIS 672 (becomes 680a research study) and LIS 675 (becomes 680b research study). This learning activity has a flexible time frame, but it must be completed as a prerequisite to the capstone course: Issues in Leading Transformation in Library and Information Services. Program faculty guide students in developing an appropriate schedule for completion of both studies. Students produce two research papers of publishable quality.

Table 7.1 The Curriculum (Continued)

Modules

3-credit foundation course	1-credit module
LIS 677, Human Resource Management	LIS 682, Human Resource Management Module
LIS 678, Managing and Leading in a Political Environment	LIS 683, Managing and Leading Library and Information Services in a Political Environment Module
LIS 676, Financial Management	LIS 681, Leadership in Financial Management Module

The content of the 3-credit courses is complex, and therefore the program curriculum also includes corresponding "modules" of 1 credit each, to provide students with the opportunity to synthesize and integrate what they have learned.

The modules are similar to small capstone projects. Instructors for each module assign a project to be completed by students independently or in groups. The project is designed to enable students to pull together the elements they have learned in the corresponding 3-credit course.

| LIS 691, Issues in Leading Transformation | This capstone course involves sustained interaction with faculty and fellow doctoral students in examining issues critical to transformational change. It draws on all the theories and applications explored in previous coursework and independent investigation to lead and guide informed conversation about and exploration of leading transformation in information services. Content is flexible in order to serve the competencies, needs, and interests of the student cohort. Assignments and activities include in-class presentations, discussion facilitation, and reflection on the group process. Work associated with this course does not extend beyond the week of class meeting. |

The final course is a capstone course that highlights major themes and introduces students to several leaders in the profession. For instance, Duane Webster leads a discussion of the scenarios that he developed for university libraries as part of his work with the Association of Research Libraries. As another example, for one of the capstone days the students must organize a presentation involving role playing. Board member Margolis attends this session and assumes different roles as he challenges the students to extend their thinking and problem solving.

Following the capstone, students take the qualifying examination, which is a form of assessment. The examination has revealed some weaknesses in student understanding of the research process, and as a result, the course on Issues in Information Policy now includes a segment on information policy research, and the capstone incorporates a new segment on the components of good social science research. Of course, the dissertation serves as the last formal assessment of each student by the student's committee members.

Finally, every fall three leaders in the profession who are not affiliated with the program conduct a program assessment. They have access to student work and program documentation and may interview program faculty and students. They provide a written report, which is shared with the faculty and the advisory board. The purpose is to use the report as a means of ongoing improvement.

CONCLUDING THOUGHTS

To maintain the program for the long-term, a number of issues need to be resolved. First, once the IMLS grant expires, additional funding will be needed to support the teaching program and the level of dedication that the professors of practice provide. Second, additional funds need to be raised to support students with their tuition. Although GSLIS provides partial tuition support, working students must cover the remaining costs of tuition and expenses related to travel, lodging, and meals, while attending courses on-site. Third, applicants to the program have a weak understanding of research and are often unaware of the research literature and of research as a formal process of inquiry whose goal is to engage in extending theory and solving problems. Students find the research components of the curriculum the most challenging and least familiar.

Fourth, although a number of prominent librarians are willing to become professors of practice, there is still a need to involve more faculty within GSLIS and Simmons as a whole. Once Hernon retires, others within GSLIS will have to provide the level of leadership and guidance that he has provided for more than five years. Whoever replaces him will have to keep the professional community aware of the program and actively involved in making it successful. Indicators of the current success of the program include the placement of student research and other papers in the scholarly literature of LIS, the advancement of students in the program to positions with greater authority and responsibility, and the graduation of students. In May 2011 GSLIS will proudly hood its first PhDs in managerial leadership in the information professions.

Because leadership is not necessarily linked to a managerial position, managerial leadership does not encompass all leadership that might occur within a library.[3]

NOTES

1.   Peter Hernon, Candy Schwartz, and Caryn Anderson, "Managerial Leadership as an Area of Doctoral Study," in *Making a Difference: Leadership and Academic Libraries*, ed. Peter Hernon and Nancy Rossiter, 253 (Westport, CT: Libraries Unlimited, 2007).

2.   Ibid., 229–50.

3.   Ibid., 255.

8

~

CASE STUDIES METHOD: AN OVERVIEW

Maureen Sullivan

There's only one way to learn the demanding art of leadership—and that's by leading. That's why a Harvard Business School education has been, and continues to be, rooted in the practical lessons of the case method.[1]

The case study analysis method for teaching and learning has proven to be an effective tool for deep learning for some time. A well-written case enables students to explore theories and concepts by relating them to an actual situation. The case study analysis method is especially useful when the issue and concepts to be learned are complex and challenging. Case studies can be developed or selected by program faculty for classroom analysis or written by students as a preassignment or an in-class learning activity.

The case method is at the heart of the curricula of many higher education programs. Among the most widely known of these is the Harvard Business School. The Harvard Graduate School of Education (HGSE) also uses the case method in the Harvard Institutes for Higher Education. These cases are extensive descriptions of complex situations, usually written by PhD students and based on real examples.

Participants in the HGSE Leadership Institute for Academic Librarians, a weeklong program held annually in August, read and discuss four or five case studies. Each participant also prepares a mini-case to describe an actual situation in her or his own experience to submit in advance of the program. This advance assignment calls for participants to focus on an event or experience that proved to be challenging for them. Each participant has the opportunity to discuss the case with colleagues in a small group, to gain different perspectives on the situation, and to consider alternative approaches. It is an excellent tool for what C. Roland Christensen, a leading authority on case method teaching, calls "discussion teaching," a method in which "every student teaches and every teacher learns."[2]

From the beginning, the curriculum for the PhD Program in Managerial Leadership in the Information Professions at Simmons College has included the writing of case studies by students. Those case studies have implications for managing and leading libraries as managers move the organization forward and deal with old and new problems. For the case studies, students select situations from their own experience and tell their stories about those situations.

There are opportunities to write case studies of varying length and complexity in a number of courses, the capstone experience, and the qualifying examination. They provide an excellent foundation for evaluating various leadership theories and styles.

GUIDELINES FOR WRITING A CASE STUDY

Choose a situation that was or is challenging for you and your organization. That situation should bring forth the complexities, challenges, and opportunities for effective managerial leadership. Organizational experiences that involve conflict, obstacles, controversy, values, dilemmas, and serious issues offer the richest opportunities for analysis and learning.

Select a situation that you know, that will be of interest to your colleagues and will enrich the collective learning experience. Choose a situation that is complex and will require in-depth discussion and examination. Provide as much relevant data and contextual information as you can.

Write the case as a story. Tell what happened. Stay with the description of events and avoid any analysis or interpretation of the events. If you are or were directly involved, tell your story in the first person. Describe the events. Include your thoughts and feelings. Relate what others said and did. Consider writing the story as a script, using quotations to enable the characters to speak in their own voices.

Open the case with a brief description of the organizational context and your role. Include relevant data that will enable the reader to understand quickly the setting of the situation.

Develop the body of the story. View this as your effort to relate the plot or heart of the story to the reader. Relate meaningful conversations. Include information about the time frame or use dates to indicate the progression of events.

Close with a statement of the unsolved problem or of the dilemma faced. Include several questions to be posed for discussion by your colleagues. These questions can be used to focus their attention on the key issues or as decision points for the managerial leader.

Identify for yourself what you see to be the key learning points in the case.

POSSIBLE STRUCTURE FOR A CASE STUDY

In general, the type of case study the students develop has five components. First, the opening, general paragraph provides an overview of the situation. Second, one or two paragraphs describe the institutional setting. Third, the body of the case is organized to tell the story of the case. Students should use headings as appropriate to organize the segments of the case description. Fourth, they are instructed to close with a statement of the dilemma faced or the problem to be solved and any lessons learned. And finally, there should be a set of questions that guide discussion about managerial leadership and lessons that might be learned.

Students can include any relevant documents as appendices. If they wish not to divulge the specifics of the organization and individuals involved, they should write the case with fabricated names and information. (The examples of case studies included in the next chapter do not reveal any specific institution. Their purpose is to frame a discussion that applies across organizations.) Students are reminded that effective case studies are well written and provide them with a foundation to communicate with different audiences in their coursework. The audiences range from administrators in higher education, to members of city government, to policy makers, to others in the library—from middle to senior managers.

USE OF CASE STUDIES

Case studies comprise a method to communication with others—not limited to the program. It is possible for students in graduate programs of library and information science, as well as participants in a leadership institute, to take the case studies and discuss complex issues. Further, as part of their professional development, library staff might review case studies and engage in role playing.

CONCLUDING THOUGHTS

An excellent model for students to emulate in writing case studies is the set that A. J. Anderson, professor emeritus at Simmons College, wrote for *Library Journal* for approximately sixteen years; the chapter appendix reprints his problem-solving model, which anyone writing case studies should review before starting to develop the scenario.[3] A number of his case studies have withstood the test of time and are known for being well written. Students, or for that matter anyone writing a case study, should review his work—not necessarily for its relevance to today but for its ability to form, structure, and foster discussion involving different parties.

Case Studies . . . are lively . . . accounts of management challenges with expert commentary from academic and practitioner perspectives.[4]

NOTES

1. Harvard Business School, "Learning in Practice: Make Your Case for Leadership" (2010). Available at http://www.hbs.edu/learning/case.html (accessed February 1, 2010).

2. C. Roland Christensen, "Every Student Teaches and Every Teacher Learns: The Reciprocal Gift of Discussion Teaching," in *Education for Judgement: The Artistry of Discussion Leadership*, by C. Roland Christensen, David A. Garvin, and Ann Sweet, 99 (Boston: Harvard Business School Press, 1991).

3. See also A. J. Anderson, *Problems in Library Management* (Littleton, CO: Libraries Unlimited, 1981).

4. Harvard Business Publishing, "For Educators" (2009). Available at http://hbsp.harvard.edu/list/hbr-case-study (accessed February 2, 2010).

AJ'S PROBLEM-SOLVING MODEL—THE STEPS TO BE FOLLOWED*

1. Identify the MP (Main Problem). It must be phrased as an open-ended question: "What could So-and-So do about _____?" Or "What should So-and-so do about _____?"

2. State the <u>Facts</u> of the case—give a very brief summary.

3. Identify and list the <u>Alternative Courses of Action</u> for the MP:

   1.
   2.
   3.
   4.
   Etc.

4. Identify the <u>Advantages and Disadvantages</u> of each Alternative Course of Action

   Alternative # 1 (PLEASE REPEAT EACH ALTERNATIVE COURSE OF ACTION BEFORE LISTING THE ADVANTAGES AND DISADVANTAGES OF EACH)

   <u>Advantages</u>
      a.
      b.
      c.
      etc.

   <u>Disadvantages</u>
      a.
      b.
      c.
      etc.

5. Select the <u>Best Alternative(s)</u> and state <u>Why</u> it is (or they are) the best to pursue.

6. <u>Implementation</u>: Outline in step-by-step specifics and detail exactly what should be done to implement the Best Alternative(s).

7. <u>Follow-Through</u>—the "<u>If/then</u>" stage. <u>If</u> the best course(s) of action will not work, or is (are) not possible to do, <u>then</u>—.

8. List the <u>Assignments.</u>

*This appendix was developed by A. J. Anderson, professor emeritus, Simmons College, and is reprinted with his permission.

From *Shaping the Future: Advancing the Understanding of Leadership* by Peter Hernon, Editor. Santa Barbara, CA: Libraries Unlimited. Copyright © 2010.

9. List the Issue/Areas (I/As).

10. List the Cluster Problems (CPs). "Cluster" or group them under separate headings.

11. List the "Things."

> Things I Would Do
> Things I Would Like to Do
> Things I Would Have Done
> Things I Would Like to Be Able to Do
> Things I Would Like to Know

HOW TO TACKLE A CASE USING AJ's PROBLEM-SOLVING MODEL

Read the case—just think about it.

Read it again, this time jotting down thoughts that occur to you—in no particular order.

Review your list of items and identify whether what you have written down is something that needs to be done (an Assignment), or that needs to be investigated (an Issue/Area), or that needs to be discussed or solved (a Problem, later to be referred to as Cluster Problem), or that you are curious about (a Thing).

Write beside the Assignments the letter "A", beside the Issues/Areas the letters "I/A", beside the Problems the letter "P", and beside the Things the word "Thing".

Make headings, or open separate windows, and list the Assignments, the I/As, the Ps, and the Things.

Select one of your problems and make it the Main Problem (MP). This is usually a problem requiring immediate action, or a problem that cannot be avoided, or that should not be avoided.

The MP should be stated in terms of how the person in the case for whom you are solving the problem should or could deal with it. The statement of the MP should start with the words "What could (the person's name) do about _____?, or "What should (the person's name) do about _____?"

Then state all the Alternative Courses of Action for the character that you can come up with.

Then generate Advantages and Disadvantages for each Alternative Course of Action.

Then select what you consider to be the Best Alternative(s) and state Why it is (or they are) the best course(s) of action for the character in the case to follow.

Then state how the Implementation of the Best Alternative(s) would be accomplished—being as specific as possible as to exactly what should be done.

Next identify what the character should do if the Best Alternative(s) might not work. This is the Follow-Through step, the "If/then" step—viz., "If Alternative #4 won't work because _____, then _____ ".

Then list the Assignments.

Then list the I/As.

Then list the Problems, but Cluster them, meaning group them under headings, such as a person's name, or a group of people, or a particular policy, etc., and use the heading Cluster Problems. Whereas the Assignments and the I/As are merely listed, please discuss the CPs, meaning give your thoughts on them.

Finally list the Things, but assign them to the following categories:
>Things I Would Do
>Things I Would Like to Do
>Things I Would Like to Be Able to Do
>Things I Would Like to Know

(You may not have something to put under each of these headings, but you most certainly will have under more than one.)

It is suggested that you, as the analyst, try to put yourself in the shoes of the person in the case whose problem you are solving. When this is not possible (because you cannot relate to or identify with the person), then consider yourself a consultant to the person. One does not have to identify with the character in this event, or like him or her, as a consultant!

When the events in the case have taken place and the person for whom you are solving the problem has made a decision that has not worked out successfully, you can "cut into" the case at some point and solve the problem from that point. The MP would then be stated in terms of "What could so-and-so have done about _____?" Or "What should so-and-so have done about _____?"

It is also possible to make assumptions and in effect add to the case as stated. No case can ever state all the facts surrounding a particular situation. If you have occasion to make an assumption, such as "I am assuming the library has security officers," please state your assumption(s) at the beginning of your analysis.

On the sheet entitled "AJ's PROBLEM-SOLVING MODEL—THE STEPS TO BE FOLLOWED" you will see an additional step not outlined here—the Facts. When handing in your preliminary analysis, after you have stated the MP, please make a very brief summary of the Facts of the case.

"The Absentee Director"
A Case Analysis

Main Problem

What could Dale do about the fact that he feels abandoned by Dorothy Kesten as his director and that he would like her to become more involved with the library staff?

The Facts of the Case

Dale is a 30-year-old Interlibrary Loan Librarian who has worked at Barger College's Hahnemann Library for the past two years. In a letter to his friend Jonas, Dale admits that he is near the breaking point of frustration with his director, Dorothy Kesten. Dorothy, at 34, has been the director of the library for four years, after serving two years as head of reference. She is very active in professional organizations, and is frequently absent from the library because of her attendance at meetings and conferences. When she is not away at conferences, she stays in her office, does not interact with the staff, offers no feedback (positive or negative), and never shares what she has learned at the conferences. Dorothy has taken her "laissez-faire" style of management to the point of neglect. Although the library is functional, the non-unionized staff of 19 (8 professional and 11 clerical) is docile and shies away from meaningful discussions at the infrequent staff meetings. Dale is desperate to express his frustration, but is afraid to approach Dorothy because she has been known to get angry and glower at anyone who mentions one of her "taboo" topics.

Alternative Courses of Action

1. Do nothing. Continue to suffer in silence.

2. Try to talk to some or all of the Hahnemann Library staff about his feelings in hopes that venting his frustrations will make them go away.

3. Try to talk to the department heads of the Hahnemann Library staff in an attempt to rally them into trying to confront Dorothy about her neglect.

4. Try to get Dorothy's attention by trying to get the staff to hold their own staff meetings and trainings, copying Dorothy on the memos.

5. Try to have an informal discussion with Dorothy, telling her that he feels frustrated with the communication among the staff (not singling Dorothy out).

6. Write an anonymous letter to the President of Barger College, stating that the library staff are frustrated with Dorothy's frequent absences and lack of leadership.

7. Try to find a brochure for a professional seminar on how to be a better manager, highlight the section on involvement with staff, and anonymously leave it on Dorothy's desk while she is away.

8. Try to get Dorothy to realize how much she is neglecting the staff by making a joke at the next semiannual staff meeting that she is gone a lot.

9. Make a list of what he would like from Dorothy as a director and try to make an appointment to discuss the list with her.

Advantages and Disadvantages

1. Do nothing. Continue to suffer in silence.

   Advantages

   a. Dale avoids conflict with Dorothy.

   b. He avoids alienating those on the staff who like Dorothy's management style.

   c. If Dorothy does "go on to bigger and better things," the staff will outlast her and they might get a better director.

   Disadvantages

   a. His resentment might build and affect his job even more than it has.

   b. The problem still exists; Dorothy's behavior does not change.

   c. His self-esteem is further eroded because he caves in to his fear.

2. Try to talk to some or all of the Hahnemann Library staff about his feelings in hopes that venting his frustrations will make them go away.

   Advantages

   a. He "solves" the problem by trying to make it go away by talking about it.

   b. He avoids conflict with Dorothy.

   c. He might build camaraderie with other staff members by sharing a mutual resentment against Dorothy.

   d. He will feel validated if others agree with him.

   Disadvantages

   a. He is likely to alienate those staff members who support Dorothy.

   b. He sets a bad example to the other staff by gossiping.

   c. He sows seeds of discontent among the staff and morale goes down.

d. Dorothy's behavior still does not change.

e. The staff might resent him for doing this.

3. Try to talk to the department heads of the Hahnemann Library staff in an attempt to rally them into trying to confront Dorothy about her neglect.

Advantages

a. Dale does not have to confront Dorothy alone.

b. He might unify and empower the staff in the common goal of confronting Dorothy.

c. He and the other staff create a tangible list of complaints, rather than just Dale's personal frustrations.

d. Involves only the professionals, not the clerks.

Disadvantages

a. Not all of the department heads might want to go along with the plan to confront Dorothy.

b. He divides the staff between supporters of the plan and nonsupporters.

c. Dorothy might feel ambushed if confronted by the department heads.

d. Dorothy might find out he is organizing the staff against her and discipline or fire him.

4. Try to get Dorothy's attention by trying to get the staff to hold their own staff meetings and trainings, copying Dorothy on the memos.

Advantages

a. Dale does not have to confront Dorothy directly.

b. It makes Dale and the staff look like they have a lot of initiative.

c. Dorothy is impressed by their initiative and is motivated to get more involved with the staff.

d. Dale shows he has leadership ability.

e. His self-esteem is increased because he takes an action.

Disadvantages

a. He bypasses Dorothy's authority.

b. Dorothy might see his behavior as insubordination; Dale could be disciplined or fired.

c.   Still does not solve the problem; Dorothy might continue her neglect.

d.   The staff might resent his taking over Dorothy's authority and acting like a director.

5.   Try to have an informal discussion with Dorothy, telling her that he feels frustrated with the communication in the staff (not singling Dorothy out).

Advantages

a.   He deals directly with Dorothy, not involving anyone else.

b.   He is doing something proactive to deal with his frustrations by going directly to the source.

c.   Gives an opportunity for the real issue (Dorothy's management style) to be discussed.

d.   He is reassured by spending one-on-one time with Dorothy.

Disadvantages

a.   His frustrations are vague and may annoy Dorothy if he does not have anything concrete to present.

b.   Staff communication might be one of Dorothy's "taboo topics"; he might be scared off by "the ray."

c.   Dorothy might demand to know with whom he is having the communication trouble.

d.   If Dorothy finds out his trouble is with her, she might lose respect for him because of his cowardly approach.

e.   He brings only his problems and complaints, not solutions.

6.   Write an anonymous letter to the President of Barger College, stating that the library staff are frustrated with Dorothy's frequent absences and lack of leadership.

Advantages

a.   Dale does not have to confront Dorothy.

b.   Brings the problem to the attention of someone who has influence over Dorothy.

c.   He feels a sense of power in going over Dorothy's head.

d.   Dorothy might be reprimanded and told to get more involved with the staff.

e.   Dorothy might be replaced with a better director (Dale?).

<u>Disadvantages</u>

    a.   Dale feels guilty for stabbing his boss in the back.

    b.   Dorothy feels that there is a traitor among the staff and becomes more distant.

    c.   Dorothy could find out Dale sent the letter, and discipline or fire him.

    d.   It would make the library look bad to the president of the college.

    e.   The president might be too busy for, or ignore, the anonymous letter.

7. Try to find a brochure for a professional seminar on how to be a better manager, highlight the section on involvement with staff, and anonymously leave it on Dorothy's desk while she is away.

<u>Advantages</u>

    a.   Dale feels like he has at least done something.

    b.   Dorothy might attend the class and become a better manager.

    c.   He avoids confronting Dorothy.

<u>Disadvantages</u>

    a.   Dale still remains ashamed of his fear of confrontation.

    b.   Dorothy could be insulted and attempt to find out who left the brochure.

    c.   Dorothy could completely miss the point and throw the brochure away.

8. Try to get Dorothy to realize how much she is neglecting the staff by making a joke at the next semiannual staff meeting about how much she travels.

<u>Advantages</u>

    a.   Might open the door for others in the meeting to initiate a more serious discussion with Dorothy about her neglect.

    b.   He does not have to confront Dorothy one-on-one.

    c.   If she gets angry he could pass it off as "just a joke."

<u>Disadvantages</u>

    a.   This is a passive-aggressive behavior and does not address the immediate problem. Dorothy would have to guess what the problem is (her traveling? her communication style?).

    b.   Staff meetings are held only 2 or 3 times per year; Dale might have to wait months to make the joke.

c. Dorothy might not get the joke, or ignore it.

d. Dorothy might consider Dale's joking to be disrespectful, and discipline him for insubordination.

9. Make a list of what he would like from Dorothy as a director and try to make an appointment to discuss the list with her.

Advantages

a. He offers solutions and not just criticism.

b. He feels good about taking direct action without involving anyone else.

c. He clarifies his concerns in his mind (and on paper) before approaching Dorothy.

d. Dorothy might respect him for speaking up in a positive way.

e. He opens a communication line with Dorothy for further issues.

Disadvantages

a. Dorothy might be too busy to meet with him.

b. He might have to endure nerves, discomfort, and possibly Dorothy's glowering (the ray).

c. Dorothy might get resentful that Dale is asking her to do more work.

d. Dorothy might respond to Dale's request by becoming over-involved with the staff, causing the staff to resent Dale.

Best Alternative and Why

Dale is obviously at a critical point with his resentment against Dorothy, as even he realizes he sometimes has trouble concentrating on his job as a result of it. Because he feels so helpless and has such a fear of confronting Dorothy, I believe Dale would be very tempted by some of the more passive-aggressive alternatives above, such as writing an anonymous letter of complaint or making jokes with hidden messages. But I think Dale's fear of the possible consequences of these alternatives (being disciplined or fired) would make them too risky to be considered as viable options.

The only productive, professional way that Dale might have a chance to bring about real changes in Dorothy's behavior is to try to speak to her directly and honestly about his concerns. Dorothy cannot change a problem that she does not know exists. Dale's best course of action would be to combine Option 9 (make a list of what he would like from Dorothy as a director) with Option 5 (try to have a discussion with Dorothy, stating his frustrations).

Dale might also be very tempted to try Option 5 only, that is, trying to have an informal discussion with Dorothy, stating some of his problem (lack of

From *Shaping the Future: Advancing the Understanding of Leadership* by Peter Hernon, Editor. Santa Barbara, CA: Libraries Unlimited. Copyright © 2010.

communication in the staff), but not all of it (Dorothy's lack of involvement with the staff). This type of vague complaint would almost surely bring about the glowering "ray" from Dorothy. Not only would he be dumping a problem on her desk without offering any recommendations for a solution, but because Dale had not defined the problem completely in his own mind, Dorothy would be left to guess what the real problem actually was. The discussion could easily become confusing and frustrating for both, ultimately end badly, and be totally ineffective.

If Dale clarifies in his mind and on paper exactly what his expectations of Dorothy are, and what he would like to see change in the library *before* he meets with Dorothy, she will be much more likely to take him seriously. His preparation will help him be more confident in his presentation and will also make him look more professional in his forethought and recommendations for a solution. It is also imperative that Dale try to meet with Dorothy one-on-one, rather than involving the staff, since Dorothy might feel ambushed if confronted by a mob of angry librarians.

Implementation

Before he does anything else, Dale should sit down and write a list of concerns that he has about Dorothy's behavior and how they affect him or the library. He should write this list at home or while he is away from the library in order to get perspective, avoid interruptions, and avoid getting so upset that it interferes with his work. The list should look something like this:

Problem with Dorothy:	Effect:
Away from office at meetings 30 days per year.	I feel "home alone"—like no one is providing leadership or direction for the library. I feel like Dorothy would rather be somewhere else.
Stays in office while here.	I do not feel comfortable approaching Dorothy. I never have any interaction with her. I feel like I am on my own.
Always on phone, not approachable.	I do not feel comfortable bringing issues to Dorothy.
Does not share what she learns at meetings.	We miss out on great opportunities to learn new things or improve the functioning of the library.
We have no measure of how effective we are.	We are left to guess whether we are doing a good job or not. We do not have any goals to strive for.
We only have 2 or 3 staff meetings per year.	Communication is poor among departments.
There are never any meaningful discussions at staff meetings.	Morale goes down because there is nothing exciting ever happening in the library.

Problem with Dorothy:	Effect:
We cannot talk about "taboo topics"—she gives us "the ray."	We feel demeaned, like children. We brush some issues under the carpet because we are afraid to bring them up.
Stays completely out of the operation of departments.	We do not get any suggestions on how to improve our operations.
Has attitude of "benign neglect."	We feel abandoned and never feel encouraged or motivated. Morale is seriously affected.
Does not ask for input on the budget.	We feel discouraged to think creatively about new ways to use money.

Dale should NOT show this list to Dorothy. This is for him to clarify his own thoughts and work through his emotions so that he can present an objective statement of what he wants from Dorothy when he speaks to her. Next, Dale should review the "Effect" column, and summarize the list into categories, such as:

> ➢ Lack of communication from Dorothy and within departments

> ➢ Lack of direction and feedback

> ➢ Feel uncomfortable approaching Dorothy

> ➢ No training or goal setting in library

Next, Dale should review the categories and, item by item, should write down what his ideal solution to that problem would be, turning the negative statement into a positive request. He should be certain to turn the "you" statements (you never give us feedback) into "I" statements (I would like more feedback). This will keep Dale from sounding like he is criticizing Dorothy. For example:

Category:	Request: "I would like . . . "
➢ Lack of communication from Dorothy and within departments	➢ More frequent staff meetings ➢ A "forum" section in staff meetings to raise new ideas or issues
➢ Lack of direction and feedback	➢ Annual reviews ➢ Occasional informal feedback about how my department is running.
➢ Feel uncomfortable approaching Dorothy	➢ More personal contact with Dorothy when she is here. ➢ To have Dorothy visit my department occasionally.
➢ No training or goal setting in library	➢ To hear about what Dorothy learns at the conferences ➢ Staff development/training in-house ➢ Clearer policy on staff attendance and involvement in professional activities.

Again, Dorothy will not see this list. Dale will simply use this list as "backup" when he offers suggestions to Dorothy on how to improve the communication in the library. Dale can make a separate list to give to Dorothy, with only his suggestions for improvement.

Next, Dale should prepare his opening statement to avoid stammering or backing away. He should start with something positive, like, 'Thank you for seeing me. In the past two years I have enjoyed my job as Interlibrary Loan Librarian, and I enjoy working with my fellow staff members. I want to do my part in providing the best service possible to our patrons and to my coworkers, and I've noticed some areas that we might be able to improve in." Dale should memorize this opening to avoid sounding stilted. He can then launch into a statement of his categories, such as, "I am concerned about the staff's communication with each other, and with you. Would it be possible to have more frequent staff meetings, and dedicate a section of those meetings to a forum for new ideas? Also, I feel like I would benefit from more feedback, both formally and informally. My department has been using the same procedures for the past two years, and I think your objective viewpoint might give us some good ideas for improvement." Dale should only cover 2 or 3 of the biggest issues to avoid overwhelming Dorothy. If he is successful in opening up communication, he will have a chance later to bring up more issues.

Now that Dale has clarified the problem, and knows basically what he is going to say to Dorothy, he is ready for action. He should go to Dorothy's secretary, tell her that he would like to meet with Dorothy, and ask when the best time would be. Dale needs to be prepared for the secretary to say "now is the best time." Because he has prepared in advance, this should not be a problem. If Dorothy is not in or available, Dale should make an appointment for the soonest available time Dorothy has.

When the time comes to meet with Dorothy, he should arrive with the list he has made for Dorothy, his notes to himself, and a pad of paper. He should be positive and upbeat, getting right into his opening statement without beating around the bush. He should state the facts exactly as he did above, when practicing. If Dorothy's response is good, he should go on; she may even encourage him to do so. If Dorothy glowers, Dale should stop, explain again that he is only making these suggestions for the benefit of the functioning of the library. When he is finished, whether or not the reception was favorable, Dale should thank Dorothy and offer to take concrete steps in helping to implement his suggestions. He could offer to do research on other library's policies and procedures, or he could offer to help coordinate the scheduling of staff meetings. This should show Dorothy that he has a sincere interest in offering a solution, not just a complaint.

Follow-Through

Because Dale has prepared his ideas in advance and presented them in a positive manner, I believe that Dorothy would be willing to listen to Dale without taking offense. She might, however, become annoyed that Dale is essentially asking her to do more work, in addition to the duties she performs at the library (budget work, book selection) and in professional associations. She might agree to more staff meetings (after all, she does like to attend meetings) and more informal contact, but discourage the formal trainings and reviews, which are time-consuming and require a lot of written work. If this happens, Dale could offer to work with her to run the trainings, doing the presentation preparation, or asking for volunteers in the staff meetings. Dale could also offer to find a template for a "Quick Review Form," which would not take much time to fill in and review with an employee.

If Dorothy listens to Dale's suggestions, and at the end of the meeting says that "everything is just fine here" and refuses to make any changes, Dale should respectfully disagree with her, ask that she think about the issues he raised (he should leave the list he prepared for her). He should then tell her that he has serious concerns for the future functioning of the library if some of the changes are not made, and ask her if she would be better convinced that something needs to be done if the other department heads of the library agreed. If she says "yes" or "maybe," he should follow through on option 3, speaking with the department heads, and then hold a staff meeting of the department heads and Dorothy in 2 or 3 days (set the date and time then). If she says "no, that won't convince me," then he should leave, stating that he is sorry she feels that way, and encourage her to think about it. The next day, after he has had some time to calm down from the meeting, he should discuss his concerns with the other department heads, and find out if they agree with him and are willing to confront Dorothy. If they are, they should request a staff meeting through Dorothy's secretary. If Dorothy refuses to meet with the staff, they should request a staff meeting in writing. If Dorothy ignores this letter, then her "benign neglect" has become "malign neglect," and the staff is facing a much bigger problem than they realized. At this point they have no other option than to go over Dorothy's head by informing the college president of what is going on. This can be done in a letter from the staff to Dorothy, with a copy sent to the president, expressing their concern about her refusal to meet with them.

If the other department heads are not willing to confront Dorothy, Dale must discern from them whether their reluctance is due to the fact that they do not believe there is a problem, or whether they just do not want to face the problem. If none of the other staff believe there is a problem with Dorothy or the library's operation, Dale must seriously reassess whether he has overreacted to the situation. If they believe there is a problem, but are not willing to face it, then I believe that Dale must back off from confronting Dorothy or informing the president for a period of six months. For Dale to act alone in "going over Dorothy's head" would, at this point, be career suicide. It would be too easy for Dale to be singled out and labeled a "trouble maker," especially if he does not have the support of the rest of the staff backing him. During this six-month waiting period, Dale can wait for the "seeds" he has planted with Dorothy (in the letter) and with the other staff (in his request for support) to take root. Dale has already raised awareness and given people ideas which, over time, they might incorporate as their own, and be much more willing to face in six months' time. Also during the six-month waiting period, Dale can try to increase his contact with Dorothy on a more informal basis, and in doing so, can note her moods when he sees her, and create a "biorhythm" chart on Dorothy. This will increase his chances of getting a positive response the next time he tries to readdress the issues with her.

In six months, when Dale again attempts to discuss the issues with Dorothy, if he still does not have Dorothy's cooperation (even during the peak biorhythm period), or the other staff's support, Dale must reassess whether he wants to, and is able to, continue working in this environment. Having had six months to let the things settle, he should be able to make a much more objective decision about remaining in the position, and if he decides to start looking for another position, at least he will know he tried everything possible to stay.

 From *Shaping the Future: Advancing the Understanding of Leadership* by Peter Hernon, Editor. Santa Barbara, CA: Libraries Unlimited. Copyright © 2010.

If Dorothy refuses to even have the initial meeting with Dale, he should request a meeting in writing, detailing in the letter specifically what he wants to discuss, listing his concerns and requests from the list he has prepared. If she does not acknowledge the letter, Dale should go to her office, ask her secretary when Dorothy is expected, and wait for her. When she comes in Dale should express his concern that these issues need to be addressed immediately. If Dorothy still refuses to meet with him, Dale should go to the other department heads at the library and tell them what he has been doing. He should tell them about his concerns, ask if they agree with him, and, if they do, would they be willing to confront Dorothy in a staff meeting? If they are willing, Dale should write another letter to Dorothy, informing her that he and the department heads would like to meet with her in a staff meeting. Dale should carbon copy the department heads on the letter.

If Dorothy ignores this letter, then again, the staff has no other option than to inform the college president of what is going on in a letter, expressing their concern about her refusal to meet with them. Again, if other staff is not willing to send a letter to the president, Dale should *not* go ahead on his own. Without the backing of the other department heads, Dale risks singling himself out as a troublemaker, and could face disciplinary action from Dorothy for going directly to the president, whether or not it was justified. Again, Dale should begin the six-month waiting period (as described above) and reassess his own role in the situation.

If the staff agrees with Dale and they do write to the president of the college, but the president ignores the letter, they must consider making repairs to the staff dynamics from the bottom up. The very act of writing the letter to the president will have already helped the staff to unify and increase their own communication. They will have raised their own consciousness of the issues and can then try to fill in the gaps in Dorothy's absence. If Dorothy ignores them, and Dorothy's boss ignores them, then they must help themselves by supporting each other. This can be done through informal trainings, increased informal interdepartmental communication, and the gathering of more facts about how other academic libraries function. If, in six months, they find that they still yearn for more formal contact with Dorothy, they should initiate the process of meeting with Dorothy again. What they may find is that through their increased communication they are functioning well enough without her, or that Dorothy has noticed a change in her staff, and is now eager to become involved.

Assignments

1. Write a list of Dale's complaints about Dorothy and what effects her behavior has on the staff and library as a whole.

2. Write a summary of the "effects."

3. Write a summary of the categories of problems and address each one in a column titled "What I Would Like to Change."

4. Draft the opening statement to Dorothy.

5. Write a copy of the final list of suggestions to give to Dorothy.

From *Shaping the Future: Advancing the Understanding of Leadership* by Peter Hernon, Editor. Santa Barbara, CA: Libraries Unlimited. Copyright © 2010.

6. Draft a policy on attendance at professional conferences: who can go, when, and who pays.

7. Draft a sample "Quick Review Policy" to show Dorothy in the meeting.

Issue/Areas

1. Find out how customary it is in other libraries for a director to be absent at conferences 30 days per year.

2. Look up sample "Professional Conference Attendance" policies.

3. Search for a sample "Quick Review Form" on the Internet as a template.

4. Look for sample Library Director job descriptions on the Internet to get a general idea of what that position is supposed to entail.

Cluster Problems

Dale

Dale has legitimate complaints against Dorothy, but it is his paralyzing fear of confrontation and his negativity which keep his resentment fueled and pose real problems. He admits to getting so annoyed with Dorothy that he has trouble concentrating on his work. He complains to coworkers and fuels the fire for his resentment by gossiping about her instead of taking action. Dale is terrified of angering Dorothy, and only thinks of bringing his problems to her, not solutions. For example, Dale says in his letter, "I can't just say 'Dorothy, I wonder if it's necessary for you to spend as much time as you do on association and committee work?' I shudder to think what she might say to that!" Dale allows his emotions to rule him, getting so flustered that he cannot sit down and figure out specifically what it is about Dorothy that bothers him so much. He can only see a "big knapsack of grievances" lumped all together, which overwhelm him and keep him trapped in his ineffectiveness.

Dorothy Kesten

If one were to evaluate Dorothy Kesten as a manager using "*POSDCORB*," her results would look something like "————*B*". It appears that the only thing Dorothy wants to do is work on the budget; the rest she neglects. She has completely avoided her responsibilities in the areas of leadership, mentoring, directing, and motivating. As a result, after four years as director of the library, she does not appear to have a close working relationship with anyone on her staff. By staying in her office all the time, avoiding involvement in the departments, not providing any feedback to staff, and holding infrequent staff meetings, she sends a clear message that as long as the library maintains its basic functioning, she does not want to be bothered. However, Dorothy's neglect goes beyond benign when she "breathes hard and glowers at 'taboo topics.'" She shames her employees into backing down from subjects she does not like and sends the message that it is not OK to communicate openly. Another blatantly irresponsible practice of Dorothy's is to return from professional meetings sharing only gossip, not information. Not only does this set a horrible example about gossiping, but it deprives the staff of important training that could improve their skills and motivate them.

<u>Hahnemann Library Staff</u>

Dale may describe the Hahnemann Library Staff as a "docile crew," but their burying their heads in the sand allows Dorothy's behavior to continue. While it is true that the responsibility lies with Dorothy to encourage open communication among the staff, it may also be that there are "never any meaningful discussions at staff meetings" because no one ever speaks up. Instead they remain suspicious of Dorothy ("to be honest we do not know what she does when she's in her office"), and appear to have spent at least the last two years spreading rumors and waiting for Dorothy to "move on to bigger and better things."

Things

Things I Would Do

1. Increase my own communication with Dorothy (formally and informally).

2. Increase my own communication with the other staff (positive communication, not gossip).

Things I Would Like to Do

1. Participate in/hold in-house trainings.

2. Attend more conventions.

3. Have an annual review with Dorothy.

Things I Would Like to Be Able to Do

1. Have input with the budget.

2. Call librarywide meetings without Dorothy's approval.

3. Have direct communication with the president of the college.

Things I Would Like to Know

1. Does the rest of the staff feel as strongly as Dale that Dorothy is an absentee director?

2. Is there a policy at the Hahnemann Library about attendance at professional conferences?

3. Does Dorothy pay her own way to the professional conferences?

4. Are there, or were there ever, formal reviews at the library?

5. How frequent were staff meetings before Dorothy became director?

6. Does Dorothy have a job description?

7. Is the president of Barger College supportive of Dorothy's participation in these professional associations? Does he require it?

8. Is the president of Barger College involved with the library? Does he give Dorothy an annual review?

9

~

STUDENT CASE STUDIES

*The actual learning with the case study method does
not take place in the mere reading of the case study, but rather
is derived from a group discussion of the case.*[1]

WHOSE RESTROOM IS IT, ANYWAY?

Patricia A. Kreitz

"Call me old-fashioned or just plain old, but I can't live with this situation," declared
Raylene Miller in a trembling voice. "Well, Raylene," said Susan Smith, director of
Agilent College Library, trying for a calming tone of voice. "I recognize that you are
very upset. I promise you, I'll look into it." A frown appeared on Raylene's face and she
raised her voice, "Wait—we need you to do something now. We all change in that
restroom before and after aerobics—I tell you, this can't happen!" She angrily shoved
the piece of paper in her hand at Susan and warned, "If you don't take action
immediately, the other women on the first floor and I will! We have rights too, and we're
counting on you as another woman to help defend us. If you won't, we will!" And with
that threat, she turned on her heel and stormed out of Susan's office.

Taking a deep breath, Susan scanned the paper Raylene had shoved at her. It was a
memo from the Head of Access Services, Don Blakely. Addressed to all women staff
members with offices or work areas on the main library's first floor, it informed them
that Robert Smith would be using the first floor women's restroom starting Monday as he
began the physical and psychological process of becoming Roberta Smith. Not another
problem with Don, thought Susan wearily, as she buzzed her secretary and asked him to
have Don come to her office immediately. As she waited for him to arrive, her gaze was
drawn to the view of the quad outside her office windows. She had felt so privileged six
months ago to be hired as library director at this small liberal arts college. With its
reputation for quality undergraduate education and its peaceful, rural surroundings, she
thought she had taken the perfect job. Now though, as she reflected on the first two
months of her directorship, she felt an increasing sense of frustration as she realized that
this was not the first time she had felt as if she were the last to know what was happening
in the library, most often in Don's areas of responsibility.

"Hi, Susan, you wanted to see me? I've got a million things on my plate, but what can I help you with?" said Don with an air of avuncular concern as he sat across from her desk and stretched his legs out, leaning back in his chair. Susan's expression was grim as she held the memo out to him. "Don, I was shown a copy of your memo about Robert Smith using the women's restroom by an upset staff member. I want you to explain this to me—including why you did not bring it to my attention. It appears the women on the first floor are quite upset," she said. Shaking his head and rolling his eyes, Don responded, "Oh, Susan, I didn't want to bother you about this. When you have as much experience as I do, particularly working with clerical staff, you'll recognize that they don't have much in their jobs to get excited about. They get into a dither about the smallest things—it all blows over quickly, particularly if you don't encourage them by making a big deal out of their complaints."

In a voice that trembled slightly from trying to hold in her anger, Susan said, "You should have told me about Robert. Why didn't you?" "Robert came to me in confidence, Susan, of course I couldn't violate that!" Don countered in a shocked voice. He continued, "However, last Monday he told me that he had been advised by his medical team that he should now make the process public. His psychologist told him he needed to start acting like a female, so he's going to be dressing as a woman at work. In addition, he would like to begin using the women's restroom since he'll have women's clothes on. I told him that the university had to treat it as we would any reasonable accommodation for a disability, thus my memo to the women who use that first floor bathroom."

Don reached across the desk and patted Susan's hand. "Besides," he said as his face assumed an injured look, "I think you'd be grateful to me for knowing when not to bother you with day-to-day issues when you've still got so much to do to learn the ropes around here. When you have as much experience as I've had, you'll know how to handle these things, too. I know what I'm doing." He jumped up from his chair. " If you'll excuse me now, I have a meeting in five minutes." And with that, he started to turn to leave Susan's office.

"Wait, Don, you're just going to have to be late to your meeting. Please sit back down." Susan gathered her thoughts quickly. "We're going to talk later about keeping me informed in advance. However, right now we have a crisis on our hands and I need some more information," Susan stated firmly. "First, tell me, do you have anything in writing from Robert's doctors about the situation and his needs? Did you consult with Andy in Human Resources or with the university's legal counsel? How do you know this falls under the Americans with Disabilities Act and merits an accommodation?" As she shot these questions at him, Don started shaking his head and shrugging his eyebrows. He replied in an affronted tone, "I don't need a piece of paper to know someone's telling me the truth, Susan." Continuing, he said, "A person's word is good enough for me and, besides, I've seen the changes happening since he's been taking hormones. Robert's lost his beard and other things are changing, too."

"And as for consulting with HR and Legal, you'd know I didn't need to if you ever read that *Manager's Legal Bulletin* that you insist on routing to all of us. I know what we have to do, and if those first-floor women clerks continue to object, they're going to leave us open for a charge of sexual harassment from Robert!" Don continued angrily, "Besides, Robert was very embarrassed about all this and nervous about how people would take it. He told me in strict confidence. How could I talk to anyone else when he specifically asked me to keep it confidential?"

Realizing she needed time to think, Susan dismissed Don to go to his meeting. Her eyes followed his departing back as she thought about the issues and what her next steps should be. Sighing with frustration, she picked up the phone. She needed to consult with Human Resources and probably university Legal Counsel quickly.

Critical Issues to Address

1. **Ethics:** The ethical concerns of a manager caught in between an employee's request for confidentiality and the organization's need to be informed so that it can respond to a situation that might present legal, fiscal, policy, or ethical issues. Does the manager's immediate supervisor or another administrator have a right to demand that the manager violate an employee request for confidentiality? Does the university have a clear set of guidelines for managers caught in such a situation?

2. **Managers speaking for the university:** What course of action should the university take when a manager may have informed an employee incorrectly concerning his or her rights?

3. **Conflicting legal rights/conflicting human rights:** When different employees' deeply felt concerns and/or legally guaranteed rights clash, how does the university resolve this? What rights does an employee undergoing a sex-change process have according to university policy, state law, and federal law? What rights do the objecting employees have? How does the concept of gender get defined for those using university-supplied and university-labeled same-gender facilities?

4. **Leadership:** The university librarian does not know what is happening on her watch and appears out of touch with staff. She permits subtle and not-so-subtle negative comments about her from a direct report. If he's making those statements to her face, what is he saying behind her back? How should she respond?

5. **Followership:** Obviously the manager appears to have a less than optimum opinion of the university librarian. In addition, he may not wish to share his leadership or may, for unknown reasons, not trust her. What is the problem? Can it be repaired, and if so, how? Leader–follower relations are mutual—never an either/or.

Discussion Questions

1. What is the university's responsibility to Robert and to the women working on the library's first floor? What issues must be considered in working toward a resolution of this conflict? Would your answer differ if the sex change had been from female to male?

2. How should Susan address the dilemma Don raised about being asked to keep an employee's statements or information confidential? What legal, fiscal, policy, and ethical issues does this raise?

3. What steps should Susan take to address Don's comments and behaviors? How can she determine if his perspective is unique or is shared by others in the library? Or, do you see this as more a question for the university than the library per se?

THERE IS NO INTEGRATION WITHOUT GOOD COMMUNICATION

Anne Marie Casey

Background

Central Valley State University is a publicly funded institution in the Midwestern United States. Formed as a state teacher's college in 1890, it grew considerably in the second half of the twentieth century to become a doctoral/research-intensive university. In addition to its traditional programs, the university has one of the oldest and largest distance learning degree programs in North America. The College of Distance Learning has been successfully delivering master's degrees to adult learners on military bases and in health-care settings since 1971. Recognizing the importance of high-quality library services in distance education programs, the College of Distance Learning formed the Distance Learning Library Services department in 1976. Funded entirely by the college, Distance Learning Library Services is a department in the library. The personnel consists of seven reference/instruction librarians, one of whom is the director, the Document Delivery Office with four staff members, and a copyright clerk. The College of Distance Learning is completely self-funded and strongly supports Distance Learning Library Services.

Gabriel, who has been the Dean of Libraries at the university for fifteen years, devotes much of his attention to fund-raising for the library and involvement in university governance. He manages the library through the department head managerial team. The department heads work well with Gabriel and generally appreciate his hands-off approach to management. He is congenial and is liked by the library staff. However, most staff members distrust him to some degree. Ten years earlier he outsourced the cataloging department and eliminated several union positions in the library. Whenever Gabriel starts looking at staffing, library employees think he is planning another major change in order to eliminate jobs.

Central Valley State has been experiencing a series of budget cuts over a three-year period due to falling state appropriations. The library has not been spared and has undergone staff layoffs, serials' cuts, and limited technology replacement. Distance Learning Library Services has remained unscathed due to the continued strong funding from the College of Distance Learning. Now going into the fourth lean year, Gabriel asked Eleanor, the Director of Distance Learning Library Services, and Ying, the Head of Reference and Interlibrary Loan, to conduct a workflow analysis of the Interlibrary Loan office and the Document Delivery office to see if they can work more closely together and combine some of their processes to free up a staff position.

What Is This All About?

Eleanor and Ying were surprised at Gabriel's request. Over their daily coffee break the next morning they speculated about what he really wanted. Did he only want this to be an information-seeking exercise? Did he intend to combine the departments? If so, which one of the two librarians would get the new assignment, and which one would be the "loser"? Is Interlibrary Loan or Document Delivery the next cataloging department? Why didn't Gabriel just go back to fund-raising, which he was good at, and leave the running of the library to the department head librarians, who knew what they were doing?

A Little History

Document Delivery is the area in Distance Learning Library Services that takes requests for library materials from distance learning users and either mails items from the library collection or sends them by e-mail or fax. In the late 1990s Interlibrary Loan and Document Delivery jointly purchased a new Interlibrary Loan platform that allowed them to run their operations on the same system and made the process much easier for Document Delivery to request interlibrary loans for distance learning users.

Document Delivery is made up of Marta, the staff supervisor, and three clerical staff members, Marie, Jane, and Kristen. The Interlibrary Loan staff consist of Susie, the coordinator, Karen, the staff supervisor, and Patty, Christine, and Lynn, the clerical staff.

The two departments are located next to each other. The door that separates them has normally been kept open during the workday to support the flow of business back and forth and a collegial atmosphere between the two departments. Interlibrary Loan and Document Delivery have worked together amiably for several years, and the staff members in the two departments have occasionally socialized.

The big difference between them is the service models under which they operate. Interlibrary Loan, as part of the university library, has traditionally had an instructional model of service. The staff generally work to educate patrons so that they will know how to use library resources by themselves in the future. The philosophy of Distance Learning Library Services has historically been more customer-service oriented. As the library support service for the entrepreneurial wing of Central Valley State, Distance Learning Library Services has a long-established culture of giving customers what they want when they want it. There has been some strain over the years between the two different service philosophies, but since Gabriel has been Dean, the tension has resolved itself into the understanding that a different approach is acceptable for a different audience of users. Until now, there has been no attempt to integrate services between Distance Learning Library Services and any other part of the library.

Discussing the Dean's Request

During their discussion over coffee the day after Gabriel requested the workflow analysis, Ying and Eleanor agreed to delegate this task to Susie, the coordinator of Interlibrary Loan, and to Marta, the Document Delivery supervisor. They both had confidence in Susie and Marta. Ying and Eleanor considered Interlibrary Loan and Document Delivery to be the easy part of their responsibilities. They spent most of their time dealing with challenges raised by the librarians in their respective areas, so they were content to let Susie and Marta handle anything that came up in their areas.

Eleanor joined the Document Delivery daily operations meeting the next day and told them about the request from Gabriel. Marta was shocked and announced that her job was on the line. She just knew that Gabriel wanted to combine Document Delivery and Interlibrary Loan and put Susie in charge of the new department. Once reorganized, they would only need one staff supervisor, and Karen had seniority! Marie, Jane, and Kristen started talking about how hard it would be to report to Karen after the two departments merged.

Although she had some private questions about what Gabriel has in mind, Eleanor assured them that as far as she knew, Gabriel had no ulterior motive and that the departments would continue to operate separately. She asked the staff to work on an analysis of their workflow.

In the meantime, Ying had told Susie about Gabriel's request. After that conversation, Susie called an emergency Interlibrary Loan meeting to discuss it. "What does Gabriel really want to do? Does he have an ulterior motive?" Christine asked. Susie said that Ying had told her that there was nothing to worry about, but Susie could tell from her facial expressions that Ying was concerned. The Interlibrary Loan staff worried that Gabriel wanted Distance Learning Library Services to take over Interlibrary Loan because the College of Distance Learning would then fund Interlibrary Loan and Gabriel could save some money to buy more serials for the Chemistry Department. Karen suggested that Gabriel viewed this as a way to get rid of her. She knew that Gabriel had been out to get her for years because she had supported the clerical strike when he was the new Dean. Everyone knew Gabriel got rid of union staff by reorganizing and eliminating jobs.

Examining the Workflow

The two departments outlined their workflow in a series of meetings over the next month. Part of the plan they developed involved job sharing, whereby each staff member would spend a day in the other department. Although the two groups were always cordial in public meetings, there was a good deal of sniping going on when they worked together during the job-sharing exercise. The door that had always remained opened during work hours now stayed closed, and the impromptu lunches and holiday gatherings between the two departments stopped occurring.

As time went on, Susie complained to Ying, and Marta complained to Eleanor, that their counterparts in the other department treated them unkindly during the job-sharing period and were spreading rumors about them. One of the constants heard from staff in both departments was that the other did not understand how to work with their students. Interlibrary Loan thought Document Delivery handed too much to students without trying to teach them to be lifelong learners, and Document Delivery thought Interlibrary Loan had a very poor customer service attitude. No one thought the other could be taught to serve their users the "right way."

Morale Is Going Down

Ying and Eleanor had remained relatively uninvolved up to this point, but they were worried about the morale in the departments and confessed to each other again that they were uneasy about Gabriel's request. It would help to understand what sort of outcome he was looking for. They were telling Susie and Marta there was nothing to worry about, but they were not so sure that was the truth. They agreed that they needed to ask Gabriel more questions and let him know how this uncertainty was affecting the morale in the two departments.

They scheduled a meeting to talk to Gabriel about the anxieties this project had raised and to tell him that the two different departmental cultures might make it impossible to integrate services. They asked what outcome he expected, and he continued to say he had no hidden agenda. He was interested in the workflow analysis, he was sure the cultures were not that different, and he knew they did the same kind of work. He did not see any problems with the departments integrating some of their workflow. He appreciated the librarians discussing their challenges with him, and he had every confidence in their abilities to carry out his request. However, he reminded them that he was the Dean and expected staff to do as he asked. He reassured them that he had no plans to force two cultures together to the detriment of good service, but he still believed that there were some redundancies that could be eliminated.

This meeting did not help as much as they had hoped it would. They were still unsure about what Gabriel wanted to do and were a bit resentful that he had told them he was the boss and they had to do as he said. In spite of this, Eleanor and Ying realized that they had to find a way to calm the fears in their two departments. They called a joint meeting and together told all of the staff members that they expected them to follow through with Gabriel's request in a professional manner. From that point on, Eleanor and Ying participated in all of the meetings related to the analysis of the Document Delivery and Interlibrary Loan workflows. They constantly reassured staff members that their jobs were safe and supported them through the analysis and development of the report.

Where They Are Now

The door is still closed between the two departments. The workflow analysis was completed and the final report recommended no staff changes. Gabriel met with everyone involved to ask some questions about the analysis and the report and seemed satisfied with the final recommendation.

In the course of conducting the analysis, however, the departments realized that the ebb and flow of work in each area was different. Susie and Marta decided that this difference might enable the two departments to collaborate to implement a long-held dream of Susie's—to scan articles from the print collection and deliver them electronically to faculty on campus. The new service was implemented the next academic year and was well-received by the faculty. Document Delivery and Interlibrary Loan staff members complain on the grapevine about who gets the credit and who does the work. The new service, however, is a success, and Gabriel is happy with it.

The Problems

Leadership seems lacking at times in this situation. Although the Dean seems to operate successfully for the most part as a team leader and collaborates with his managerial team to lead the library, he becomes autocratic when he does not get the response he expects. When his department heads report problems, he is somewhat dismissive and tells them they have to do what he asks because he is the one in charge.

A major problem he has is the lack of trust staff members place in him due to the memory of the outsourcing of the cataloging department and the subsequent elimination of union positions. This may have been the best solution to the situation at that point in time, but it was probably never explained well and has left Gabriel with a legacy of distrust among staff. He may not have had a hidden agenda, but everyone assumes he does based on past experience.

The department heads have fallen into a trap that is common in organizations where there are fewer employees than needed. Both Ying and Eleanor are responsible for a professional department (general reference for Ying and Distance Learning reference and instruction for Eleanor). They trust the staff members who supervise the Document Delivery and Interlibrary Loan teams. However, they forget that sometimes these teams need the leadership of the department head librarians who understand the big picture better and trust the Dean enough to ask him the tough questions. The fact that they stepped in to reassert leadership of the Document Delivery and Interlibrary Loan teams when they were aware of problems is positive, but they should have been paying closer attention all along. In the beginning they seemed to have a more laissez-faire attitude but demonstrated good team skills and leadership when problems came to their attention.

Poor communication in this library is another major problem. The Dean has ideas about investigating and trying out new things but is vague in his expectations. In the beginning, no one questions his ambiguous directions. The staff members do not speak to supervisors about the fears and suspicions they have at first. They assume the worst and communicate by spreading rumors or complaining. Serious problems arise before they ask for clarification or help.

Different organizational cultures present some problem, but this one should not have been insurmountable. There are effective ways of establishing common objectives that would enable both sets of users to be served. Developing a common service model requires good communication, trust, and some hard work. This library seems to be lacking in the first two especially.

Lessons Learned

Those in a leadership position should communicate directly and honestly. Sometimes leaders in upper management lose sight of what is important to the average staff member. They tend to look outward to the larger community of the institution and forget that staff do not see or often care about the big picture. Upper-level administrators need to explain reasons for changes, as far as possible, and to encourage questions. They also need to understand that a major change, such as the elimination of a department, will remain in the collective consciousness of an organization for a long time and be sure to address fears this legacy may continue to bring up.

Middle managers need to consciously assume leadership from their different vantage points. They need to take responsibility for clarifying ambiguous commands from higher up the chain. They also need to explain changes to their teams professionally and to support the people who report to them thoroughly in carrying out what the Dean asks.

Everyone needs to communicate better. This means continuing to ask questions until one understands. It also means expressing doubts and concerns professionally so they can be addressed. No one is a perfect communicator, so it is important to discuss new ventures until there is a good understanding on all sides.

The clash of cultures needs to be addressed. An academic library with two such different service cultures is probably not a healthy one. Both cultures in this library should be analyzed, and a new service philosophy that accommodates flexibility for different types of users should be adopted.

Discussion Questions

1. How could open and honest communication up front in this library have made the results different?

2. How can a leader who makes a major change in the organization, which affects many jobs negatively, be effective on an ongoing basis?

3. What sort of leadership model would make this library more effective?

4. When is it right for a team leader to back off, and when is it appropriate for that person to be a true leader?

5. How can two seemingly disparate service cultures be brought closer together to form one library service culture?

SOLUTIONS CHASING PROBLEMS: A CAUTIONARY TALE

Kathleen De Long

The Organizational Context

The University of the Prairies Library is one of the largest members of the Association of Research Libraries in the country, with approximately 350 staff and a collection of over ten million volumes. The library is organized along traditional, hierarchical lines, with a director of libraries and three associate directors who are responsible for access services, bibliographic services and collections, and human resources and finance. There are eight subject libraries that report to the director through heads of the libraries, who are responsible for the day-to-day management of their various public service areas (circulation and reference). The director, associate directors, and heads of the libraries compose the senior administration team and take responsibility for the overall management of the library.

This case highlights a particular issue, the library's response to dealing with a decline in circulation transactions as a result of the impact of electronic collections. The need to deal with the change seems evident to all, but the reactions of those involved differ substantially. The issue starts an inquiry into how the library might change its service model. The key players involved with the issue and proposed change are also stakeholders, and as time progresses we find out a great deal about the organization's culture and the relationships among various groups. The key issues and events are as follows:

- Change in the service model prompted by decline in volume of circulation transactions. Technology, budget, demographics, union presence, and process improvement are all factors considered by the key players as the events unfold.

- A decision to implement self-serve technology, followed by lack of support on the part of some of the senior administration team, the heads of the libraries.

- Relationships between heads of the libraries and library administration and between those heads and circulation staff and supervisors. At issue are loyalties, trust, and hidden agendas.

The Situation

Oh No! We Have a Problem! The University of the Prairies Library knew there was a problem, and the senior administration team was sure it had a strategy to deal with the problem of declining circulation.

For the past three years, circulation statistics had been steadily dropping. The Health Sciences branch had been the first to see dramatic changes in its volume of circulation as the branch moved aggressively into e-journals; about 85 percent of the serials collection was now available online, and circulation statistics had dropped to such a low that only one staff member was scheduled on the circulation desk at a time. Although the Health Sciences situation was the most dramatic, circulation staff in other libraries could also see their volume of transactions was declining. Some of the staff were relieved that circulation statistics (and the number of people lined up for service) were dropping. As one put it, "I don't need to stand on my feet any more than necessary, thank you. I've worked in circulation for the past 28 years, and not having a constant lineup is good news for me!"

Life went on . . . but when the Associate Director for Access Services put the topic of 2006 annual circulation statistics on the meeting agenda of the senior administration team, she sounded an alarm about increasing staff costs (the last two collective agreements had provided healthy cost of living increases) and declining volumes of work. The heads of the libraries agreed that they had noticed it, too. "It makes sense as we transition to electronic from print," was the rationale that was expressed, and, "Well, we still need to staff the service desk no matter the volume," was the stance of the heads of the libraries. With some persuading, the heads of the libraries agreed that an in-depth look at circulation activities was needed. Dropping circulation transactions seemed but a symptom of even greater changes.

The head of the Humanities and Social Sciences Library stressed any support for staff would be welcomed. The average age of her circulation staff was fifty-four, and she was deeply concerned about the incidence of repetitive strain injuries among staff as a result of their wanding barcodes and desensitizing materials. She assumed that self-serve technology might relieve staff of highly repetitive tasks; if this were so, she was all for it! The head of the Law Library concurred but added that reducing the number of staff scheduled at the circulation desk was problematic. The question that she posed to the others was, "What were staff to do if they weren't needed to circulate library materials?" No one contemplated laying off longtime members of staff, and the union would certainly oppose any move to do so. There were no answers to her question, but there seemed to be general agreement that it had been a very long time since workflow and processes had been examined in any of the circulation areas, and that it was high time that this was done.

The senior administration team decided to form a circulation task force (composed of circulation supervisors and led by the associate director for access services) to examine workflow in the circulation areas and investigate how other libraries use self-serve technology. The director also agreed to address the case for self-service circulation in the strategic plan that was being readied for submission and begin building a budget case for seed money to pilot a self-serve option. As she pointed out, "If we don't ask now, we won't get any project funding for the next fiscal year."

Nine Months Later—We Have a Solution! When the task force submitted its report, there were a number of recommendations for the senior administration team. Those recommendations addressed implementation of self-service technology, the scheduling of staff in a new service model that included use of self-service technology, and possible reallocations of staff after the new model was implemented and had proven itself.

There was not a lot of discussion when the recommendations were presented to the senior administration team. In presenting the recommendations, the associate director addressed all of the points that the heads of the libraries had raised when the topic of declining circulation statistics was first broached. She referred to the continuing shift to e-resources, the change in workflows that was resulting and, most important, how aging staff could be supported by automating highly repetitive tasks such as circulation/discharging through self-serve technology. It would mean fewer circulation staff and probably reallocating some staff to other areas of the library. Those staff remaining would become problem solvers working with users who needed extra service help rather than performing nonstop transactions. Service hours would be retained, and circulation staff would be happier working fewer evenings and weekends as well as taking up higher level problem solving. She exclaimed, "It is win/win! How could you disagree with that?"

The heads of the libraries were tasked with working with their circulation supervisors to communicate the recommendations to staff and marketing the new service to the faculties they were responsible for. However, when the heads met for lunch after the meeting, as they often did, the mood was tense and unhappy. This time the conversation did not begin with trading information on shoe sales and gourmet recipes as it usually did. "I wish I knew how we got to this point," the head of the Education Library observed. "I have had two circulation staff retire, and all I am going to get in return is a self-service machine that I am supposed to be marketing! I'm sure our users won't want to use it; they prefer the personal touch every time. And what am I supposed to say to staff? How are they supposed to feel valued if we don't even replace them when they retire?" The other heads nodded in agreement.

The head of the Science and Technology Library spoke up, "I've talked to my circulation supervisor, who tells me that we really don't need to replace the staff member slated to retire in the fall. Machine or no machine, we just don't need more circulation hours from staff." Several others looked askance, and the head of the Humanities and Social Sciences Library finally said, "We've got to be united on this; you see what is happening, don't you? We're losing our staff resources and our staff complements could continue to fall even further. Fewer staff means fewer resources, which means less clout. We lose positions to the detriment of our own roles as managers of large libraries with large staff complements."

A lot of head nodding followed this trenchant observation. "Well, library administration got us into this; let's see them get us out," the head of the Humanities and Social Sciences Library continued. The comment that seemed to best sum up the lunchtime conversation was: "As long as we stay close to our own faculties and keep them happy, the machines can stay or go. It doesn't mean they will be used."

It seemed clear to staff that a major change in the service model was coming. Circulation staff could see the shiny new self-service machines that were being installed. Some of the staff were worried that their jobs were in jeopardy and contacted the union. As one staff member explained to the union representative, "Between the machines and the drop in circulation we don't know where we stand." The representative reassured them that library administration had contacted the union "to tell us that the situation was being monitored." Circulation positions would not be filled as staff retired until it was seen how the service demand was balancing out. This strategy was keeping jobs safe, and no layoffs were planned. Still, the staff were uneasy and the coffee chatter was increasingly negative. As one longtime circulation staff member said to her colleagues, "I've worked at this job since I was eighteen; I don't know how to do anything different. Are machines going to take away the only job I know how to do?" Although her fears found support, some members of staff were eager to see what the self-service machines could do, and what they would mean for scheduling. Each of the major libraries received two machines, and the smaller libraries got one each.

What Is the Plan? "I really wish I knew the plan" was becoming the plaint of the circulation staff. The self-service machines were installed; what did it mean? Would library users know how to use them? Who was supposed to show them? When appealed to, circulation supervisors assured their staffs that the senior administration team had done the planning, and everything would work out. The supervisors, however, were themselves uneasy. Most of them had participated in the task force, thought the recommendations made sense, and noted that the machines were here.

It was not until late summer, when the Director of Libraries met with the associate director for Access Services, that more pointed questions began to be asked: "What was the plan?" Things had been on track until now. The money was found, the machines were bought, the strategic plan outlined the service change, and the task force had reported. Where was the local planning and excitement leading up to the anticipated fall launch? Everyone had agreed that this was necessary! In fact, the heads of the libraries were the biggest supporters. The associate director agreed to do some investigation.

Leadership Dilemma and Discussion Questions: Where to Begin?

- Transformational leadership, according to Bernard M. Bass, conveys factors, particularly idealized influence and inspirational motivation, that are intended to motivate followers to improve their performance by developing their understanding about the importance and value of goals and transcending their own self-interest for the sake of the organization.[2] Avowed self-interest is a powerful force allied to lack of agreement about goals. Can this library director become a transformational leader? Why or why not?

- What decisions and actions should the library director be contemplating in order to diagnose problems and take action to correct what is happening?

- The library service environment is going to continue to change. Falling circulation volume is just one example of this. How do libraries continue to focus on performance outcomes while paying attention to team process variables such as planning, adapting, structuring, learning, and trusting?[3]

Lessons Learned: Something to Think About

There are two lessons that management or administrative groups must learn if they are going to be successful at working as a team. The first is the importance of communication, and the second is that of relationship building. In this case study we see examples of failure in both areas. Building relationships and opening channels of communication are not going to be easy to do or to maintain, because this group lacks trust and exhibits reluctance to try new approaches or develop more innovative ways. Effective managerial leadership is needed, and it is difficult for leaders to be effective when organizations are operating in an environment of great change and have many individuals who are invested in the status quo. The discussion questions above should help this library organization acknowledge the change environment and the leadership that is necessary and address the need to develop team processes that include constructive channels of communication and trust relationships.

REDEFINING UNIVERSITY PRESIDENTIAL LEGACY LEADS TO A NATIONAL ELECTRONIC DATABASE

Jon E. Cawthorne

Context

Since her appointment as university president in 2001, M. Joyce Tisdale had accelerated Green University on a path toward recognized excellence in undergraduate education, teaching and learning, and community partnerships. Like fund-raising and building projects, there were many areas in the university that could use presidential leadership to remake old systems and in the process create a national and international impact. She was convinced that future presidential legacy would require a new way of thinking about collaboration and partnerships. Instead of focusing on the already large endowment, she would work toward the establishment of a national shift in higher education.

She decided her legacy would be to create the largest research knowledge database in the world. That database would have to meet the needs of other institutions and be part of a national vision that redefines a core educational function. A few factors she thought would have long-term implications were

- the millennial generation's technological savvy and interest in their own educational experience,

- redefining course and degree requirements to support and drive new jobs and the local and national economy, and

- addressing areas that suffered from annual rising costs.

Tisdale had supported libraries throughout her career, but she realized that serials' costs would continue to increase in academic libraries. Bundled electronic packages made cancellations politically difficult, if not impossible. Over the years, many libraries had purchased more electronic serials, but canceled duplicate print subscriptions as a cost-saving measure. With annual inflation, collections budgets would continue to shrink each year. New faculty want electronic access; however, humanities and social science tenured faculty prefer material on library shelves.

She wondered what the future university library would look like, not just at Green, but at institutions across the country. She also thought about the increasing cost of scholarly publishing. The library, she decided, must be a part of the solution; it was, after all, a key resource on campus. If she worked at a national level, she would not only address a problem at Green, but her work could benefit institutions elsewhere.

After much thought, consultation, careful planning, and a tremendous amount of courage, Tisdale decided to set out her vision for a comprehensive national electronic knowledge database in a speech entitled, "A national vision for university libraries," delivered at the Conference on Education, Economy and Society held in Washington, DC. This conference brings together academics, researchers, professionals, administrators, policy makers, and industry representatives interested in education. The following week she planned to deliver the same speech to the American Library Association and the American Association of Publishers conferences respectively.

At each conference Tisdale proposed to transform "our universities, our libraries and the nature of scholarly publication and research. We are experiencing open access movements, but we all need to lean on deeper collaborations, the likes of which this country has never seen. Let's expand our vision of what we can create together for the benefit of all."

She captivated the audience with stories woven from current driving forces to establish a future vision of university excellence. She touched on Google Scholar, publishers and vendors, the millennial generation, traditional faculty versus Web/personal publishing, physical library versus virtual library, and the pending retirement of the baby boom generation. Library collections, books, and services, she noted, are part of the foundation of any excellent university. With a few more flattering words about the library, librarians, and staff, she launched into a discussion of the database. "In the next ten years, I challenge all of us to look across and beyond our divisions to develop a national electronic knowledge database. Librarians, vendors, faculty, computer scientist, students, and national policy makers must be stakeholders in a knowledge database filled with full-text research articles. Our common goal must provide library research material that's open to all. Access to research collections in all higher education institutions will lift faculty/student research capability. All students and faculty, no matter their institutional affiliation, will benefit from our work to create this deep partnership across the country. Together, we can accomplish so much more than we can individually."

Her speech was well received, and the comments centered on the logistics and positive responses to her idea. To address some of the more specific questions, she mentioned the Canadian Research Knowledge Network, http://researchknowledge.ca/en/index.jsp. Some of the conference participants, especially the presidents, legislators, and librarians, thought her vision would never become a reality. There were too many moving pieces to coordinate it all.

Still, following the conferences support for her idea gained momentum, as did the opposition. Publishers worried about an untested financial model, and they envisioned steep financial losses. At the height of the discontent, several editorials appeared in major newspapers, calling for Tisdale to resign. The Green University Librarian enlisted help from her colleagues, leaders from the national library, and the executive director of the Association of Research Libraries. When a number of academic presidents came out in support of Tisdale's vision, the mass attacks subsided. The librarians convened several meetings with publishers, vendors, and teaching faculty to discuss specific issues and make the vision a reality. Other presidents acknowledged the problem of individually funding library operations and supported new, collaborative models.

Over the next three years, Tisdale spoke before numerous conferences and professional associations and garnered support. Once she received seed money from several prominent granting agencies, her vision was well on its way to becoming a reality. At the same time, a symposium on the future of the academic library was held at Holy Names University, during which the creation of the knowledge database, its funding, and its governance structure were announced. With this success, many supporters of Tisdale's vision privately began discussing possible options for recognizing her achievement. One idea was to rename the database the Tisdale National Knowledge Grid.

Closing Analysis

Tisdale created a vision for the future of higher education and academic libraries. Conversations with colleagues led her to the idea, but she also drew strength and conviction from rethinking her own legacy. As with most large visions, she endured criticism. Even though some of the comments were negative, she became the spark that academic library leaders needed to stretch their vision of partnerships and possible futures.

Although this case study is purely fictional, the achievement of Tisdale's vision demonstrates the need for deep collaboration across different regions of the country, different financial accounting systems, and, most important, different approaches to fixing the financial uncertainty of the rising costs of maintaining access to print and electronic resources.

Discussion Questions

1. What form might deep collaboration take in the future?

2. Is Tisdale a transformational leader?

3. How might she have gained buy-in to her vision?

4. Her vision has political implications; what are those implications, and how might she have dealt with them?

5. In the near future, will these academic libraries be able to maintain (justify) untouchable areas of the collection and remain central to their institutions?

JUST WHEN YOU NEED THEM THE MOST

Adriene Lim

Background

Childers University is a public university serving the largest student population (30,000 FTE) in a state ranked last for funding of higher education for the decade. Within the next five years, another 5,000 students are expected to enroll. This situation has produced chronic problems for the library (i.e., inadequate staffing, poor technology and facilities infrastructure, and operational dysfunction related to policies, procedures, and communication). At the same time, there is a universitywide hiring freeze, and the library has lost a major portion of its staff due to low retention and attrition. Making matters worse, Virgil Casey, the newly hired university dean, faces a crisis when the library receives a 5 percent budget cut, with little hope of it being offset for at least five years.

Technical Services, with seven librarians and fifteen staff members, is bogged down with original and high-quality copy cataloging, original authority work, and processing large gifts for the library's special collections. Public Services, with eleven librarians and sixteen staff members, handles an increased instruction load, growing virtual and in-person reference demands, expansion of collection development initiatives, and other projects. Library Systems has one librarian, Kim Roberts, who is the head, and two staff members, although the unit manages eleven servers, administers four large mission-critical systems, leads and participates in numerous Web 2.0 and digital library projects, and supports over 120 public computers and 85 staff workstations.

Coping with the Situation?

The Library Management Group—consisting of Casey; Sheila Wright, the tenured assistant university librarian (AUL) for public services; Jason Tester, the tenured AUL for technical services; and Roberts—holds a weekly meeting. At one of these meetings, Casey raises the idea of a strategic planning process to address the current and future challenges. He begins by stating: " I think that the library is floundering and inefficient. We're trying too hard to be 'all things to all people.' A strategic planning process will bring us more focus. My idea is to bring in a consultant to lead the process right away, and I have a person in mind. His name is John Stark. He's advised me to form a committee comprised of twenty faculty and staff, all representatives of the library's units and departments. According to John, no AULs should be appointed so that staff can speak and share their ideas freely."

Sheila and Jason give each other surprised glances but otherwise remain silent. "But what will managers' roles be in the planning process?" Kim asks. "I'm not sure," says Casey. He adds, "We'll have to see what John Stark recommends."

Strategic Plan Produced. Casey brings in the consultant to lead the strategic planning process, which results in a substantial five-year plan that seems to move away from the unworkable model of the past and emphasizes three areas of focus: a concerted shift from print to digital resources; an expansion of instructional services for students; and strengthening of digital services and systems in the library. Casey approves the plan without asking other members of the Library Management Group to review the document and to identify any possible problems or changes. Casey and the provost are thrilled because the library is the first and only unit in the university to formulate a strategic plan.

Plummeting Morale. One year after the library adopted the plan, faculty and staff are still stretched to the breaking point. Many new services and systems have been implemented as laid out in the plan. However, no services or tasks have been disbanded or reduced to accommodate these changes. Casey and the Library Management Group have reallocated only one additional staff position to the Library Systems team, due to a technical services staff member's retirement. Two other fixed-term public services librarians and two other technical services paraprofessionals have been eliminated from the roster as a result of additional budget cuts, just when they were needed the most to cushion the worst of the shortfalls. Staff and faculty notice that they are often called on to work long hours, absorb additional duties and tasks, and stay innovative and energetic, although these extra efforts are rarely recognized. Other than members of the Library Management Group, Casey only sees the faculty and staff once a month at all-staff meetings, and he rarely walks through the library's operational areas or attends staff functions.

At a Library Management Group meeting, Kim proposes the formation of a task force to explore restructuring the organization to match the strategic plan, solve the workload impasse, and raise morale. The task force, she thinks, should examine organizational models of comparable university library systems, especially those that seem to move the organization beyond the old-fashioned concepts of public and technical services as two large and separate silos.

Jason disagrees: "I was hired to manage technical services, and if you think we need to examine my area at all, then it's obvious that you all don't trust me to do my job." "The same goes for me," Sheila shouts.

Kim is taken aback by the objections, because the library's present operations seem to be unsustainable in the current model, and she thought the other administrators would agree with an open *inquiry* into the possibilities, at least, of what a restructuring would offer. She implores both Jason and Sheila to reconsider their positions, advocating for a holistic approach in their attempts to solve the resource and staffing problems within the organization.

Later, Casey decides not to support the proposed examination of the organization's structure, believing that, without the support of both AULs, any efforts to restructure the organization will fail.

Considering a Vote of No Confidence

Throughout the next year, the Library faculty and staff continue to voice complaints about the lack of direction, while Casey and the Library Management Group focus on improving and documenting internal staff and faculty procedures and policies related to promotion and tenure, travel, and equipment requests. Casey moves two public services staff positions that materialized due to attrition to create a new AUL for administrative services. The library faculty view this move as the last straw. They regard the focus on administrative procedures as an inordinate amount of attention on bureaucratic details, and they no longer have any confidence that Casey can move them through the crisis they are experiencing.

Just as they begin to formulate a plan to submit formal complaints about the Dean to the university's administration and to discuss the idea of a vote of no confidence, Casey abruptly announces that he is hiring a team of outside consultants to analyze the library's operations and recommend how a reorganization and restructuring of the library should take place. Because of the lack of trust among the library's faculty, the AULs, and the Dean, and the contentious relationship of all parties, everyone is skeptical that the consultants' recommendations will help the situation. Besides, they wonder, "Where is the money coming from to hire the consultants?"

Discussion Questions

1. What aspects of transformational leadership would work best for Kim in her attempts to persuade the rest of the Library Management Group of the benefits of a restructuring/staff reallocation plan?

2. How should a transformational leader have handled this situation? Outline the key steps in a process.

3. How does having tenured, possibly entrenched administrative staff make the job of a transformational leader tougher, especially when there is no flexibility for hiring new staff? What might be done to address these factors?

4. Explain the reasons why the AULs' reactions are understandable or not, given the type of leadership style they are experiencing from Casey.

5. In what ways could outside consultants have a positive influence on the situation in this case study?

6. Given the crisis faced by the university, how could the money for paying the consultants be justified? From where might the money come?

INFORMATION POLICY

This section of the chapter adds one case study related to information policy, which is defined as a set of interrelated laws, regulations, guidelines, and other policy instruments concerned with the life cycle of government and other types of information and records. These instruments shape agency responsibilities during that life cycle. Information policy brings librarians into contact with policy makers at the national and international levels as well as at subordinate levels. The goal is to influence policy making and the policy instruments that emerge. Information policy also addresses how policies work internally within organizations.

CYBERSPACE PRIVACY

Patricia A. Kreitz

The Whitehall University Library has recently decided to increase its fund-raising efforts by establishing its own development office. A development director was recently hired from another institution. However, for the position of assistant development director, the library staff identify Jane Erickson, social sciences curator, as the top candidate. In the past three years, Jane's grant and donation figures have been outstanding, and she has recently completed a certification in development management. Jane's supervisor supports her application, and several donors have written strong recommendations. But Jane does not get the job.

Introduction

"Thank you for seeing me, Mr. Moreno," Jane Erickson said to the library's Human Resources director as she sat down across from him. "I am very upset that I wasn't chosen for the assistant director position. I believe I am the most qualified candidate, and I don't understand what happened." Juan Moreno glanced at the papers in front of him before starting. "Ms. Erickson," he began, "at a university library like ours, it is extremely important to choose someone for this responsibility who can 'be' our face to very important and wealthy donors—carrying our reputation on his or her shoulders." Nodding in agreement, Jane interrupted, "Yes, and I hope my track record and recommendation letters show my ability to do that." Ignoring the interruption, Moreno continued, "If the assistant director's reputation is tarnished, it brings the library into question, and we have information disqualifying you for this position."

Surprised, Jane said, "Whatever do you mean?" "An Internet search," he answered, "turned up a report in the university's *Campus Crier* that you and others were charged with a series of campus thefts." Shaking her head, Jane asserted, "But how did those old issues get out on the Internet? Anyway, it was when I was a freshman—truly, it was a prank. The charges got dropped," she pleaded. "Don't I even get to explain?" Shaking his head negatively, Moreno said, "The article only has the basic facts. It says you were arrested for theft. Donors can research people, too. We can't have someone involved in theft asking people to give the library money."

"This is wrong," said Jane in a rush, "I shouldn't have my reputation ruined and lose out on a job that everyone says I'm perfect for because of something I did as a freshman." Standing up, she continued, "This is an invasion of my privacy that never would have happened if the library hadn't put my name out on the Internet. I want that issue removed. I won't let the library ruin my reputation forever."

Case Analysis

Privacy Rights and Employment Practices. Employers are increasingly using information found in cyberspace to select among job applicants. A quarter of human resources managers in a recent survey have disqualified candidates based on personal information found online.[4] While researching job applicants online is legal, using the results to discriminate based on U.S. Equal Employment Opportunity Commission protected characteristics is illegal. Treating applicants differentially is also illegal. In this case, Jane would have legal recourse if she were the only applicant who had been searched, or if her age, race, sex, or other protected status were used to reject her.

Because digital content varies in granularity, it can lack context. As the campus newspaper article demonstrates, a significant amount of personal information found in cyberspace can be incomplete. Other information can be inaccurate, or, at worst, malicious. Emerging best practices suggest that employers should use Internet searching as only one of a suite of tools to select a candidate who best fits the job and that employers should give a candidate an opportunity to explain negative information before making a final hiring decision.

Jane, however, is guilty of net naiveté and, perhaps, poor judgment. Career counselors and recruiters advise job seekers to search for themselves on the Internet before job hunting. If needed, they can try to have negative information removed or try to provide balance to their cyberspace identity by adding positive and professional Web pages and e-information. These experts also advise applicants to address past negative net information proactively. Jane would be in a stronger position if she had brought up the incident herself, particularly since it occurred at the same institution. She could balance the information by stressing her successful track record with donors.

Privacy Rights and Library Collections. New communication and publication media, such as search engines, social network Web sites, blogs, and Internet communities, are transforming patterns of information sharing and exposing what was formerly private or physically restricted information.[5] Libraries contribute to this transformation by digitizing older print materials, such as this campus newspaper, or by preserving and making accessible culturally significant born-digital works such as Web pages, blog archives, and news feeds. In the age of "search," the mission of libraries to curate and make accessible society's print and digital cultural heritage results in public access to an increasingly detailed level of personal information.

Library collections have always contained potentially damaging personal information, such as "yellow journalism" newspapers, or memoirs that reveal information about others. In the past, most of this information was physically restricted by its publication medium. Does the combination of Internet accessibility and powerful search engines change libraries' ethical or legal responsibilities? Does Jane have a right to expect the library to protect her privacy?

Privacy Protections. Some e-privacy advocates suggest that laws should be passed allowing individuals to exercise a legal "take down" demand similar to copyright holders, who are allowed to ask Internet sites to remove copyrighted materials posted by users. This removal process protects hosting sites from legal action if copyrighted or libelous information is posted by end-users and, as such, may protect libraries. However, other e-privacy experts warn that take-down demands are overused and can subvert free speech rights. Such requests may be appropriate for malicious or incorrect information, but it is harder to argue for a legal right to force removal of self-published or factual materials. Though privacy laws need to be altered to balance privacy protections with free speech in an electronic world, experts do not agree on the extent of the alterations needed.[6]

Arguing for caution in using legislative or administrative controls, some researchers point out that our understanding of foolish or negative digital pasts is already growing more sophisticated and that distinct rule sets will evolve.[7] In particular, they argue that current employment law is sufficient and all that is necessary is to wait out the generation gap. In time, employers will become more tolerant as the cyberspace generation moves into the workplace as both employees and employers.

Discussion Questions

The Whitehall Library management must respond to two issues. First, what policies should they apply to Internet job applicant information? Did they treat Jane fairly? If not, what should they do? Finally, what policies should they establish to ensure fair treatment for future job applicants? Second, how should they respond to Jane's demand to remove this information? Should digital content containing sensitive personal information be treated differently than print content? The library's decision should be incorporated in its collection development policies.

At a broader level, should the library profession, perhaps partnering with museums and archives, develop policies or best practices addressing how to balance increasingly searchable digital collections containing potentially damaging personal information? Does current law protect libraries, or will new legal rights evolve out of lawsuits?[8] As libraries, museums, and archives collect and preserve social cyberspace—archiving social network sites, blogs, the content of Internet communities, Web sites, or other Internet-accessible information—what responsibilities do they have, if any, to protect individuals' privacy from exposure by researchers, journalists, employers, or the simply curious or malicious? Archives often enforce privacy protection agreements through professional best practices or legal contracts with donors. Could those agreements be a model that would balance access and privacy for digital content? How should the profession balance an individual's privacy rights with its deeply held value of intellectual freedom? Would restricting information be censorship or, are there cases, such as malicious information or minors' privacy, in which protections should be imposed by libraries?

Conversations and reflections on case studies . . .
[help] people see assumptions, consequences and
options.[9]

NOTES

1. Anne Roselle, "The Case Study Method: A Learning Tool for Practising Librarians and Information Specialists," *Library Review* 45, no. 4 (1996): 30.

2. Bernard M. Bass, *Leadership and Performance beyond Expectations* (New York: Free Press, 1985).

3. Daniel R. Ilgen, John R. Hollenbeck, Michael Johnson, and Dustin Jundt, "Teams in Organizations: From Input-Process-Output Models to IMOI Models," *Annual Review of Psychology* 56 (2005): 517–43.

4. YouGov, *What Does Your NetRep Say about You? A Study of How Your Internet Reputation Can Influence Your Career Prospects*, commissioned by Viadeo (Spring 2007). Available from http://www.viadeo.com/NetRep//NetRep%20by%20Viadeo%20-%20Spring%202007.pdf (accessed December 8, 2009).

5. Daniel J. Solove, *The Future of Reputation: Gossip, Rumor, and Privacy on the Internet* (New Haven, CT: Yale University Press, 2007), 29.

6. Ibid., 113.

7. Danah Boyd, "Social Network Sites: Public, Private, or What?," *Knowledge Tree* (2007). Available from http://kt.flexiblelearning.net.au/tkt2007/?page_id=281 (accessed December 8, 2009); David R. Johnson, and David G. Post, "Law and Borders: The Rise of Law in Cyberspace," *Stanford Law Review* 48 (1996): 1367–1402.

8. Andrew Albanese, "Digitization Suit at Cornell: Alumnus Claims Newly Available Article Constitutes Libel," *Library Journal* 133, no. 4 (March 1, 2007): 17–18.

9. Impact Assessment, "Academic Leadership Case Studies" (2009). Available at http://www.insightassessment.com/cases.html (accessed January 6, 2010).

10

~

SCENARIO PLANNING

Joan Giesecke

Scenarios are "a set of organized ways for us to dream effectively about our own future.[1]

Coping with constant change has become a standard part of any library position. Successful leaders find ways to cope with and manage change. Unsuccessful leaders may feel that the best they can do is move from crisis to crisis. Successful leaders use a variety of tools to manage the change process. One such set of tools is planning techniques and processes. Planning can be defined as applying rational thought to the future. It is a continuous process rather than a one-time activity. Planning done casually and haphazardly does not lead to success. In times of continuous change, leaders and managers find that standard forecasting techniques such as strategic planning models may not provide enough guidance for planning when so little is certain. To complement strategic planning techniques, leaders can use scenario planning processes to bring creativity and intuition to the process of data analysis.

Scenario planning is a technique that uses stories to describe possible futures to help managers think about how surprises and discontinuities can be examined in the planning process. The stories help managers consider a number of possible futures and assess alternative strategies that can be effective in a variety of circumstances. These scenarios or stories are then used to develop strategies that will increase the chances of success for the organization as it responds to a changing environment. Scenario planning is not a process for predicting the future or developing preferred futures. Rather, the process asks participants to imagine multiple futures and then design plans to respond to changes depending on how the future develops. Scenarios can help an organization evaluate its progress and course of action, as it answers the following question: Are we headed in the right direction given the most probable scenarios and the alternative options?

BRIEF HISTORY OF SCENARIO PLANNING

The military has used scenario development as a planning technique since the 1940s. By thinking through various options that could develop in the world, officers develop plans for responding to changing events. In the corporate world, in the early 1970s Royal Dutch Shell successfully used scenario planning techniques. The planning team recognized that trend analysis and long-range planning techniques would not help the company succeed if the price of oil changed dramatically. Instead, the team developed a series of scenarios for corporate managers to consider different futures depending on what happened to the price and supply of oil. As a consequence of these planning exercises, Royal Dutch Shell reacted quickly when oil prices changed. It was one of the few oil companies to remain profitable during the oil and gasoline crisis of the 1970s.

Scenario planning has resurfaced as a planning technique as profit and not-for-profit organizations cope with a volatile environment. Whether coping with the changing global political environment, the global financial crisis, the changing technology world, or the aftermath of natural disasters, today's organizations need flexible strategies that help them succeed despite such uncertainties.

SCENARIO PLANNING PROCESS

The scenario planning process is a structured process that results in key stories the organization can use to describe possible futures. To be effective the scenarios that are developed must resonate with people. The stories have to speak to the readers to help them develop responses to the scenarios that can move the organization forward.

As outlined by Peter Schwartz, the scenario planning process involves eight basic steps:

1. *Identify the decision to be addressed.* Managers decide what questions they wish to evaluate in the planning process. This is one of the most crucial steps in the process. Without a clear focus the scenario process leads to vague results that will not help the organization cope with change. The focus of the decision should be a strategic concern for the organization. Scenario planning is the appropriate tool when the stakes are high and external events influence the outcomes for the organization.

2. *Identify the key forces in the environment.* As in strategic planning, participants outline strengths, weaknesses, opportunities, and threats that the organization is likely to face. The analysis covers both internal and external factors that may have an impact on the organization.

3. *Identify the driving forces.* Based on the environmental scan completed in the previous step, participants identify those trends and pressures that will have the most impact on the organization or department. Driving forces usually come from one of five categories: social, economic, political, technological, or environmental.

4. *Rank the forces.* Participants review the forces to decide which are most important in relation to the question asked, which are most certain and likely to occur in any future plans, and which are most uncertain and difficult to predict. The process of ranking the forces enables participants to identify those forces that are likely to have an impact on the organization in a variety of futures and those that are more unlikely to occur or to influence how the organization develops.

5. *Choose the main themes for developing the scenarios.* Participants narrow the forces to choose the one that is most uncertain and the one that is most important. Both forces form the matrix that will determine the different themes for the scenarios. Each force should be described on a continuum of options to frame the scenario plots. The process of identifying the two significant forces can help

participants avoid thinking in terms of worst case, best case, and average scenarios. Instead, they develop four unique stories to describe possible futures.

6. *Write the scenarios.* Stories, developed to outline possible futures, are the core ideas that managers should consider in making decisions about future directions. The plots need to capture the imagination of decision makers without overwhelming them with details.

7. *Review the implications of the scenarios.* From the stories that have been developed, participants outline possible strategies that will help the organization to respond to changes should the future develop as outlined in the stories. Participants look for strategies that are applicable to more than one scenario as well as strategies that help if the future yields big surprises that are unlikely to be anticipated in traditional planning efforts.

8. *Identify ways to monitor change.* Participants outline those indicators they will use to review the scenarios to determine if the future is developing as they described. The indicators help managers know which strategies might work in response to the changes the organization may experience.[2]

A MORE DETAILED OUTLINE OF THE PROCESS

For anyone new to scenario planning, Bill Ralston and Ian Wilson provide a more detailed outline of the steps to take in using scenario planning in an organization.[3] They describe eighteen steps for organizations to follow, and they recommend that organizations develop support for scenario planning and communicate the results of the process.[4] They cover how to pick a facilitator for the planning session and how to form a scenario planning team. They also offer advice on constructing the environmental scan and address trend research, the data-gathering processes, and communication techniques for the team. Their handbook fills in the activities that need to occur as the organization conducts a large scenario planning exercise.

Another good resource for those learning to use scenario planning is *Scenario Planning*,[5] in which Mats Lindgren and Hans Bandhold use a framework called TAIDA to describe the process of scenario planning.[6] The steps in that framework are:

Tracking—identifying trends, changes, and forces that may have an impact the organization;

Analyzing—choosing the most important and uncertain forces and creating scenarios;

Imaging—creating a vision for the organization;

Deciding—developing strategies to attain the organizational vision and meet the threats or changes identified in the scenarios; and

Acting—implementing the strategies and making adjustments in response to the developing environment.

These steps cover the planning and implementation process so that the organization can benefit from and use the knowledge developed during the planning process. Lindgren and Bandhold also note typical problems that organizations experience in using scenario planning.[7] These include having an unclear question to begin the process, using too short a time frame, taking too narrow a perspective on trends, or identifying so many trends that analysis becomes impossible. In the analysis phase organizations may choose the wrong forces to develop scenarios that look at uncertainties. The resulting scenarios may be too general or not comprehensive enough to be helpful to decision makers in the organization. Decision makers may develop a vision that is unrealistic or that does not resonate with the members of the organization. Planners may pick strategies that are safe rather than look at ways to address the uncertainty of the scenarios. Finally, the organization may go through the process, forget the plans, and return to a business as usual mindset. To be effective, as Lindgren and Bandhold note, scenario planning must result in plausible, believable scenarios that challenge leaders to think creatively about how to advance their organizations despite the many unknowns in the environment.

A MINI-SCENARIO PLANNING PROCESS

For those organizations that are familiar with and practice a variety of planning processes, David Mercer describes an abbreviated form of scenario planning that organizations can use.[8] He assumes organizations already have done much of the analysis of the external and internal environments that is needed in any planning process. Based on having usable data for planning, he recommends a six-step process:

1. Determine the drivers for change.

2. Create a framework for analysis or pick the most uncertain and most important drivers.

3. Produce initial mini-scenarios.

4. Pick two or three of the stories to develop.

5. Write the scenario.

6. Identify issues arising from the discussions.[9]

Following these steps, an experienced planning team can develop scenarios that enable leaders to think about the alternative futures that might emerge.

WRITING THE SCENARIOS

Effective scenarios tell stories that are believable and yet challenging enough to enable decision makers to think creatively about the future. Unlike forecasts, which are judged by how well they predict trends, scenarios are judged by how well they help the organization develop strategies to face uncertainty in the environment.

In a good story, the reader can relate to the plot, which addresses the issues identified in the planning process. If the plot is too mundane, the scenario may be ignored. If the plot is too outlandish, the scenario will be viewed as unrealistic and not worthy of consideration. When the plot captures the imagination of the readers, scenario planning becomes successful.

A number of standard plotlines may be used in scenarios:[10]

• Winner and Losers—where the future is a zero-sum game

• Challenge and Response—challenges are faced head on

• Evolution—change comes from today's systems

• Revolution—a radical or dramatic change that has an impact on the organization

• Cycles—coping with events that recur, such as budget woes for public institutions

• Infinite possibilities—the most optimistic view of the future

• Lone Ranger—one character or group defeats adversity alone

Once the basic plot has been chosen, the writer of the scenario needs to craft a well-written and intriguing story. The beginning of the story may describe the forces at work. Next, the writer may examine how the forces evolve or interact, and note new forces that may materialize in the future. Finally, the writer needs an ending that helps the reader view the story as a valid description of the future. Scenarios are usually written in the present tense, even though they are describing events as if it were five or more years in the future.

Within a group of scenarios some elements may appear in each of the individual stories. These are the trends or elements that are seen as most likely to continue. Differences in the scenarios reflect the different values of the uncertain and important forces chosen for the planning exercise. Generally scenarios are two to three pages in length. They are long enough to provide a good story without being so detailed that the reader loses focus.

REVIEWING THE PLOTS

Once the scenarios have been written, the planning process involves the development of strategies to cope with change and evaluate options for the organization to pursue even as it experiences some of the changes noted in the scenarios. The advantage of scenario planning–based strategies is that the process gives the organization time to create options that can be implemented under uncertain conditions and to make adjustments in strategic direction as the future becomes clearer.

SCENARIO PLANNING FOR STUDENTS

Using scenario planning techniques in the classroom is one way to help students think creatively about the future and to learn techniques they can apply in their own organizations. For most students, using the five-step scenario planning approach (related to TAIDA) is sufficient to teach the technique and to begin to develop plausible scenarios describing the possible future for libraries and other information organizations. Most doctoral students are familiar with environmental studies that have been done extensively in library and information science (LIS), are aware of the research and readings on future trends, and understand the need for change if organizations are to remain vital and supported in tough economic times. With an experienced group of graduate students, who are also LIS practitioners and who have read background materials on scenario planning, it is possible to complete a mini-scenario building process in a half-day class. The class begins with a brief review of the scenario planning process. Students are then given a question to address (e.g., "What might be the future of children's services in public libraries in an era of decreased funding?" or "What might a twenty-first-century engineering library at a large research university look like in five years?). Questions that relate to the students' own experiences, where different opinions exist for how the question can be addressed, and where there is an element of conflict, are also effective as teaching examples.

Once the question is set, students identify the major driving forces and trends that have an impact on the environment and the context or the focus of the decision. Next they pick the most important and most uncertain of the forces. This step can generate a lively discussion as students try to figure out which trends are most likely to apply to almost any choice made and which trends are truly uncertain. They often struggle with separating important but known issues from important issues that may have multiple values. For example, coping with serials inflation is an important trend in looking at collections issues. Because costs are unlikely to decrease, this element will be a part of any collection-based question.

Conversely, predicting continued public support for summer reading programs may be more difficult. Once students have identified the two forces that form the axis of the matrix for the scenarios, they begin to outline key plot elements. In the classroom setting, they pick the title for each of the four scenarios and identify the main plot elements, and the instructor provides them with ideas on how to write scenarios. Although class time is not taken to write scenarios, a concluding discussion of possible strategies for the organization to consider is useful in clarifying how an organization can use scenario planning in its own planning processes.

CONCLUDING THOUGHTS

Today's leaders face many challenges and uncertainties. Fortunately there are techniques to assist them in thinking creatively about the uncertainties they face. Scenario planning is one such technique. With scenario planning they can ask "what if" questions and develop strategies to guide the organization in coping with possible changes in the environment. By looking at plausible, multiple futures, leaders are less likely to develop tunnel vision and miss key changes that will have an impact on the organization. Participants in scenario planning have the opportunity to reconsider assumptions that may be part of a standard planning exercise and to consider opportunities to reinvent the organization as needed.

The resources cited in this chapter will help leaders develop scenario planning processes for their organizations. The processes will work for those individuals with little planning experience as well as for those who have participated in a number of planning exercises. The organization can build on work already done by others that identifies trends and forces that will have an impact on the organization. Leaders, however, should be careful not to just accept scenarios developed by other organizations. Rather, they should tailor the process, the scenarios, and the strategies to the unique factors in their own organizations.

Scenario planning can be a very creative way to engage members of the organization in planning processes. Staff can use their imagination to create stories to help them think about change. The process encourages people to keep an open mind about possibilities and to develop strategies to address possible changes. A good scenario is creative and has a touch of surprise that helps leaders and staff plan for change in a complex, uncertain world.

Scenario driven planning helps managers identify their assumptions about the future and the organization, . . . and then use that information to review and renew the organization.[11]

NOTES

1. Peter Schwartz, *The Art of the Long View* (New York: Doubleday, 1991), 4.

2. Ibid.

3. Bill Ralston and Ian Wilson, *Scenario Planning Handbook: A Practitioner's Guide to Developing and Using Strategies to Direct Strategy in Today's Uncertain Times* (Mason, OH: Thomson, 2006).

4. Ibid., 52.

5. Mats Lindgren and Hans Bandhold, *Scenario Planning: The Link between Future and Strategy* (New York: Palgrave/Macmillan, 2009).

6. Ibid, 49.

7. Ibid., 112–14.

8. David Mercer, "Simpler Scenarios," *Management Decisions 33*, no. 4 (July 1995): 33.

9. Ibid., 35.

10. Schwartz, *The Art of the Long View,* 147–64.

11. Joan Giesecke, *Scenario Planning for Libraries* (Chicago: American Library Association, 1998), viii.

11

~

STUDENT SCENARIO PLANS

*Scenario planning is not about predicting the future. Rather,
it attempts to describe what is possible.*[1]

This chapter presents five scenarios written by students in the MLIP program. Joan Giesecke selected these particular scenarios for inclusion. The final scenario plan, developed by students in the fourth cohort, shows how four different scenarios on the same question can generate different strategies.

SCENARIO ONE: THE STUDENTS' EDUCATIONAL AND TRAINING (SET) INITIATIVE—AN ANALYSIS OF SCENARIO PLANNING FOR THE LAS VEGAS–CLARK COUNTY LIBRARY DISTRICT

Felton Thomas Jr.

Introduction

The Clark County School District, the fifth-largest district in the United States, has seen tremendous population growth. For the past decade, the Las Vegas–Clark County area has averaged over 5,000 new residents per month; many of them are children of immigrants. The increased number of new students with limited English language skills has been a strain on the school district.

Nearly 30 percent of the schools in the district are designated as "needs improvement" schools under the standards of the No Child Left Behind Act of 2001 (P.L. 107-110). In the West Las Vegas community, where half of the community is African American and 40 percent is Hispanic/Latino, the schools are doing even more poorly. The school district has asked for help in finding innovative and creative ways to assist in educating the students.

Recognizing the need for the library district to participate in the educational process, the Executive Director of the Las Vegas–Clark County Library District has asked his executive leadership team to develop a strategy that meets the needs of the community at large and the library's community. The library leadership team decides to take a new and innovative approach to addressing this problem.

The group decides that the geographical area with the greatest need surrounds the West Las Vegas (WLV) Library and that the WLV library will play a critical role in a program known as the Students' Education and Training Initiative (SET). An eight-member committee consisting of four library employees (two of them are from the WLV library), a school district member, a PTA member, a member from the local Councilman's office, and a community student is charged with creating the process and the plan. The hope is that the committee, which is to be chaired by the Public Services Director, will receive district and community support.

The committee members are appointed, and they gather information to understand the problems better. To stimulate new ideas they also review examples of innovative approaches that other library systems have used. At the first committee meeting, a local consultant discusses the process of planning scenarios and asks committee members to familiarize themselves with assorted materials and create a list of forces that will define the success of the SET initiative. The following section mentions each driver for change that is important to the scenario-planning process.

Identified Drivers for Change

1. The education and training that the staff need to start a student education and training program.

2. The level of need for a librarian-based educational initiative within the community.

3. The level of political support for the initiative required from elected officials, which may depend on the types of educational training provided.

4. The level of support needed from community activists, who may think the plan is "too little too late."

5. The level of support needed from the professional staff.

6. The willingness of the professional staff to teach classes in collaboration with the educators in the school district.

7. The need for the library district to change the job description for a youth services librarian. (How will this affect those already on the job?)

8. Possible union efforts to propose pay raises for staff involved in the initiative.

9. The possibility that the school district could cut school librarian positions to save money.

10. The level of support from parents, especially homeschoolers if there is a homeschooling element.

11. The level of support from students, depending on the level of tutorial services.

12. The possibility that the state library association may argue the professional's role is to be a facilitator and not an educator.

13. The possibility that a conservative local newspaper may conclude that taxpayers' monies should be spent traditionally or differently.

14. The possibility that adult customers may look on the plan as a competition for resources that would be used for the materials or services that they prefer.

15. The possibility that board members may seek immediate results to calm debate.

16. The level of support to be expected from parents and teacher associations.

17. The type and level of collaboration possible with the school district so that substitute teachers might serve as tutors.

18. The possibility that Sylvan and other fee-based tutoring agencies may actively lobby against the plan or to be the agency that provides the service.

19. The possibility that the initiative could spawn a larger education initiative for adults.

20. The possibility that technology services may make the initiative less staff intensive.

21. The possibility that national library associations and other state programs may offer support or opposition to the plan.

22. Responsibility for creating the initiative (staff based or bringing in consultants).

23. The possibility that the district could charge for more extensive tutoring services.

24. Technology, staffing, and capital expenses.

Once the SET team begins the process of determining the most important and most uncertain elements, its members decide that community and staff support for the initiative are the most important elements and that the types of educational services provided are the most uncertain. The two elements then become the axes of a matrix on which the scenarios are built (see figure 11.1).

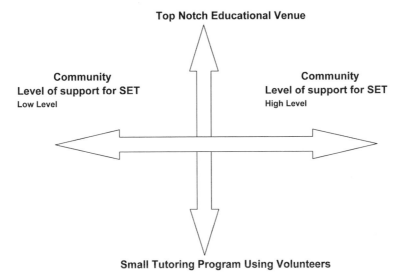

Top Notch Educational Venue

Community Level of support for SET Low Level

Community Level of support for SET High Level

Small Tutoring Program Using Volunteers

Figure 11.1 SET Scenario Matrix

At another committee meeting, the purpose of which is to reassess their progress and to start developing scenarios, committee members review the level of success that they have achieved in communicating their work to the library district staff and the community members of West Las Vegas. They write articles for the district's newsletter *The Circulator*, scheduled to be published in two weeks. The *Las Vegas Sentinel*, the local African American paper, and *El Tiempo*, the largest newspaper for the Spanish-speaking community, have both been approached, but neither has contacted any committee member.

The committee then begins the task of mapping a list of possible services for students to judge the community's level of support against the matrix (see table 11.1, p. 166). These items are then used in the development of scenarios.

Table 11.1
Possible Services Provided by SET

Possible services to be provided for students	Community—high level support/basic tutoring	Community—high level support/ed. venue	Community—low level support/ed. venue	Community—low level support/basic tutoring
Library research class	X	X	X	X
Online tutoring	X		X	X
Basic tutoring	X		X	X
Mentoring program for self-esteem		X		
Homework help center	X	X	X	X
Reading, math, and science classes		X		
Gang intervention program		X		
Head Start center	X			
Textbook repository	X	X	X	X
Parent/teacher learning center	X	X	X	X
Student technology lab with testing software	X	X	X	X

Scenario Plots

The services to be provided assist in the refinement of the SET matrix (see figure 11.2). This section provides two scenarios.

Top Notch Educational Venue

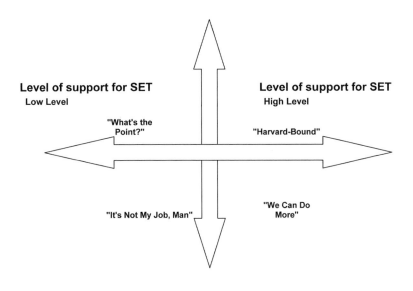

Level of support for SET
Low Level

"What's the
Point?"

"It's Not My Job, Man"

Level of support for SET
High Level

"Harvard-Bound"

"We Can Do
More"

Small Tutoring Program Using Volunteers

Figure 11.2 SET Matrix Refined

Scenario 1: It's Not My Job

Young people's librarians Dolly Nelson and Sandra Kelly walk into the restaurant calm but a little uneasy about the meeting they are about to lead. A quick look around the table confirms that every Las Vegas–Clark County Library District (LVCCLD) young people's department head is in attendance. "We'd like to thank everyone for attending," Dolly starts, but then Sandra interrupts, "Remember this meeting is not to be discussed with anyone, especially your branch managers." Sandra takes a deep breath and continues, "Listen, none of us wants to be here, but the District has failed to listen to us. We now have very few options." Dolly regains center stage and declares, "We don't have a lot of time, let's vote. We are either going to go before the board of trustees and protest, or we are going to stage a walkout."

Dolly has started in the district as a Young People's Assistant (YPL) and received a stipend fifteen years ago to attend library school. She has loved her job for many years until recently, when the district started to talk of changing its philosophy toward educating children. Her beliefs are very simple: if it ain't broke—don't fix it. Children have benefited for many years from the assistance that library workers have provided them and will continue to benefit for many years in the future. She cannot understand the district's preoccupation with working with the school district. After all, she was a teacher for five years in Portland before she came to Las Vegas. She left teaching to get away from the stress, and now she is starting to feel it again. How misguided can the "suits" be, "don't they realize that librarians do educate people, just in a different way than the schools?"

Sandra, on the other hand, just recently relocated to Las Vegas from Los Angeles. Six months earlier, when she took the department head position, she found the district's movement toward educating young people to be refreshing and innovative. But now it has become clear to her that they are trying to change things before the infrastructure is in place. In her mind, the district has done a poor job of getting the YPL department heads to support the change and, until they do, she is going to side with the department heads.

Despite the fact that the staff of the West Las Vegas Library have decided to embrace the SET initiative, both Dolly and Sandra appear before the board and speak eloquently of their history in the district. They speak about the hardship that the initiative will cause staff members and that librarians have never been trained to be educators. After telling the board that educating children simply is not their job, both sit silent when a board member retorts, "Well, whose job is it?"

Scenario 2: Harvard-Bound

Deborah Kincaid stands up and applauds loudly when she hears the board member's response to the two staff members. She is shocked that the librarians are allowed to keep their jobs after this showing of what she thinks is the ultimate insubordination. Her eight-year-old son Jake is sitting next to her, somewhat oblivious to the chaotic scene around him. On one side are the staff members holding signs that say, "It's Not Our Job" and "No More Pay, No More Play." On Deborah's side is an eclectic group of supporters for the SET initiative. Assemblyman Carl Wilson and community activist Reverend Lerone Reed told Deborah that they would picket the District if the initiative was somehow derailed. Officials from the Clark County School District and the University of Nevada–Las Vegas are preparing to speak when Jake suddenly falls off his chair.

Jake is Deborah's reason for being at the meeting. When Deborah's husband was promoted to a high-paying management job at his casino, the two decided that Deborah would quit teaching and homeschool their son. Deborah is shocked by the lack of support provided to her by the school district. One of the SET committee members has approached her for advice from the homeschool perspective, and she has become excited about the program. She is excited by the possibility of the school district actually providing credit for a class that will be held in the library district. Jake is only eight, but she and her husband have already determined that Jake is going to attend Harvard Law School. Anything that they can get provided to them for free on this journey will be worth fighting for. Deborah's attention is brought back to the meeting when the councilman and minister rise from their chairs and move toward the podium.

Each has only three minutes to speak, but both speak passionately in favor of the initiative. The assemblyman talks about the number of teenagers who have died as a result of gang violence in the community over the summer: "For those young people it's too late, but this initiative is saying to all the other young people that we have not given up on you. Please support the initiative, fund it to the maximum level, and show the community children that we will make a difference in their lives."

The reverend echoes the assemblyman, but adds this warning, "If you fail our children today, how can we trust you with our tax dollars tomorrow?" The board then tells the attendees that they have a difficult decision to make and that they will look at the recommendations made by the executive director and staff for guidance.

A Managerial Leadership Approach

Strategies for solutions to the two scenarios become simpler using scenario planning. The process eliminates the approaches that only appeal to small numbers of people and helps make rational decisions. In the scenarios where there seems to be only a "lose-lose" ending, however, a final vetting process may be helpful.

If the overriding function of management is to provide stability to an organization, while the overriding function of leadership is to produce change, then there would seem to be one primary approach to both scenarios. That approach is to follow the direction that initially leads to change but works quickly to produce a more stable organization. This approach requires the committee to recommend the services under SET that have the highest level of acceptance from all four quadrants. It would also require that services needing a great deal of lead time or extensive capital outlay be left out of the initial SET proposal. Finally, a creative solution that allays the staff's fears but provides the community with the same service should be explored.

From this approach the committee should recommend three services within the SET proposal: the library research class, the homework help center, and the textbook repository.

SCENARIO TWO: FACING THE CROSSROAD—REDEFINING THE WORK OF LIBRARIANS IN THE TWENTY-FIRST CENTURY

Jon E. Cawthorne

Central Question

Can academic libraries recognize the need for change and integration of the librarian's work into the overall teaching, learning, and social fabric of the university?

Setting

Our librarians, Richard Shelby and Dina Rankin, work in the main library at Steeple State University, which was recently named a doctoral I level institution. Although the university administration pushed for this status, Richard and Dina know the library is not funded adequately to support faculty research. In their view, this is an excellent library for undergraduate students. Richard has thirty years of experience and Dina has eight. Trent, the student, is beginning his third year at the university. The exchanges in both scenarios among Richard, Dina, and Trent occur toward the end of the school term.

Driving Forces (Table 11.2)

Table 11.2
Driving Forces

Economic	Political	Social	Technological
University budgets	Faculty embrace of library change	Millennial students	Wikipedia, Google, Facebook, blogs, My Space
Creation of hybrid courses	Campus political environment	Workforce demographic changes	Increasing e-content digitization, full-text electronic
International-ization of universities	Perception of worth by upper administration	Library as positive force: "good will"	Changes to teaching and learning process
Distance education/exten ded studies	Union contracts	Social networking	Faculty as content publishers
State funded vs. state located	Higher education organization	Image of librarians; roles of librarians	Constant innovative applications, hardware
Grant funding for innovation	Change: culture and communication	Everyone publishes	Web redesign for better service

Scenario Grid

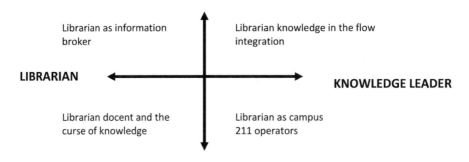

VIRTUAL FUTURE
LIBRARIANS ABLE TO CHANGE

Librarian as information broker

Librarian knowledge in the flow integration

LIBRARIAN

KNOWLEDGE LEADER

Librarian docent and the curse of knowledge

Librarian as campus 211 operators

TRADITIONAL LIBRARY
LIBRARIANS UNABLE TO CHANGE

Most important: The library remains central to the mission of the university.

Most uncertain: Librarians' ability to recognize and adapt to change.

Scenario 1: Librarian Docent and the Curse of Knowledge

As a college junior, Trent can count the number of his visits to the library on one hand. He vaguely remembers the library tour. Once he checked out a book using the library's self-check-out machine. Although the library is centrally located, he (and others) does not view the services and resources as essential to the entire university. He finds other places to study. Some of his friends boast they do not need to enter the library given the availability of Google and the Internet.

For a writing assignment, the instructor asks the class to reflect on the role of librarians on campus and to factor into the answer the cost and value of libraries:

- What do they do?

- How do they support teaching and learning?

- Should the library continue to exist in its current form?

She wants students to incorporate the viewpoint of librarians into their answers.

Trent thinks he knows everything important about the subject. What surprises can he expect? After all, since he transferred to the university in his junior year he has only visited the library a few times. To confirm his understanding, he goes to the library and approaches the reference desk to request an appointment with one of the librarians. Both Richard and Dina are on the phone, one engaged in personal communication (text-messaging his family) and the other discussing an upcoming departmental meeting. When Richard is done with his text-messaging, Trent asks if he would consent to an interview about the library and what librarians do on campus. Richard is willing to do so once he concludes his reference desk assignment. Although Trent does not understand why he cannot ask the questions right away, he agrees to return later.

Trent meets Richard in his office and is amazed to see a Web cam mounted on a computer right next to a laptop. There is an iPod connected to the laptop. Trent gets excited because he has similar technology. For the first question, Trent asks how the equipment helps Richard do his job and is surprised by the response: "Well, I have the Web cam to communicate with my librarian colleagues." Richard adds, "Occasionally, we do use it to discuss work without leaving the office, but primarily I like to discuss lunch or vacation plans." He explains how the technology was easy to learn, but it does not have much practical application to his job because "technology can never replace a live person at the reference desk. This profession is built on people serving other people." Trent thinks the answer makes sense, even though it does not match how his friends use technology.

Next Trent asks, "What do librarians do on an average day?" In response, Richard says:

We review our e-mail for reference questions from faculty and students. Throughout the day, some of us spend time at the reference desk, usually in two-hour blocks. When we get off the desk, we check more e-mail and review new book selections. We also order new books that the faculty request. We serve on library and university committees, and spend a lot of time giving tours of the library to classes that request it.

Trent thinks the tours convey useful information, but he wonders how the work that librarians do connects with what goes on in the classroom. "How do you support teaching and learning?" he asks. Richard replies:

We support faculty by providing the material they need to teach their classes. We also staff the reference desk during the day and two evenings so that students and faculty can ask questions. Occasionally, we give a lecture on the library materials. I want to stress that these lectures do not focus on the stuff you find on Google. Rather we help you find information in the books you see throughout the building. We prefer to do more in-depth instruction with graduate students, not with the large undergraduate classes. We find that we cannot present the material effectively in an auditorium of fifty or more students. We encourage faculty to let us offer tours so that we can get students into the building.

Trent thinks Richard has made good points, and there is probably contact between students and librarians through the tours and students asking questions at the reference desk.

Trent asks his final question, "Will the library, in its current form, exist in the future?" Richard has a ready answer: "Of course, libraries have been a part of campuses throughout history, and Steeple State is no different. Even though we have new gadgets, the book is still the library's most important resource." Richard continues, "Being able to find and interpret information not necessarily found in books is what separates the educated from the uneducated person. There's no real reason to change as I have been doing the same thing for 30 years." Surprised by this comment, Trent asks a quick follow-up question, "So nothing will change?" Richard reflects a moment before saying, "Libraries are so much a part of the university; they are the heart of the institutions so, no, I don't see them changing. We have weathered changes over the years, but the basic service has remained the same. Besides, I will retire next year. I know the library will remain a support unit to the institution, but if, by chance, it does change, I won't be here to see it!"

Richard asks Trent about his major and his summer plans. Trent thanks Richard for his time. As he walks away, Trent is forming a mental image of his paper. Librarians, it seems to him, see no real urgency in implementing new services or changing what they have done for years. He does not see how they can be central or vital to teaching and learning, especially for undergraduates. Trent has no idea about how books are selected, but he does not care. The truth is that he can answer the questions for the assignment.

Scenario 2: Librarian Knowledge in the Flow of Technology Use

As a college junior, Trent sees the library as central to his academic and social life. If he is not in his dorm, or in class, he visits the library physically or virtually. Without leaving the library's home page, he can check his e-mail and calendars, reserve seating for campus events, participate in ongoing chat sessions with the university administrators, and of course, do research. Whether with individual or group work, the library staff are extremely helpful in person; they are equally engaged via e-mail, IM, chat, blogs, social networking sites, and wikis. Librarians are willing to engage students however they connect.

For a class project, one of his instructors asks the class to reflect on the librarians' role on campus and to include comments from librarians:

- What do they do?

- How do they support teaching and learning?

- Should the library continue to exist in its current form?

Although Trent thinks he knows enough about the topics to do the paper, he decides to make an appointment with a librarian. He meets Dina in the library as she is on her way to the faculty technology committee of the college of education. As they walk, Trent finds Dina open, friendly, and focused on his question: "What does a typical day look like?" She answers, "What I love about being a librarian is that my days are never the same. Even when we used to work on the reference desk, there was tremendous variety in the questions students asked. Now we get even more questions through different forms of communication." Trent mentions that he has asked a question through IM and was delighted to get a response so quickly. Dina invites him to stay for the brief meeting and promises to spend more time with him afterward.

During the meeting Trent notices that Dina fields most of the questions and leads the discussion about the library's role in connecting with students. After the meeting Trent asks, "How do you support teaching and learning?" "Well, what I just did in that faculty meeting was support teaching and learning," she replies. Further,

I love to talk with the faculty, especially when they are planning important shifts in the way they teach. The library was one of the first to try IM, chat, MySpace, and blogs. Because we were very successful I tell our story to other colleges. Next week, I'm going to the curriculum committee in the business college and will explore ways for the faculty to integrate technology into classroom instruction.

Talking about student learning, Dina says:

Today, we live in a society with greater access to information than ever before. The Internet makes everyone a librarian. Sure, many students don't know the theory behind searching, but does that really matter if they find what they need? Just think, Trent, the library spends tremendous amounts of money to purchase books and to put them on the shelves. We also ask students to sit in class for lecture. Is such learning still viable for higher education? If people want the answer when they want it and the library is not available, what impact does that have on their decision the next time they need a question answered? I am working for a library that tries to keep the knowledge librarians have, offer, and share in the flow of the new ways people are using technology.

Dina goes on to describe a grant she is working on to partner with the college of education and social networking sites. The grant will allow the college of education and her to create learning applets for MySpace and Facebook. "Like I have said several times," she muses, "librarians have to change their approach to service in order to create a viable and relevant future for libraries."

Trent asks about how the library supports teaching and learning. Dina is not sure she has the whole answer, but replies, "I think the library has a great deal to contribute to teaching and learning. Our support should go beyond the physical and traditional roles we are well known for." Trent thinks librarians are already quite innovative, but Dina goes on, "What if librarians promoted a deeper understanding of how students learn? Our attention in this area and our knowledge of students could help faculty design more effective courses." Dina wants librarians to become integrated, high-level knowledge consultants who support teaching and learning by helping all people design more effective knowledge tools. "The Internet," she explains, "provides an excellent canvas for us to create these tools. People who set up blogs or contribute to wikis are excellent examples of new knowledge creators whom we can assist. Let academic libraries be a resource center for bloggers and other independent content providers." Trent finds the conversation very interesting. He is learning about how librarians think of change and the new service roles they can play.

He asks his final question, "Should the library continue to exist in the current form?" Dina says,

Well, the library has always incorporated new technologies, yet it remained focused on printed books. At one time only a few people were published in book form; now anyone can be published on the Internet. Libraries broadened their collections and access to resources, and created archiving robots to collect and preserve new pages on the Web. They receive electronic documents from students and help them build their own life experience collections. Our outreach to faculty and re-engineering our profile on campus as knowledge consultants has been very deliberate. There is a new way of thinking about the expert. Academic libraries all over the world are collaborating more than ever.

Trent could easily talk with Dina much longer, but he has to write the paper. Realizing that he has all the information he needs to write it, he thanks her for her time and insights. He sees the possibilities for the library as endless. Trent is even more impressed with the library and excited about its future than he was before he met with Dina. He likes being a student at Steeple State University.

Team Leadership Strategies an Academic Library Might Use

- Discuss new technologies that improve service to students.
    - Create focus group interviews with students.
    - Encourage experimentation that leads to new services.
    - Improve design and functionality of the Web site.
- Maintain constant communication with students, faculty, and staff.
    - Establish a student advisory panel.
    - Invite speakers to expand future ideas and develop partnerships.
    - Celebrate success, no matter how small.
- Revamp the hiring process.
    - Decide what skills and talents will make the academic library more effective and part of the flow of university life.
    - Redefine requirements for position announcements.
    - Develop new procedures for screening candidates.
- Developing a strategic plan that ties back to Steeple's mission:
    - Design discussions that extend people beyond what they know.
    - Include people outside the library on planning committees.

Conclusion

The "curse of knowledge" is a problem we must all guard against; it does not allow for creative thinking.[2] Knowledge is a key element in both scenarios. In the first plot it is difficult for Richard to see beyond what he already knows about the library and its services. Even with all the technology around him, he cannot see any use for newer technology. He holds on to past accomplishments while the world changes around him. The way people search and relate to information is dramatically different. Richard seems not to notice or care.

Discussion question:

- Do the values that we hold in librarianship inhibit us from seeing opportunities around us?

In the next plot, Dina is very connected. She envisions new roles for librarians: knowledge consultants helping at all stages of knowledge creation. There has been a tremendous influx of people tagging and organizing pictures, documents and videos, and so forth. The success of Google and Wikipedia signals a new digital order that has an impact on library collections, organization, and services.[3] Working in this new digital order will require a deeper examination of the values and services for the twenty-first century.

SCENARIO THREE: WHERE HAVE ALL THE PEOPLE GONE?

Anne Marie Casey

Central Question

In a time of uncertain state funding and a change in Carnegie classification to doctoral/research-intensive, how can a public university library plan to adequately support users?

Background

Public funding for colleges and universities depends on the state economy, which rises and falls with changes in business and population shifts. The state of Michigan has been suffering a declining economy for most of the last decade. Dependent for the most part on the auto industry centered in the greater Detroit region, Michigan had a thriving economy for much of the twentieth century, while the American car held world supremacy. In the last decade, this has changed as the "Big Three" began slipping in global auto sales and the state had little to take the place of the declining auto industry. State funding for public education and services is threatened more each year. Central Michigan University (CMU) has experienced several years of declining financial support and anticipates more as the state economy continues to weaken.

CMU started as a normal school in 1892. It has grown steadily to become the fourth largest public university in the state of Michigan. In 2000 the university received a new Carnegie classification of "doctoral/research-intensive university" (see http://en.wikipedia.org/wiki/Carnegie_Classification_of_Institutions_of_Higher_Education). Following the new classification, the university saw an increasing emphasis on research. The strategic planning document, *CMU 2010* (http://www.planning.cmich.edu/), lists as number three of its five priorities the university's need to enhance the infrastructure for research and creative activity. Although teaching and learning are still the number one priority at CMU, research is increasing in importance.

The University Library at CMU has been affected by both the decline in state funding and the new emphasis on research. In the last decade, library staff positions have been cut and technology replacement funds have been used to meet shortfalls in other areas. The acquisitions budget has remained intact, however. Although yearly increases have not always matched inflation rates, the acquisitions budget has only been cut once in the last decade because of the high value the academic division places on library materials. The loss of library staff or technology money that has been part of the budget cuts does not seem to have registered with faculty. The library management team is uncertain of the best way to proceed with the possibility of reduced funding and the need to support the traditional undergraduate curriculum and increase support for graduate programs and faculty research.

The leadership at the Central Michigan University Library is team based; the dean leads a team of managers, who in turn lead departmental teams. The decision-making process is participative and collegial. This leadership style worked well for many years while the economy was strong and external conditions did not change so rapidly.

Driving Forces

Most important: Providing library services and collections that support the continuum of users, from the freshman general education major to the experienced faculty researcher (see figure 11.3).

Most uncertain: State funding.

Stakeholders

- Undergraduate students
- Graduate students
- Teaching faculty
- Faculty researchers
- University administrators
- Librarians
- Library Staff

Quadrants

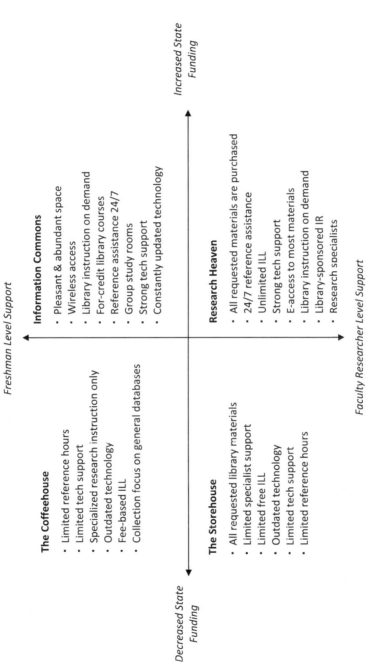

Freshman Level Support

Information Commons

- Pleasant & abundant space
- Wireless access
- Library instruction on demand
- For-credit library courses
- Reference assistance 24/7
- Group study rooms
- Strong tech support
- Constantly updated technology

Research Heaven

- All requested materials are purchased
- 24/7 reference assistance
- Unlimited ILL
- Strong tech support
- E-access to most materials
- Library instruction on demand
- Library-sponsored IR
- Research specialists

Increased State Funding

Faculty Researcher Level Support

The Coffeehouse

- Limited reference hours
- Limited tech support
- Specialized research instruction only
- Outdated technology
- Fee-based ILL
- Collection focus on general databases

The Storehouse

- All requested library materials
- Limited specialist support
- Limited free ILL
- Outdated technology
- Limited tech support
- Limited reference hours

Decreased State Funding

Figure 11.3 Quadrants

Scenario 1: The Storehouse

Mary Ann and Wayne are faculty members as well as husband and wife. After raising a family, they both threw their energies into teaching and research in their respective fields. They were happy when the university administration increased support for faculty research beginning in 2000.

Wayne, the chair of the Biology Department, has been the prime mover at the university in the growth in enrollments in that department by establishing a master's degree program in environmental studies that has attracted outstanding faculty and students. His dream is to establish a doctoral program in environmental studies before he retires. He is in the process of developing a plan for new courses that will be part of the proposed doctorate. Mary Ann, who teaches writing in the English department, oversees the university's writing center. Her research focuses on nineteenth-century British fiction writers. She has just been invited to edit an issue of a prominent journal on Dickens. Her most recent book has received a prestigious award. With all of the work they do during the academic year for their courses and departments, Wayne and Mary Ann have fallen into the habit of "living" in the university library over the summer so that they can work on their research.

On their way to the library, Wayne and Mary Ann hear another news report on the radio about the worsening state budget. The latest news is that the state cannot make its budget for the current fiscal year and plans to call back funds from the public colleges and universities. This will mean more cuts for the library, which is totally funded by state appropriations. They are not worried about their research. Both the president and the faculty senate agreed that library acquisitions funding would not be cut because faculty need immediate access to books and journals for their research. Mary Ann and Wayne are sure that no matter what else happens at the university library, the environmental biology journals and everything published on Dickens will be there. They go their separate ways and settle into their research routines. Only it is not quite what they expected. After a week of constant challenges, they vent to each other.

Mary Ann tells Wayne that she is frustrated because she had trouble finding some of the newest books on Dickens she needs for her review article. She knows that they were ordered. She has been sending her orders over to Alice, the English literature bibliographer, as she finds new titles, and she has not heard back that there is a problem. Mary Ann says that she tried to discuss this with Alice one day during the week, but Alice was always busy answering e-mail reference questions. She assured Mary Ann that she had put through the orders as quickly as she could, although it was harder now, with staff shortages. Alice had handled all of the e-mail reference questions over the summer.

Then, Mary Ann says, as if that were not a big enough problem, she could not find the new books that were listed in the catalog. She estimates that she wasted four hours over the course of the week trying to track down books that had not been shelved. The head of circulation, Dianne, had apologized and said her department would do better in the future. They had lost a lot of student employee hours in the budget cuts and were having trouble keeping up with shelving.

Mary Ann grows angrier as she recounts her week's frustrations to Wayne. He joins in and says that he has run into similar shelving problems with the journals. Some individual issues were missing because the library had decided to stop binding volumes to save money. Even the electronic journals are a problem. Sometimes the link does not work from the catalog, and when he tried to locate Dave, the science bibliographer, to get some help, he found out that Dave, an academic year library faculty member, was not granted a summer appointment for the first time in recorded memory. Wayne had been planning to ask Dave to do some in-depth research for him on the new courses he was proposing for doctoral students, and no one else in the library comes close to Dave's knowledge of the biology resources.

The more they talk, the more problems they remember and the angrier they get. The couple decide to go talk to the library director, Jenny, an old friend of theirs. She is happy to talk to two great library supporters. As she listens to their report of the many problems they have encountered, she grows sadder. When they are done, Jenny apologizes for all of the challenges they have faced and promises to do her best to rectify what she can. She confesses to them that she feels like she is barely able to hold the library together these days. The increase in research at the university has focused attention on the collections. President Smith and the academic senate have told her that the budget cuts, forced on the library by the state economy, cannot be taken out of acquisitions. Smith has also told her that the faculty constantly tell him that buying new library materials is the most important job the library has.

Jenny had argued unsuccessfully that access to collections could be accomplished for expensive items through interlibrary loan in order to save services, but the faculty disagreed. When researchers are in the mood to discover new information, they cannot wait a couple of days to get the books or articles. They want them when they locate the references.

Jenny's only recourse is to cut student employees and lay off staff. Since the faculty librarians are tenured, she cannot let them go, so she is transferring them to other departments to fill vital positions of people she has let go. Jenny understands how the lack of staff is starting to have an impact on the university's researcher community. They have the money to buy the books and serials, but have lost many of the people who ordered them, processed them, shelved them, and kept links to them alive. The library can no longer guarantee subject specialists to help researchers because they cannot afford to pay summer supplements to the academic-year bibliographers. She promises to do her best with what she has.

Wayne and Mary Ann are quiet on the way home that day. They have a lot to think about. This is the first time either of them realize how much they take for granted in the library. They have always assumed that buying the books and journals they need is the most important thing the library can do to support their research.

Scenario 2: The Coffeehouse

Todd and Justin are freshmen who met in Professor Greenberg's Survey of Ancient History class and became friends. They both have twenty-page term papers due in November and decide to get a head start on them in mid-October. Todd's mother is a librarian at the community college back home and has always impressed upon him how many resources the library has, not just in books and magazines, but in people who can help you find information. Todd tells Justin that they need to start their research for their term papers in the library. Justin is convinced that they can find everything they need by searching Google, and they will not have to go out in the cold. After a lengthy discussion, Justin finally agrees to go to the library because the coffee shop there has the best java beverages in town.

After buying some lattes in the library coffee shop, Todd and Justin head to the reference desk. They are surprised to see Olga from their dorm sitting behind the desk. They ask to speak to the reference librarian, and Olga tells them that the librarians leave at 6:00 p.m. now. With all of the budget cuts in the last couple of years, the reference librarians have been moved to other departments to cover for laid-off staff. The few reference librarians left are only there during the day. Olga tells them she will try to help, and, if they still need more information, they can come back tomorrow during the day or e-mail a question to the librarians.

They discuss with Olga the topics Professor Greenberg assigned them. They are not quite sure how to get started. Todd asks Olga where to start looking for articles on ancient Rome. His paper is on how Julius Caesar changed the Roman Republic, and Justin's is on the effects of Sulla's actions on the Roman Republic. Olga tells them to search ERIC. No matter what the librarians say, she swears by ERIC. "And," she says, "you can access ERIC from your dorm room, so you never have to come to the library."

Back in the dorm later that night, Todd and Justin check out ERIC but do not find much information. Todd has e-mailed the librarians for some more information but wants to get started that night. He and Justin decide to search Google.

Justin searches for "Effects of Sulla" and finds a ton of great articles on the effects of different chemicals on a kind of bean, named "sulla." He thinks this is an odd topic for a history class, but what does he know? He is only a freshman! Todd stumbles on an incredible find. There is actually an essay on Google called, "The Heart of Change: Julius Caesar and the End of the Roman Republic" by a scholar. It has great references too.

The next day Todd gets an e-mail message from a reference librarian with information that differs from what he found on Google. Rob, the librarian, suggests some databases for Todd to search and as well as some search terms. Rob also sends links to an online encyclopedia of Roman history and suggests Todd read the article on Caesar. He finishes his note with a link to a tutorial he has written to help students find information on history topics. Rob tells Todd to contact him or come in during the day if he has any questions. Todd shows the e-mail message to Justin. The two freshmen decide to call Rob and have him help Justin and answer a few more questions for Todd. Rob tells them that Google is a good source of information for some topics but not usually for academic research papers. Although Todd found something on Google that was actually on his topic and that he could possibly use, what Justin found had absolutely nothing to do with Roman history. Todd and Justin continue to check their research by e-mail with Rob and hand in papers with authoritative information on their assigned topics.

Conclusion

Educating faculty to become library advocates. People working within a profession tend to forget how little everyone else knows about how they work. To most people who use a library, it is all about the collections. As long as we have the materials they want, they do not think too much about how they got there. Academic administrators and faculty need to understand that access to collections is much more complicated than buying things and putting them on a shelf or a server. Librarians and the library administration need to engage with teaching faculty regularly through orientation, training, and liaison meetings to help them understand all library resources available, and they need to learn what the faculty members need to help them teach and do research. The library management team needs to lead liaison work with faculty and university administrators as well as empower librarians and staff to engage with faculty wherever possible in order to educate them on all the library has to offer and to enlist their support in educating students and colleagues.

Reevaluating traditional collection development practices. Acquisitions budgets at academic libraries can be complicated and subject to political forces external to the library. In a situation where funds are allocated to departments or disciplines, it is diffficult to redistribute these funds when the focus of the educational mission changes. Everyone wants more money for library materials; few, if any, want to give up funds. However, there may be ways to realign a historically based budget without stirring up negative political problems.

The library can conduct an analysis of the collection that includes such components as usage, perceived needs, and costs. After the collection analysis, when patterns are better understood, a variety of new options may be obvious. Among them might be participation in consortial and group collection building; investigating whether aggregated databases with full-text article access may be as effective for undergraduates as multiple journal subscriptions; and using interlibrary loan and document delivery services to obtain copies of articles of little-used, expensive subscriptions. In addition, library bibliographers can consult with teaching faculty to learn whether other types of materials might be more useful to a department than the serials subscribed to previously. (For example, access to a product such as *MD Consult* might be more useful to an allied health department than a number of more expensive subscriptions.) If the library offers something more currently useful to the department in place of serials that are minimally used, the department may be more willing to authorize serials' cancellations and more open to changes in historical funding patterns.

Adapting services. Budget cuts are inevitable in public and academic libraries in states such as Michigan. Staff cuts might mean a change in service quantity, but they do not have to mean a change in the quality of service provided. Offering reference services by phone and e-mail and getting back quickly to answer questions can alleviate some of the frustrations caused by cuts in staff hours of coverage. Placing good tutorials and pathfinders on the library home page can enhance the learning experience of undergraduates in lean budget times.

Rethinking staff assignments. When libraries are forced to lay off staff or are not able to fill positions as people leave, there are a number of ways that they can deal with the reorganization of work other than by reducing services. To maintain the quality of primary services, it is important to first decide which are the most essential. Once those are determined, it is important to maintain in their current positions the librarians and staff who are most vital to continuing those services. Next, the senior management team might determine if some staff assignments can be outsourced to other areas in the institution, such as having the institutional technology department host the library Web site. Finally, the team should educate substitute staff to do the work they are trained for and to refer work that is more difficult. For example, if students work on the reference desk at times, they need to understand what they know how to answer and what they need to refer to librarians. Thinking creatively about how to get the job done well rather than about who has always done a particular job can help maintain quality service when there are fewer employees than needed.

Innovating services. Library services remained relatively constant for more than a hundred years. In the last two decades, changes in technology have required libraries to change many of the ways in which they deliver services and access. However, there are traditional ways of providing services that libraries tend to cling to, even in the face of severe funding challenges. One way to continue to provide quality service is through methods that reach the greatest number of users who need those services. To maintain traditional staffing patterns and hours at a reference desk may be an inefficient use of human resources when the users who most need the instructional support of librarians, the undergraduates, often prefer to request reference assistance overnight and online. Academic libraries are discussing plans to do away with the reference desk, joining consortia to provide reference assistance online for extended hours, and investigating ways to provide access to collections and reference assistance through newer technologies such as hand-held devices and MP3 players. Targeting users with services that are delivered in current formats and cutting traditional, less-utilized services may be a way to provide necessary materials and services across the spectrum of users in lean economic times.

Learning from the Scenarios

In the current climate of severe reductions in state appropriations, rising serials' costs, the constant evolution in technology, and other challenges, this library must become proactive in its vision of the future, move beyond the team approach, and explore the adoption of transformational leadership. The goal is to position the library to develop a collection that transcends historical funding allocations, offer services that are responsive to meeting the current and future information needs and information-seeking behavior of faculty and students, and motivate staff to accept and engage in change management.

SCENARIO FOUR: A FUTURISTIC VIEW OF A HEALTH SCIENCES LIBRARY

Mary Piorun

Central Question

What will the University Medical Library (UML) look like in 2013?

Background

The University Medical Library (UML) serves the students, faculty, and staff at the University Medical Center, which includes the Medical School, School of Public Health, and the School of Dentistry. As a public institution, UML also provides access and services to the hospital's patients and their families, students from local schools, and the general public. The UML staff currently include twenty-five professional staff and fifteen support staff. The library houses just over 400,000 volumes; the UML is categorized as a medium-sized academic health sciences library.

Academic health sciences libraries and medical librarians are facing many changes and challenges, some of which are in response to our customers' needs, others a result of changes within our larger institutions, and still others a result of the way the libraries are viewed. The International Campaign to Revitalize Academic Medicine identified twenty drivers of change in academic medicine (see table 11.3). At the top of the list are new fields of scientific study and technology, particularly in genetics and information technology, and the rise of sophisticated consumers.[4] As the primary clientele reacts, the UML needs to be positioned to support any pending changes and make the library an indispensable part of the university.

Drivers

Table 11.3
Driving Forces Affecting the LSL

Staff	Economic	Environmental	Political	Technological
Retirements, staff turnover	Funding	Evidence-based medicine	Research agenda	Infrastructure to support e-science
Single point of service	Licenses restriction	Limits on class size	School/ clinical relationship	Gap in skills between profession and support staff
E-only collections		New program development	Space	Online learning
Services offered		Pressure to multitask	Partnering with other schools	Web 2.0
Working with patrons outside the library		Assessment focus	Changes in administration	

Matrix

LIBRARIAN AS RESEARCH PARTNER

	I didn't go to library school for this.	Overworked and highly valued	
LIMITED SERVICES			**WIDE VARIETY OF SERVICES**
	Sorry I would like to help you, but . . .	I can help you with this and this but not that.	

Traditional Reference Librarian

Most important: Range of services provided

Most uncertain: The extent UML is involved in the research process

- **Limited Services/Librarian as Research Partner:** *I didn't go to library school for this.* Library staff are more involved in conducting research and less so in educational services.

- **Limited Services/Traditional Reference Librarian:** *Sorry I would like to help you, but . . . .* Library services are limited to what they have always been; staff are unable to keep up with users' demands for services.

- **Wide Variety of Services/Librarian as Research Partner:** *Overworked and highly valued.* Library staff are involved in everything (inside and outside the library); staff are starting to burn out.

- **Wide Variety of Services/Traditional Reference Librarian:** *I can help you with this and this but not that.* Library services are expanded to include many of the latest technologies and teaching methods, but patrons are still unable to get help where and when they need it most.

Key Stakeholders

- Researchers
- Faculty
- Clinicians
- Library staff
- Library administration

Key Term

- *Translational research*: often referred to as "bench to bedside." Translational research is the process of taking bench research and translating it into patient care.

Scenario 1: I Didn't Go to Library School for This

The year is 2013. The Medical School has just celebrated its seventy-fifth anniversary. The library has come a long way since it first opened; some say it is going in the wrong direction.

The renovation is finally completed. The 50,000 journal volumes that occupied the third floor are now in remote storage. In its place are group study rooms, two classrooms, and the Office of Translational Research. There has been a lot of staff turnover in the past three years, including the head of Research and Information Services. Traditionally this position was held by a librarian. Today Anna, who has a PhD in biology and a master's degree in information technology, leads the department. Anna does an excellent job engaging researchers on campus and offering support. She takes on more than she can handle at times. At the moment, she is included in two grants that combined cover 30 percent of her salary; on Mondays Anna spends the day in the Cancer Biology Department assisting with project management on a new breast cancer grant from the National Institute of Health. On Fridays she spends most of the day preparing for Institutional Review Board meetings; she is just starting a three-year term as a primary reviewer.

Not everyone is happy with the changes. A few staff members have decided to leave, but there are still a few who are holding on. Yesterday Anna overheard a conversation between John and Ruth. Ruth said, "I remember when this department was called Outreach and Education Services." John responded by saying, "I didn't go to library school to work in a lab. I'm a librarian, not a graduate student. I'm lucky if I get to teach two classes a month." Two years ago all library-based education courses were converted to WebCT. Librarians teach one-on-one or small group classes only by request. As staff leave, Anna has rewritten job descriptions and in some cases changed the degree requirements. The most recent hire, Larry, has an MS in chemistry and no formal library training. Some librarians are embracing the changes. Jill, who has a second degree in public health, worked with the School of Public Health to write a grant that was funded; she now works one day a week on the grant. On the downside, one staff member who left had a strong relationship with the Department of Infectious Diseases, Radiology, and Emergency Medicine. Since her departure no one from the library attends Morning Report, Grand Rounds, or Chart Rounds. As a result, the clinical system has reduced its financial support of library services from 15 to 6.5 percent. The library, in turn, has eliminated three smaller clinical databases in order to keep the most expensive and most desired clinical database, Up-to-Date.

The implementation of the single service desk was a big change for everyone working in the library. Reference librarians are no longer sitting at the reference desk seventy hours a week waiting for patrons to come to them. Instead, they are out in the labs supporting researchers by offering training on how to create databases, manage large datasets, and apply metadata tags that allow the data to be shared worldwide. Support staff members now answer basic reference questions, provide technical support, and do all of the daily tasks performed in a library such as ordering materials and reshelving materials. They also report complaints from library users who cannot wait twenty-four hours for off-site journals to be retrieved. Staff are very concerned that the library doors are no longer locked at night; although nothing has been stolen yet, they say it is only a matter of time. With the addition of the café last year, many staff say the library is more like a student center than a research library.

Scenario 2: Overworked and Highly Valued

The year is 2013. The Medical School has just celebrated its seventy-fifth anniversary. The library has come a long way since it first opened; some say it is better than ever. The library renovation makes a much better use of space. All staff offices and classrooms have been moved to the third floor. The first floor has a variety of study options for students: group study, quiet study, and open area seating (tables, couches, and booths). Journals and books from pre-1995 were moved off-site. A bookstore and café have moved in. The Office of Translational Research shares space on the third floor. This location has been convenient for librarians who collaborate on the new translational research Web portal.

Then again, what are the librarians not involved in? With the same number of staff the library is doing more now than it has ever done. It is not unusual for a librarian to be assigned to a grant outside of the library at least one day a week, teaching evidence-based medicine, attending chart rounds or morning report for the clinical system, and answering the advanced reference questions. Three librarians at the moment are working on a systematic review for a faculty member; another librarian is managing the newly developed scholarly communications office. Librarians are also encouraged to conduct research in library and information science, but many believe there just isn't enough time to get everything done. They view library research as a low priority.

Next week the library will be sponsoring a two-day symposium on e-science. The keynote speaker is internationally known. The administration is excited that the program is taking place at the University. Over 200 researchers have signed up. When the idea of hosting a symposium was suggested, Mike, the director of the library, stepped in and volunteered library staff, resources, and space. All staff members have been working extra hours to ensure the program is a success.

The library staff have pulled together in the last few years. With the implementation of the single service desk, support staff take on more responsibilities. Extensive training programs were developed to make sure everyone working the single service desk has the skills needed to provide the best possible customer service. The response from patrons has been encouraging; students and residents love having twenty-four-hour access. Staff are happy that they do not have to staff the library twenty-four hours a day; security comes by every hour for a walk-through.

Working with security is one example of the many new partnerships the library has formed. As the university has expanded its program offerings, updated the curriculum, and started merging services with the clinical system, the library has been in the forefront as an example of reaching out and collaborating with others in any way possible. Mike noticed that staff members are not as quick to volunteer for new assignments lately. Two months ago a clinical librarian was on leave for five weeks; her absence created a disruption in services to the clinical staff, so Mike had to fill in at morning report for the five weeks. When reading the annual report last week, Mike was amazed at how much the library accomplished last year. On closer examination, he realized that over 90 percent of the new programs were his ideas. The only program that originated with the staff was an electronic system to make and track vacation requests.

Leadership Strategies Scenario I

Communicate the vision: In this scenario the library is heading in a new direction (e.g., changing job descriptions, increasing the hiring of professional staff who do not have an MLS, and emphasizing staff need to find grant work and spend time outside the library). The library has started moving in the new direction without any formal communication of a new direction/vision to staff. Staff see the change on a piece-by-piece basis. (The library director needs to gather all the staff together and communicate the new priorities, tell staff what their new roles will be, and set clear expectations.)

Staff commitment: Because the staff do not have a clear picture of the future direction of the library, they are not committed to seeing new efforts succeed. They hold on to past activities and do not understand the importance of what they are being asked to do. (Including staff in planning sessions as well as asking and listening to feedback on programs would help the staff become more involved and committed.)

Support staff: Some staff meet stated expectations. Leaders need to acknowledge those who are flexible and find ways to contribute without being told what to do. For those who are unsure if their skills transfer to the new direction in which the library is headed, managers need to counsel them, point out their strengths and weaknesses, and help them determine if they need to upgrade their skills through education and workshops, or if they need to leave.

Repair damaged relationships: In the first scenario the clinical system has become disenfranchised. Because those working in the clinical system believe they receive fewer services, they have reduced their financial support to the library. This situation has a direct impact on the library budget and the institution as a whole. The library director needs to repair this damaged relationship. To begin with, he can meet with representatives from the clinical system and discuss library services in the past, present, and future. Together they can identify what services are most important (Is it databases, or having a librarian at morning report?) and come to a consensus regarding what services can be provided and how often.

Leadership Strategies Scenario 2

Maintain focus and identifying activities that add value: In the second scenario it is evident that the library is involved in many different projects and the staff take on more than they can handle. The director's realization that he is the only one advancing new ideas makes him realize the staff are overwhelmed. Maintaining a balanced list of services can be difficult for a library. The list of programs and the strength of those programs are often tied to the current staff skills and interest. When hiring new people, it is the job of the director to think of the staff as a whole and the services that need to be provided. The director must also stay focused on what is important, remains relevant, and adds value to the library and larger organization. The director in scenario 2 needs to step back and focus on the staff and the list of services provided.

It is important for the director to make the library services indispensable to the university. In scenario 2, the library is moving beyond traditional library services. The director needs to ask whether assuming these new roles serves the library and the institution. The library does not want to take on every volunteer opportunity. It needs to be selective and choose those opportunities in which the skills of library staff can be displayed and valued.

Collaborate: Building alliances across campus is a vital role for the library director. However, linked to the above comments on staying focused and adding value, the director should spend time strengthening and nourishing the relationships that are already established and not be so focused on building new relationships.

Listen to staff: The staff show signs of burnout. The director and managers need to have a greater awareness of how the staff react to changes. In scenario 2 the staff support new initiatives and want to please the director; the director, however, needs to understand the limits of what the staff can do.

Learning from the Scenarios

The team approach that has been successful in this library for many years may not be as effective as the predominant leadership style in this time of conflicting changes. In the current climate of prospective reductions in state appropriations, a changing academic focus at the university, rising serials' costs, and the constant evolution in technology, the library leadership needs to be more proactive in creating a vision for the future of the library. Currently the library reacts to outside pressure and is slow to change due to the team process, which has historically tried to obtain buy-in from everyone.

The managerial leader in this scenario may need to adopt an additional leadership style that fits well with the team approach but focuses on a vision and its achievement. Transformational leadership may be the style that fits best. The transformational leader recognizes the followers' needs and inspires them to facilitate change and fulfill higher order needs. The director and the management team need to plan for the future rather than react to changes caused by external factors. By leading the staff through a process of creating a new vision and empowering them to achieve new goals, the transformational library leader guides a library to achieve its mission. The library needs to be in a position to develop a collection that is up to date rather than based on historical funding allocations and to offer services that are more responsive to current and future information-gathering behaviors and less based in tradition.

SCENARIO FIVE: FOUR FUTURES FOR CHILDREN'S PROGRAMMING, ANYTOWN PUBLIC LIBRARY

Central Question

With declining revenue and looming budget cuts, what is the future of children's programming at Anytown Public Library in 2013? (This question guides the remaining scenarios, all of which apply to the Anytown Public Library.)

Background

The Anytown Public Library (APL) serves the City of Anytown, Illinois, a midsized suburb of Chicago incorporated in 1950. Numerous educated professionals choose to locate to Anytown, because there is an efficient public transportation network that results in a short commute to workplaces throughout Chicago. Anytown is also attractive to young families due to its inexpensive housing and excellent school system. The city is diverse in its makeup, with a growing immigrant population that began moving to the area in the last ten years. New citizens are drawn to Anytown because it is relatively affordable, extremely safe, and is situated in close proximity to an urban center. With a population of 150,000, Anytown is a bustling, young city served by a medium-sized public library system.

APL is comprised of three small branch libraries (East Branch, North Branch, and South Branch), each of which serves distinct neighborhoods. A larger central library is located in the heart of the downtown district. The entire library system employs seventy-five staff members, with a mixture of paraprofessional and professional staff. Presently, APL boasts a budget of $8 million per year.

APL administrators are concerned about looming economic hardships. The Friends of Anytown Public Library (the Friends) is an organization that works to raise money for the library's supplemental needs and programming. In fact, the Friends have provided the majority of funds for children's programming over the past two decades. Friends' members are mostly older, retired Anytowners. Over the years membership has declined as many Friends have either moved away or become too frail to assist in fund-raising activities, such as book sales.

In addition, due to a decline in the overall economy, APL is facing a major budget cut of approximately 20 percent. Commercial and property tax revenues are down, forcing Anytown to decrease the budgets of all city agencies. Finally, the whole community is feeling the effects of two major employers in the area recently having gone out of business.

Scenario Factors

Forces (Drivers)

- Demographic shifts

- Political environment: How much community support (parents, community groups, the Friends) does the library have for children's programming? (This one is relevant to the scenario.)

- What are (or are not) the schools providing? If they go to a year-round system, is there a need for a summer reading program? Are there new standards/requirements for the kids with regard to testing or school accreditation?

- Competition from other sources for programming (Barnes & Noble, YMCA, etc.)

- Technological literacy of the community

- Technological offerings of the library: What kind of programming is possible with new technology?

- Friends of the Library: Do they exist? How vibrant are they? How much money are they raising?

- Mindset, morale, and motivation of the staff (This is also relevant to the scenario.)

- Number of children's/youth services staff

- Community organizations/volunteer groups: How vibrant are they? What kind of cooperative efforts has the library developed with them?

- Current library resources/funding streams

- Any alternative funding options the library has developed or is investigating

- Socioeconomic level of the community

- Literacy level of the community

Axes

Most important: Mindset/morale/motivation of staff

Highly motivated staff ————————▶ Unmotivated staff

Most uncertain: Community support

High community support ————————▶ Low community support

High Staff Motivation/Low Community Support (The Little Engine That Could)	High Staff Motivation/High Community Support (Pollyanna and Her Friends)
Low Staff Motivation/Low Community Support (The Dirty Dozen)	Low Staff Motivation/High Community Support (Beauty and the Beast)

First Scenario: The Dirty Dozen, by Cynthia Chadwick

Low Staff Motivation/Low Community Support: The Dirty Dozen. The year is 2013. The last four years have been difficult for the staff at APL, particularly for the twelve remaining professional librarians. This group of opinion leaders, with a combined 200 years' experience in libraries, has taken to calling themselves the Dirty Dozen. They think many of the recent changes at APL made in response to budget cuts are grievous mistakes. First, there was the centralization of collection development, stripping branch librarians of their collection duties and placing all collection decisions in the hands of a manager who lacks an MLS and was most recently employed as a buyer for Barnes & Noble. Soon after, to no one's surprise, came the gutting of the Dewey Decimal system at Central, in favor of a "subject neighborhood" (bookstore) arrangement. According to the librarians at Central, most patrons, particularly the older Friends members, hate the new arrangement and are just as confused as staff about where to find anything. Finally, and most hurtfully, there has been a steady whittling away of their positions. As librarians retire (three in the last four years), paraprofessionals are hired to replace them, with their professional duties either being taken over by the un-degreed newcomers or reassigned to the remaining librarians.

Of these twelve professionals, the three children's librarians are perhaps the most demoralized. The recent budget cuts have hit staff training particularly hard. In a field as specialized as children's librarianship, these librarians know that newer staff do not have the training or continuing education opportunities they need to be successful. Plus, the new staffing model (another cost-cutting measure) moves paraprofessional staff all over the libraries rather than letting them specialize. This means the children's rooms are frequently staffed by people who lack the deep knowledge of the collection that patrons such as teachers and homeschoolers require. With inadequately trained staff, the professional librarians are expected to take on mentoring duties, even as their own workloads increase. In addition to mentoring, they are required to be on the floor more to serve as backup for more detailed reference questions. As a result, these librarians do not have time to attend to their off-floor duties, top among them being children's programming. All three are die-hard believers in the importance of children's programming and are deeply frustrated that they do not have a spare moment to think about it.

Ten years ago APL boasted an awarding-winning children's summer reading program. Thanks to the then-vibrant Friends, there were adequate funds for a summer reading program as well as for the year-round children's programming that ALP was known for. Due to a steady decline in Friends' membership and fund-raising ability over the last decade, there is no longer the money needed for programming. Seasonal programs, for Independence Day and Halloween, were the first to go; then supplemental materials and craft projects for story times were cut. Just this month the decision was made to eliminate the summer reading program and reduce the popular family story time to once per week. Staff members are distraught by the loss of the summer reading program and by the most recent cut in story times. Morale is at an all-time low, with everyone feeling paralyzed, just wondering when the bad news is going to stop.

The schools in Anytown have also been hard hit by budget cuts. Teachers are grateful to still have their jobs, as many saw firsthand the effects of the closure of two major employers in town. But teacher morale is sinking as teachers know they will have to do more with less; even as the budget shrinks, the school population is climbing with the growing immigrant population. Teachers barely have time to reminisce about the partnerships they once enjoyed with the library, such as visits from librarians to teach the kids about new databases or having on-site story times. In addition, with the elimination of the library's summer reading program, teachers are discouraged that the hard-won reading levels of kids will likely drop over the summer.

With the recent close of two major employers, Anytown is now pressuring the library to redirect its resources to helping folks find jobs. The mayor is very interested in seeing the library focus its programming on job searching and resume writing and has even hinted to the library director that some of the computers dedicated for gaming might be better used by job seekers. The local Rotary and Lions clubs are also focusing their resources on job creation, and recently turned down the library's request to fund a series of science programs. The parks and recreation department has experienced even deeper budget cuts than the library and has laid off most of its programming and outreach staff.

In the wake of these cuts to children's programming, library staff have to admit that there hasn't been much of a public outcry. As their membership and advocacy efforts wane, the Friends do not seem to have the energy to advocate for much of anything, nor do they have the political pull or membership crossover they once had with service organizations. As the immigrant population rises, Anytown's new Americans have a greater need for English as a Second Language (ESL) classes than they do for programs for their kids, who they believe are generally well-served by the schools. Most of the these new immigrant families are impressed that the library offers one family story time each week, and they are happy when second-job work schedules permit them to attend. They believe the library is doing a good job and are grateful for what they offer. Other members of the community, those who remember the glory days of library programming, are disappointed, but they have bigger problems, like the threat of unemployment. Besides, in tough economic times, isn't a summer reading program a bit of a luxury? The library's great, but given the choice of cuts to police or fire, the library will just have to do without.

Strategies and Implications. With low community support and low staff morale and motivation, Anytown Public Library is at a crossroads. A major factor in this scenario is that staff expectations differ radically from community expectations. While the broader community is focused on employment, and is in general satisfied with APL's reduced children's programming, the children's librarians (and all of the Dirty Dozen) are stuck in a past that no longer exists. The future of children's programming at APL will likely be less grandiose, but more targeted, and perhaps will even better meet the needs of the new Anytown community. These are a few options APL could consider to re-energize staff and spark community interest:

• A strategic planning process that involves community members and library staff to craft a vision for the next three to five years. This process might be built around the questions: What are the needs of Anytown, and how can the library play a role? Having a hand in crafting this vision enables staff to see beyond the narrow issue of children's programming and even beyond the unpopular service delivery changes. Getting staff, including members of the Dirty Dozen, at the table to think about community needs might help reset staff expectations and get them on board with a new reality. It could also help community members understand the library and its role in a new way.

- In conjunction with the strategic planning process, an internal Appreciative Inquiry process could be very helpful in nurturing hope for the future. Asking everyone at APL questions such as, "What do we do best? What about our services is most important to retain?" might help allay fears that what they value about the profession is going to be lost. Developing a process for taking the best of the present into the future has been shown to be an effective way for organizations to cope with fear of change.

- If the community's focus is (appropriately) on employment and work readiness, the library staff, including children's librarians, must mobilize around that need. Children's programs, including an on-site summer reading program, could be held during the job-searching and resume-writing classes for the children of the job searchers. As parents attend classes and fill out online applications, children could read and win prizes or do activities or crafts relating to their reading. These job search classes would see their attendance rise if child care were provided, and restoring the summer reading program, even in a modified way, would be an energizer for staff.

- Politicians (and voters) sometimes wonder why public libraries and public schools do not partner more. Why are my tax dollars going to pay for both? APL could experiment with this idea by ending programming at the libraries and doing programs only at day-care facilities and schools. At the schools, story times could be incorporated into the school day as part of English and reading classes; special programs, for science or local history, could be incorporated into these subjects. As overburdened as the teachers seem to be, they would likely welcome the library's support. Family story times could be held at the schools as well, scheduled in conjunction with parent–teacher conferences and family education nights. APL could even look into the possibility of closing one of its branches and relocating staff and materials to one of the school libraries, forming a joint public–school branch.

- In the short term, the library director could make reinvigorating the Friends a top priority. Many people will contribute their time and money to a cause only when they perceive the need to be dire or when there is a clear risk of losing something. With looming budget cuts and cuts to programming already a reality, the library director has a great opportunity to rally community support. New Friends' members may appear, ready to lend their time and money, if the library director can identify what programs or services are likely to be on the chopping block with the upcoming 20 percent budget cut. Once community members see that their local branch may be closed one day a week, or literacy services for new immigrants may be eliminated, or whatever they care about may be cut, a new generation of supporters and advocates may emerge, ready to answer the library's call for help.

- With even a few committed new volunteers, a full-scale, volunteer-run summer reading program might be able to get off the ground. Perhaps some of the new immigrant families, who may not be familiar with a reading program, could be recruited to help and to build support in their communities. High school students in need of community service hours for graduation and local student councils looking for service projects could also be recruited. A grassroots summer reading program, particularly one organized by students, might have more luck attracting donations than one seen to be run by the library and funded by the city.

Second Scenario: Beauty and the Beast, by Renée Di Pilato

Scenario Forces

Most important: Staff motivation

Most uncertain: Community support

Low Staff Motivation/High Community Support. Allison Worthington is the mother of two children, ages one and three, who works from home as an accountant. Allison's husband Bill was recently laid off from a well-paying job at one of the local automotive suppliers. He now commutes to a new job in Chicago, but his salary in the nonunionized company is much lower. Allison takes her children to several of the weekly children's story time programs at the South Branch Library. Attending programs is a good way to get out of the house and socialize with other young mothers. Allison views story times as educational and entertaining programs that are crucial to building important social and verbal skills in her children. During these tough economic times, she relies on the services of the library more than ever. For instance, she no longer purchases books but borrows them, and rather than going to the theater, she checks out movies.

At the Tuesday story time for families, Miss Linda, the children's librarian, informs her audience that the popular program will be reduced from three times a week to once a week. She also tells the patrons that there will be no special summer reading programs this year. Allison is disappointed and distressed, especially given that these visits to the library are a critical supplement to the educational and economic quality of her family life. She approaches Linda afterward and asks, "I'm sorry to be forward, but may I ask why you are reducing your program schedule so drastically?" Linda shrugs her shoulders, "I just don't have the staff to organize multiple story times anymore. The mayor has instituted a hiring freeze, so I can't replace my librarians who recently retired, and it's just me in the Children's department. Plus, our Friends' group barely made any money at their last book sale." "I don't understand," Allison replies. Linda scowls and says, "The Friends used to pay for summer reading initiatives, but their funds are having to go toward other things these days, like books." Allison feels awful. "Oh, I see, I'm so sorry, we love your programs and will miss attending." Allison walks away, aware that Linda is in no mood to discuss this further.

Allison meets the other caregivers who were chatting in the children's area. They are all discussing Linda's announcement. "I can't believe they would cut children's programs," Mary exclaims. One of the nannies, Kathy, chimes in, "Yeah, the story times are always full, they could have programs every day, and they would always have a packed house." Allison puts forth an idea: "Maybe we should all get together and write letters to the mayor and the city council members. We can talk about how much we value the library and its services and how important these programs are to our kids. I know times are tight, but we should make a statement." Mary and Kathy agree, and the three women speak to the other mothers and caregivers. By the time the group leaves the library, they have spoken with the branch manager and exchanged phone numbers and e-mail addresses, and have a plan to rally support for children's programs.

Strategies and Implications. There are many strategies that library administrators can employ to address this particular situation. The need and desire for children's programming in this community is uncontested. Moreover, the popular story times have an educational function and are meant to reinforce library use as an ongoing routine. Since these programs attract patrons to the library and presumably increase library usage during periods of economic duress, it is important to maintain children's programming despite cuts in funding and low staff motivation.

First, in order to reinvigorate children's programming at the South Branch, APL administrators should resolve several issues relating to personnel. Recognizing the lack of employees at that location, they could rotate librarians from more fully staffed branches to assist with the shortage. Children's librarians from the other locations could alternate weeks and travel to South Branch to provide an additional program at their sister library. Next, a trainer or counselor should be hired to assist with morale issues and reinvigorate staff. The trainer should emphasize the Public Library Association's public library service responses, especially those that highlight children's services and their importance to library sustainability. By accentuating the significance of community needs, the administration reminds staff of their mission and purpose in their roles as public employees. This would certainly bolster the children's department, and it would affect other staff members in a positive manner.

If additional staffing or training is unavailable to assist the children's librarian, there are certainly other options to pursue. The branch manager could investigate a partnership with a local college or university. Perhaps there are graduate students in library science or even early childhood education who could offer programs at the library and receive course credit in return. This would take some strain from the lone children's librarian. Working to build a strong volunteer force is another option. Retired librarians or teachers could be recruited to offer supplemental programs that the children's librarian is unable to provide.

The administration could investigate and arrange to partner with local agencies, such as nonprofit institutions, to provide educational programs for children. Other city agencies, such as the animal welfare league, often maintain outreach departments that offer educational workshops. These groups could be invited to host programs at the library in return for publicity in the library's calendars of events and newsletters.

The library administration could also make a more concerted effort to research and write grants to fund children's programs. Although economic downturns narrow these possibilities, there are numerous foundations and governmental grants available for children's educational programs. Library advocates are also possible sources for skilled assistance, such as providing grant-writing resources.

Finally, it is imperative that library administrators work to rebuild the faltering Friends of the Library organization. The loss of children's programming inspired advocacy efforts from those who partake of that service. This is an ideal opportunity to recruit those individuals to join the Friends and take an active role in the group's leadership. In general, Friends' organizations are essential advocates to have during difficult times, because their fund-raising efforts are a significant source of supplemental income. The angry parents and caregivers are a potential force for positive change if their energy and efforts are funneled toward the aims and goals of the Friends.

Conclusion. If harnessed correctly, high levels of community support can be a powerful tool for the APL. Library administrators, who can bring staff motivation into alignment with their community's needs, will be especially successful. Other options, such as partnering with local nonprofit, educational organizations, creating a strong volunteer force, and rebuilding the Friends of Library organization, are the first steps toward ensuring that children's programming maintains a solid future at APL.

Third Scenario: Pollyanna and Her Friends, by Monique le Conge

Scenario Forces

Most important: Mindset/morale/motivation of staff

Highly motivated staff ——————▶ Unmotivated staff

Most uncertain: Community Support, i.e. parents, FOL, city officials, other community organizations

High community support ——————▶ Low community support

High Staff Motivation/High Community Support. It is 2013, and the APL has weathered the economic downturn and developed a robust children's program. The two children's librarians meet regularly with their new Junior Friends group to discuss children's programming. They work with the children and teens to develop new programs based on what the participants are interested in doing. To help fund the programs, the Friends host a small café and bookstore where the Junior Friends can work and gain valuable work experience. Through book sales, café receipts, memberships, and other special fund-raising events, the Junior Friends are revitalizing the library.

The community sees the children's librarians frequently at festivals and fairs, so everyone knows them and the library's mission. One of the children's librarians serves on the program committee of the chamber of commerce, helping to plan children's activities at appropriate events. Motivated by the community demographics, another of the children's librarians made sure that he had learned to speak Spanish, so they are comfortable attending any event and communicating easily with Anytown residents. They are reliable, responsive resources to the schools and other organizations, and they are viewed as helpful to others when needed. The library has won allies among nonprofits because of their willingness to help others out when needed in the past, and their bookmarks, stickers, and other giveaways are popular.

The two librarians also appear at the local schools, telling stories, checking out books, and signing up children, parents, and school staff for library cards. The children's librarians meet regularly with teachers and school administrators to plan the library's homework help club, ensuring that volunteer tutors know what the curriculum for the students will be each quarter. The homework club meets at the library and has satellite locations at some elementary schools in this collaboration. This is convenient for children who cannot travel to the library every day and helps the library reach more students who need the help. Because the collaboration is so successful, the children's librarians work with a "super volunteer" who coordinates the other homework help tutors, and the schools provide curriculum resources, including access to an online homework help program.

Because the children's librarians want to be sure that as many families as possible know about the library and its services, they are partners with the recreation department for special programs and events and a local nonprofit, Anytown Cares, which helps the library with outreach to doctor's offices, clinics, shelters, and other need-based organizations. They provide information electronically to the service providers, creating book lists and other helpful information so that they can e-mail them to clients or print them out. In addition, they take information prepared in Spanish and English to distribute, bring the laptop to register participants for library cards, and hand out free books to pre-readers and their parents.

The library director convenes a quarterly breakfast meeting with a blue ribbon panel made up of business leaders, elected officials, nonprofit directors, and other community activists. In addition to the library board, this group gives its feedback about library services, the economy, and marketing advice. The library director knows that the community will be supportive if they are involved in planning and think they are part of the solution. She looks forward to hearing from the outside voices that provide her with good information to help plan and make the most of her resources.

As part of the city's management team, the library director also works closely with the city manager and other department heads to plan how to maintain services equitably, develop teamwork, and commit to regular communication regarding budget issues. She has developed a strategic plan for the library within an overall city plan, guiding the city three years into the future; any longer will not make sense in a quickly changing world. The department heads meet regularly to discuss their progress, obstacles, and solutions through scenario planning.

The library director chairs a fund-raising subcommittee of the Anytown Rotary Club. Each year, through a fund-raising competition with other service organizations, business leaders show that they recognize that education for the community is vital to maintaining a strong city. The funds raised are used primarily for children's homework support, and for the literacy program, which works with children through family programs. As of 2013, nearly $22,000 has been raised for homework help and school curriculum support. In addition, several of the clubs have members who volunteer as tutors in homework clubs on school sites after school and others who have joined the Friends, ensuring that the group will continue as a force in the APL.

Strategies

- Shore up city resources:
  - Library director meets with city manager and other department heads because this affects all departments; agree to work together, not at cross-purposes; plan strategic and creative solutions that help everyone maintain their services.
  - City staff receives training about scenario planning and collaboration to ensure that teamwork is emphasized in all departments.
- Gather outside support:
  - Library director and children's librarians approach the Friends to begin a Junior Friends of the Library group, attracting children and teens interested in planning and presenting programs, and learning about fund-raising.
  - Service clubs are challenged to raise funds, and introduce volunteer opportunities in the library and membership in the Friends as ways to support activities.
  - Recruit volunteers and use such resources as volunteermatch.org to recruit reliable and qualified volunteers and volunteer managers.
  - Survey service clubs to find out what kinds of fund-raising challenges they would enjoy and participate in.
  - Create a blue ribbon committee of supporters and influential "detractors" to advise the library director from a variety of viewpoints; have breakfast from two to four times per year to get ideas and talk about the library.

- Talk about the library:
  - Participate in community events, groups, committees, and school functions regularly to learn the city's needs and create a sense of reliability with everyone—this can speak louder than words.
  - Prepare information about programs in services in languages that reflect the community demographics and make everyone feel welcome in the library.
- Learn:
  - Train all staff to understand cultural diversity and offer language training assistance to anyone wishing to learn.
  - Train librarians to issue library cards and check out materials at remote locations.
  - Provide needed technology and training to interact with the online homework help program.

Fourth Scenario: The Little Engine That Could, by Rachel Rubin

Scenario Forces

Most Important: Staff motivation

Most Uncertain: Community support

Matrix

High Staff Motivation

Low
Community
Support

High
Community
Support

Low Staff Motivation

High Staff Motivation/Low Community Support. Unfortunately for APL, the decline in support for the Friends is indicative of the general attitude toward financial support offered to the library by the community in 2013. Despite the fact that library users continue to make use of library services, especially events and programs for children, sentiment among community members is high that funding for the library should come from the city and their existing taxes, not from additional revenues generated by the community via book sales or other Friends' fund-raising activities. This attitude has not been helped by the steep downturn facing the Anytown economy and the 2009 layoffs. The population guardedly protects its expendable income. Although the library administration has campaigned for community support and attempted to demonstrate the value of the library, the members of the service district have not responded.

The lack of financial support from the community, the shrinking funding levels from the city, and the continued disintegration of the Friends have forced the library to examine its options for continuing to do library programming. In a difficult series of discussions, library administrators, working closely with the librarians on staff, decide to implement a hiring freeze and to forgo all adult programming. The sole focus of library programming funds and energies is now on continuing to provide programming for children. Children's programming is to remain a priority because of the large number of young families in the community, in addition to the fact that the staff feel very strongly that children are the most important population for the library to serve. Early literacy, developing and retaining young readers, providing supplemental educational assistance for students, and keeping the summer reading program are all top priorities.

Anytown's push to save children's programming is helped exponentially by the optimism and positive attitudes of the staff. Hansel and Gretel, two of APL's Children's Department managers, create a plan to implement revised children's services. With their encouragement and the support of administration, staff at all levels can clearly see the plan for moving forward.

Hansel and Gretel's first strategy is to develop and implement a cross-training program that trains adult librarians to effectively cover children's service points. They also train interested adult librarians to do basic story times in order to ensure that a backup staff person is always available. This sharing of roles is the only way that the children's librarians can take the time away from their service points to plan and do programs. Having extra desk coverage also allows them to go out into the schools to teach library research skills and to visit preschools where they can do early literacy story times. The staff training is so successful that it is expanded to include cross-training across multiple branches: staff eagerly step in to assist at other locations when staffing shortages affect service capabilities.

Other staff are also ready to pitch in however they can, and the administration encourages them to be creative and financially responsible. Many take the initiative to make contacts in the business community and develop relationships with local suppliers of food and craft materials. One of the local grocery stores agrees to donate cookies for each of the library's three summer reading club programs in exchange for hanging a sign advertising the bakery. For the remaining programs, exempt staff in various departments create a sign-up sheet to bake and supply cookies for the young participants. Hansel and Gretel are also able to forge a partnership with the local JoAnne Fabrics, which agrees to donate all of their fabric scraps and damaged or unsold products for children's programs.

Though the staff are successful at creating some partnerships, it is difficult for many local businesses to contribute because of the economic situation. Realizing that sustainability is crucial, Hansel and Gretel also seek to secure grant funding for future summer reading programs. They succeed in obtaining a Target grant that will allow them to continue the summer reading club for the next three years.

Despite the fact that library funding is tenuous and the community does not wish to further burden itself financially by helping to support the library, the dedication and innovative ideas of the library staff keep Anytown Public Library's children's programs afloat.

Strategies and Implications

• Rally the troops:

  – The administration must continue to show its support for the staff and to communicate frequently to maintain a common and clear vision of the future. The staff's optimism will only continue to be a source of innovation as long as they know where they are going and that they are aligned with the mission supported by the administration. Especially in times of economic uncertainty, a unified message from above helps to decrease staff anxiety and lets them focus on their jobs.

- Take the show on the road:
    - By finding ways to let the children's librarians go out into the community through preschool visits and other school visits, the library can shore up support by being visible. The librarians should take any opportunity they can to talk to parents and teachers about how the library can help them, the unique services the library offers, and the volunteer opportunities offered by the Friends.

- Reach out:
    - The administration should organize community forums or focus groups to hear from the community. They should try to ascertain the needs of their constituents in order to better serve them. If the library tailors services to the needs of the community, the community may be more likely to see the relevance of the library in their lives, and subsequently be more likely to support it in future.

- Think long term:
    - No one can predict when the economic situation will improve, nor when the attitude of the community will change. Seeking grants, private donors, or other alternative funding sources may be crucial to the continued provision of children's services. The library will have to weigh the benefits of continued services and the implications of alternative funds—especially those offered by private or corporate donors.

- Tell the story:
    - The library administration and its marketing team must communicate regularly with the community to inform them about APL's activities and to try to raise awareness and interest. They need to find ways to tell stories about the library that resonate with community members. Members of the administrative team should attend town hall meetings, build relationships, and maintain a presence at community events.
    - The administration should also work with the remaining members of the Friends to make it easy for people to find information about the group by hanging recruitment fliers on bulletin boards in coffee shops, grocery stores, and other public venues. A technologically savvy Friends' member should make sure they have a Web presence.

[Scenario planning] . . . encourages knowledge exchange and development of mutual deeper understanding of central issues important to the future of your . . . [organization].[5]

NOTES

1. NetMBA (Business Knowledge Center), "Scenario Planning" (Internet Center for Management and Business Administration, Inc.). Available at http://www.netmba.com/strategy/scenario/ (accessed December 16, 2009).

2. Chip Heath and Dan Heath, *Made to Stick: Why Some Ideas Survive and Others Die* (Audio CD) (New York Random House, 2007).

3. David Weinberg, *Everything Is Miscellaneous: The Power of the New Digital Disorder* (New York: Times Books), 10.

4. Shally Awasthi, Jil Beardmore, Jocalyn Clark, Philip Hadridge, et al. *The Future of Academic Medicine: Five Scenarios to 2025* (New York: Milbank Memorial Fund, 2005), 8. Retrieved from http://www.milbank.org/reports/0507FiveFutures/0507FiveFutures.pdf (accessed June 25, 2008)

5. "Scenario Planning Resources." Available at http://www.well.com/~mb/scenario_planning/ (accessed December 16, 2009).

3

~

CONCLUSION

12

~

RESEARCH ON LEADERSHIP— ADDING TO KNOWLEDGE

Peter Hernon

Promoting past success or defending [the] status quo is a recipe for disaster.[1]

Looking back in time we can revisit the mental image of a library. What is the image of a library's exterior and interior that emerges when one thinks of one of the approximately 2,500 public or academic libraries built with money donated by Scottish American businessman and philanthropist Andrew Carnegie between the years 1883 and 1929? Add to that image the longtime association of libraries with collections of books, perhaps held in a noncirculating collection, serving a captive audience, and being called the heart of the college or university. Now fast forward to the present day and the belief that everything, including books, is online. Academic libraries may contain information or learning commons and undertake massive digitization projects. University research libraries may be engaged in staff reengineering and moving more resources to digitization projects, digital publishing, and digital collections. Neither academic nor public libraries define their service roles solely or largely in terms of those who visit and expect to find print collections. Complicating matters, the larger organization or institution of which the library is part may question the value of the library itself and not see how it fits in or advances the broader mission. What image of the present-day library then emerges, and who holds that image?

SOME CURRENT TRENDS

"The value of college endowments," Goldie Blumenstyk notes, "declined by an average of 23 percent from 2008 to 2009, socked by the one-two punch of record investment losses and a precipitous drop in giving."[2] Furthermore, "the average investment return for the 2009 fiscal year was minus 18.7 percent . . . [, and as] investment income decreased, debt grew, particularly among the wealthiest institutions."[3] In *Beyond Survival*, Elizabeth J. Wood, Rush Miller, and Amy Knapp provide an excellent analysis of current trends in academic librarianship,[4] but their book was published before the decline in value of the endowments and the increase in debt. Still, they underscore the importance of academic libraries quickly adapting to change to remain relevant in the future. Although *Making Cities Stronger* does not address the current economic downturn, this publication of the Urban Libraries Council argues that "public libraries are logical partners for local economic development initiatives that focus on people and quality of life" and that "public access to digital information and technology is a draw for libraries. Their open structure, combined with the power of new digital collections, technology, and training, position them to help communities make the transition from manufacturing and service economies to high tech and information economies." [5]

Updating some of the findings of the well-known Pittsburgh study on collection use,[6] Rush G. Miller, Hillman University Librarian and Director, University Library System (ULS), University of Pittsburgh, reports that from 1987 to 2007,

- over 2.1 million books representing 63% of the ULS collections have never circulated
- 95% of items in ULS collections have circulated fewer than 10 times
- 99% of items in ULS collections have circulated fewer than 25 times[7]

In the changing landscape of information provision and seeking, there are new alternatives for the public in finding books, especially older ones. Google, for instance, is bringing a number of the world's books online:

In-copyright and in-print books. In-print books are books that publishers are still actively selling, the ones you see at most bookstores.

- In-copyright but out-of-print books
- Out-of-copyright books.[8]

At the same time, in response to growing public demand and changing patterns of information use, academic libraries are purchasing more e-books and e-readers, while public libraries are also acquiring audiobooks and playaways, which come with the digital content already preloaded on them, batteries to make them play, and earbuds to listen to the content.

Both academic and public libraries are experiencing an upsurge in the number of visits the public makes to their home pages. Some libraries, including ones whose institutions are members of the Association of Research Libraries, report a sharp decline in the number of questions asked at reference desks and an increase in the number of questions asked electronically and in the number of questions taking longer than fifteen minutes to answer.

Looking beyond the libraries to their broader organizations or institutions, there is greater expectation of accountability and assessment. Libraries themselves are developing a culture of assessment and evidence-based decision making, and, in some instances they are naming a staff member as assessment librarian. As the economic downturn illustrates, more academic institutions and municipalities are decreasing the funding of libraries as a percentage of their budgets. Libraries are forced to align their service expectations with reality. In academe, a number of branch libraries are closing, and there is even discussion of the library as "living on borrowed time."[9] In such a climate, Miller asks, "How do we survive?" and challenges libraries to demonstrate their value to their constituencies and institutions.[10]

Johann Neem, who concurs, sees declining budgets as part of the problem. For him, the perfect storm arises when libraries do not demonstrate how they advance student learning and the institutional mission. Undoubtedly he overestimates and does not document the extent to which he believes that libraries view themselves as ends rather than means. He wants them to maintain their core mission. After all, "the other services can be provided cheaper and better by student unions, residential halls, athletic centers, computer laves and coffee shops."[11] Although part of his argument is contradictory, this message does appear in *Inside Higher Ed*, a prestigious online newspaper. The message is a clear reflection of the fact that either he is resistant to change or he has not bought into the vision that campus leaders, it is hoped, are making.

CHANGE

Although both academic and public libraries face growing threats and competition, there are increased opportunities to help their institutions or broader organizations meet their missions more effectively. Change, which is central to success, requires leadership. It should not be assumed that all libraries have leaders, either at the director or subordinate levels. Still, the extent to which libraries undergoing transformation due to the economic recession have managers, leaders, or something else merits analysis. Where true leadership exists, there may be broad dissatisfaction with the status quo and avoidance of a rigid mindset in which library staff resist change.

Most likely libraries are currently engaged in re-missioning or rethinking their missions so that they can concentrate on their priorities. Such a concentration most likely requires some reengineering of the budget, personnel, operations, facilities (space use), collections (greater shift to digital ones), and services. At the same time, decisions about what comprises library quality shifts from a historical focus on collection size—an evaluation of what the library has or what the library does (contains information and knowledge)—to what the library should be doing. What are the high-priority activities, and what new relationships are critical to forge? Further, an increase in gate count does not mean that the public uses the library in the same way they did in the past. Will this mean that some services will be created and others downsized or eliminated? For most libraries, the future is one with an expanded digital presence, one in which many people will be using library resources but unaware that they are doing so! Databases are a good example. They may be widely available across campus and to remote users, but they may not be found on library Web pages, or other places may link to library Web pages, but users do not make the association.

The workforce must realize that the job as they performed it even six months ago has changed. Those preparing for careers in academic and public libraries must accept the fact that the job they want may no longer exist. Some of the qualities that workers will need are flexibility, acceptance or joy of change, being entrepreneurial and innovative, the ability to engage effectively in critical thinking and problem solving, excellent communication skills, delight in working with people and not being confined to a particular service area, an ability to forge new partnerships and relationships, and a willingness and ability to lead change.

LEADERSHIP

Effective leadership is required to make the transition from the present and time-honored tradition to a new future, one that perhaps addresses the results of the re-missioning and the priorities associated with it and the guiding vision. James M. Kouzes and Barry Z. Posner see leaders as role models, creating compelling visions that guide worker behavior, able to challenge the status quo, effective in working with others, and motivating others to achieve substantial accomplishments.[12] Leadership is not limited to those in managerial positions, but can apply to anyone engaged in team or group activity. Leadership, therefore, can be viewed in part in the context of team problem solving.

A General Definition

Although the research reported in chapters 3 and 4 does not produce consensus around a definition of leadership, it seems that key components of leadership include a vision, buy-in to that vision, and successful action to achieve successful follow-through on that vision. The vision and a commitment to it must be ingrained in the organizational and institutional culture. Buy-in refers to followers but also to subordinate leaders. In other words, leadership should exist at all levels of the organization, especially in those assuming a managerial function. Still, others should be encouraged to serve as both leaders and followers.

Complicating the definition, leadership should not be viewed as simply a linear process starting with the setting of the vision and ending ultimately with its achievement. The process is in fact fluid. Gaining buy-in may be neither easily accomplished nor permanent. Furthermore, as some of the directors interviewed note, leadership occurs within a context—situations—and that context shifts. Clearly, leadership as a process is not static, is complex, and encounters both problems and opportunities. For this reason, the process defies simple characterization in the form of a figure, perhaps a flow chart. It might be beneficial to probe the definition of leadership that respondents offer and to request examples of each component. The probing might focus on particular situations.

Case Studies

Beginning in 2000, Blackwell's Book Services has provided the Association of College and Research Libraries (ACRL), American Library Association, with "funding for an Excellence in Academic Libraries Award program to recognize an outstanding community college, college, and university library each year. This award . . . [recognizes] the accomplishments of librarians and other library staff as they come together as members of a team to support the mission of their institution. Blackwell's gift of $12,000 provides a $3,000 gift to each of the three winning libraries and $3,000 to support travel by an ACRL officer to the three award ceremonies."[13] Through 2009, there have been twenty-nine recipients of the award; in 2006, there was no community college library recipient. The applications of the winning libraries are available at http://www.ala.org/ala/mgrps/divs/acrl/awards/excellenceacademic.cfm.

As stated in the guidelines, granting an award is based on three factors:

1. Demonstrate how academic librarians and staff work together as a team to develop an academic library that is outstanding in furthering the educational mission of its parent institution.

2. The criteria for recognizing excellence through the Blackwell Award Program will emphasize "outcomes" rather than "inputs" as the best measures of quality. "Outcomes" are defined by the ACRL Task Force on Academic Library Outcomes and reflected in the philosophy of Standards for Libraries in Higher Education. Potential nominees are referred to these documents. An academic library may demonstrate excellence as a team of librarians and staff in furthering the educational mission of its institution through one or more of the following, or in other ways that reflect the purpose and philosophy of this award:

   – Creativity and innovation in meeting the needs of their academic community.

   – Leadership in developing and implementing exemplary programs that other libraries can emulate.

   – Substantial and productive relationships with classroom faculty and students.

3. Agree to take responsibility for organizing and funding a recognition ceremony on campus to receive the award.[14]

For the purpose of clarification, outcomes are defined as

the ways in which library users are changed as a result of their contact with the library's resources and programs. Satisfaction on the part of a user is an outcome. So is dissatisfaction. . . . [We consider] simple satisfaction a facile outcome, however, too often unrelated to more substantial outcomes that hew more closely to the missions of libraries and the institutions they serve. The important outcomes of an academic library program involve the answers to questions like these:

- Is the academic performance of students improved through their contact with the library?

- By using the library, do students improve their chances of having a successful career?

- Are undergraduates who used the library more likely to succeed in graduate school?

- Does the library's bibliographic instruction program result in a high level of "information literacy" among students?

- As a result of collaboration with the library's staff, are faculty members more likely to view use of the library as an integral part of their courses?

- Are students who use the library more likely to lead fuller and more satisfying lives?[15]

Previously I examined the twenty-three applications covering the years 2000 through 2007,[16] concluding that "the documents focus mostly on management and do not fully explain the leadership component. The assumption might be that any significant accomplishments would not have occurred without the presence of leadership, perhaps throughout the organization."[17] Instead of extending the content analysis of the documents, future research might treat the sites or a subset of them (e.g., the colleges) as case studies and look more closely at leadership as a process and the outcomes. What visions, if any, guide the reported accomplishments and change? Here is an excellent opportunity to examine buy-in and follow-through, while seeing if there are levels of leadership, from the director downward and from the staff upward. Turning to the outcomes specified in the guidelines, do the actual outcomes correspond to the definition in the guidelines, do the outcomes conform to outcomes assessment, and, for academic libraries, would the outcomes meet the expectations of accreditation organizations?[18] Accreditation organizations tend to ignore satisfaction as an outcome; for them it is merely an output.

Returning to the definition, which theories and styles guide the leadership process at each site? Are there similarities across sites? Is there, for instance, evidence of transformational leadership, emotional intelligence, resonant leadership, situational leadership, and so on? Perhaps, in some instances, we are witnessing contingent theory, defined as a leader-match theory, which matches leaders to appropriate situations. The effectiveness of leaders depends on how well their style fits the setting—the workplace.[19] Central to the theory is the least-preferred coworker (LPC) scale, which asks leaders to think of all the persons with whom they have ever worked, and then to describe the one person with whom they worked the least well. This person can be someone from the past or a current colleague. From a scale of 1 through 8, they describe this person on a series of bipolar scales such as:

Unfriendly	1	2	3	4	5	6	7	8	Friendly
Uncooperative	1	2	3	4	5	6	7	8	Cooperative
Hostile	1	2	3	4	5	6	7	8	Supportive
Guarded	1	2	3	4	5	6	7	8	Open

The responses to these scales (usually sixteen in total) are summed and averaged: a high LPC score suggests that leaders have a human relations orientation, whereas a low LPC score indicates a task orientation. Presumably individuals who rate their least-preferred colleague in a relatively favorable light on these scales derive satisfaction from interpersonal relationships; those who rate the coworker in a relatively unfavorable light get satisfaction from successful task performance.

As an alternative, researchers might use the Leadership Dimension Survey, a thirty-two-item survey that examines four leadership competencies (profound knowledge and strategy, purposeful direction, and purposeful behaviors) to probe leadership development and other aspects of leadership.[20]

If the case studies show the presence of leaders, these individuals might be asked to complete the LPC scale. Again, the purpose is to measure the impact of situations on leaders. The research should investigate the situations in which people with certain leadership styles are effective and how much similarity exists across case studies. Research might also go beyond the sites and look at libraries that are not coping well with the recession and the alignment of vision and follow-through on the achievement of strategic planning priorities. Are any of these organizations and institutions unionized? If they are, how did leaders—assuming their presence—function?

Because there is no equivalent award for public libraries, researchers might substitute the organizations managed by the past presidents of the Public Library Association or presidents of the American Library Association associated with public libraries as case study sites. In addition, these "leaders" might be asked to participate in a survey using the instrument in either chapter 3 or chapter 4. Perhaps instead of a one-on-one interview, researchers might invite a group to participate in one or more focus group interviews. This way, participants interact as they comment on the individual questions.

CONCLUDING THOUGHTS

As organizations change and transform themselves and their workforces, leadership becomes a multifaceted concept, one that may embrace different theories and styles. Numerous institutes exist to create awareness of leadership and try to transform those in attendance into leaders. Graduate leadership programs have emerged in various academic settings. Within library and information science, there is the Simmons Managerial Leadership in the Information Professions, which has been the recipient of two grants from the Institute of Museum and Library Services (IMLS). As the profession prepares the next generations of leaders, the importance of contributing to research should not be ignored. The purpose is to add to knowledge about leadership as practiced in the information professions. Equally as important, future leaders need to develop the skill set and knowledge base associated with research, namely problem solving and critical thinking. How successful can leaders be, if they do not have the good grasp of evidence-based planning and decision making that comes from having a good and broad grounding in research? This is a weakness of leadership institutes and a strength of the Simmons program. We see applicants with an insufficient understanding of research as an inquiry process. Most likely they have not read published research studies, and these individuals are no different than many practitioners in library and information science.

The question arises, How well can they complete satisfactorily the sentence, "Research is . . ."? In conclusion, the profession should continue to encourage a better grasp of leadership theory and practice, but should not ignore the role and importance of research to managerial leaders and in maintaining effective organizations.

Some readers might enjoy reviewing the discussion questions depicted in figure 12.1 as they apply a formal research process to the study of leadership. Before reviewing the questions, however, they might benefit from reading the following:

- Peter Hernon and Candy Schwartz. "What Is a Problem Statement?" *Library & Information Science Research* 29, no. 3 (2007): 307–9.

- Juris Dilevko. "Reading Literature and Literature Reviews." *Library & Information Science Research* 29, no. 4 (2007): 451–54.

- Peter Hernon and Candy Schwartz. "A Research Study's Reflective Inquiry." *Library & Information Science Research* 30, no. 3 (2008): 163–64.

- Peter Hernon and Candy Schwartz. "Procedures: Research Design." *Library & Information Science Research* 31, no. 1 (2009): 1–2.

- Peter Hernon and Candy Schwartz. "Reliability and Validity." *Library & Information Science Research* 31, no. 2 (2009): 73–74.

- Peter Hernon and Candy Schwartz. "Writing an Abstract." *Library & Information Science Research* 32, no. 3 (2010): 173.

- Danuta A. Nitecki. "Finalizing a Research Paper—Findings through Conclusion." *Library & Information Science Research* 32, no. 1 (2010): 1–3.

There are also various textbooks on the research process. The important point is to understand the process before attempting to answer the questions and to know the difference between basic research and both evaluation and assessment research. Basic research, which applies to the study of leadership, generates new knowledge and adds to theory. Still, when MLIP students engage in basic research, their findings also have value to managerial leaders; after all, the students are practitioners. Evaluation research examines the effectiveness, efficiency, and utility of library programs and services, and it provides feedback to organizational planning and change. Assessment research produces evidence for accountability, and it may focus on outcomes—impacts—and using the evidence gathered for program improvement. For instance, in academic institutions, assessment focuses on student learning and enhancing the ongoing effectiveness of such learning throughout a program of study.

The academic library is threatened.[21]

1. A number of the directors interviewed for chapters 3 and 4 view leadership as situational. How might we apply social science research to investigate which theories and styles leaders most often use in certain situations? In other words, how do we capture those situations, identify the leadership theories and styles most prevalent, and view followership?

2. In chapters 3 and 4, the directors define leadership. Is there a definition you use the most and the least? Explain. If you are dissatisfied with a definition, what changes would you make, and why?

3. How do you complete the sentences "Research is . . . ," and "Leadership is . . ."?

4. Returning to chapters 3 and 4, how important is transparency as a leadership quality? (How important is transparency to gaining and maintaining staff or community trust in a leader?)

5. How would you select case study sites to investigate the impact of the economic downturn on public libraries located in cities facing significant budgetary cutbacks? At these sites, how would you determine if there are leaders or merely managers?

6. How would you select case study sites to investigate the impact of the economic downturn on academic libraries facing significant budgetary cutbacks? At these sites, how would you determine if there are leaders or merely managers?

7. Chapters 3 and 4 show that judgment is a component of leadership. Instead of asking participants to comment on judgments they have made, participated in, or seen, how might a researcher examine in actual incidents where the director applies (or applied) judgment?

8. Examine the data collection instrument depicted in Figure 4.1. Would you make any changes to it? What and why? Now write a problem statement and a set of objectives to guide a study using that instrument.

9. Continuing with the previous question, how would you revise that instrument for use in a focus group interview? Remember such interviews have only five to seven open-ended questions. What questions would you ask? Whom would you select to participate in a focus group interview? How would you select the participants? Whom would you have as moderator, and how would you train that person?

10. Take any one of the studies depicted in table 6.1 and discuss how you would adapt it to examine leadership in academic or public libraries. Because you want the study to ultimately be published in a peer-reviewed journal, what original twist would you add so that you are not merely replicating the original study? Write a problem statement for this study.

Figure 12.1 Discussion Questions. Source: *ebrary, *The Economic Downturn and Libraries: Survey Findings* (2009). Available at http://www.ebrary.com/corp/collateral/en/ Survey/CIBER_survey_2009.pdf (accessed December 28, 2009).

11. You are the director of a library and the provost has decided to take the entire universitywide budget cut of $4 million from the library so that the rest of the campus can be spared budget cuts. What would you do? How would you demonstrate leadership among the library staff and try to avoid losing their trust?

12. Returning to the previous question, let us assume an interim director made the budget cut. You are invited as a candidate for the directorship; what would you say and expect?

13. Some of the directors interviewed (see chapters 3 and 4) referred to follow-through on the vision. Follow-through, in part, implies feedback—the gathering of evidence and its application to service improvement. Feedback might take the form of outputs, which point to the degree to which the library and it services are used, or outcomes, which indicate the impact or effects of library services on an individual and ultimately on the library's community (they might occur at the program or institutional level). How would you ensure that the evidence is correctly gathered and interpreted?

14. An advantage of LibQUAL+ (for service quality, http://www.libqual.com) and LibPAS or LibSAT (for satisfaction, Counting Opinions, http://www.countingopinions.com/) is that libraries have help in designing, executing, and analyzing the results. Let us assume that, as part of the culture of evaluation and assessment, an academic (or public) library director wants to engage in original data collection relating to the library's strategic priorities—goals, objectives, and activities (e.g., see http://www.suffolk.edu/files/SawLib/2005-2010-strat-plan.pdf). How would you go about collecting that evidence?

15. Revisiting question 14, perhaps the library wants to assume a campus leadership role in program level assessment for information literacy. How might the library work with the entire faculty of an undergraduate program to determine what the students learn throughout their program of study? In other words, are the graduates truly information literate? As you answer the question, address campus leadership.

16. The report, *The Economic Downturn and Libraries: Survey Findings*, notes that libraries worldwide face "some fairly deep and painful cuts, not just a continuation of the attritional gains in library efficiency that have been driven for years by below inflation budget rises. Our survey suggests that academic libraries will be the hardest hit by these budgetary pressures, with 34.3% of them expecting to receive a smaller budget in two years' time than they do currently." This quote suggests the need for both planning and research. Discuss possible research topics and write both scenarios and case studies based on the quote and the report.

NOTES

1.   Elizabeth J. Wood, Rush Miller, and Amy Knapp, *Beyond Survival: Managing Academic Libraries in Transition* (Westport, CT: Libraries Unlimited, 2007), xvii.

2.   Goldie Blumenstyk, "Average Return on Endowment Investments Is Worst in Almost 40 Years," *The Chronicle of Higher Education* LVI, no. 21 (February 5, 2010): A22.

3.   Ibid., A22, A23.

4.   Wood, Miller, and Knapp, *Beyond Survival.*

5.   Urban Libraries Council, *Making Cities Stronger, Public Library Contributions to Local Economic Development* (Chicago: Urban Libraries Council, 2007). Available at http://urbanlibraries.org/associations/9851/files/making_cities_stronger.pdf (accessed November 19, 2009), 2.

6.   See Allen Kent, *Use of Library Materials: The University of Pittsburgh Study* (New York: Dekker, 1979).

7.   Rush G. Miller, "Beyond Survival: How Can Libraries Maintain Relevance in the Digital Age?" (unpublished PowerPoint presentation at the ALAO Conference, October 30, 2009).

8.   "Google Books Settlement Agreement" (2009). Available at http://books.google.com/googlebooks/agreement/#3 (accessed November 19, 2009).

9.   Miller, "Beyond Survival."

10.   Ibid.

11.   Johann Neem, "Reviving the Academic Library," *Inside Higher Ed* (November 19, 2009). Available at http://ww.insidehighered.com/views/2009/11/19/neem (accessed November 19, 2009).

12.   James M. Kouzes and Barry Z. Posner, *The Leadership Challenge*, 3rd ed. (San Francisco: Jossey-Bass, 2002).

13.   American Library Association, Association of College and Research Libraries, "Excellence in Academic Libraries Award" (Chicago: Association of College and Research Libraries, 2009). Available at http://www.ala.org/ala/mgrps/divs/acrl/awards/excellenceacademic.cfm (accessed November 23, 2009).

14.   American Library Association, Association of College and Research Libraries, "Excellence in Academic Libraries Award: Guidelines" (Chicago: Association of College and Research Libraries, 2009). Available at http://www.ala.org/ala/mgrps/divs/acrl/awards/excellenceguidelines.cfm (accessed November 23, 2009).

15.   American Library Association, Association of College and Research Libraries, "Task Force on Academic Library Outcomes Assessment Report" (Chicago: Association of College and Research Libraries, 1998). Available at http://www.ala.org/ala/mgrps/divs/acrl/publications/whitepapers/taskforceacademic.cfm (accessed November 23, 2009).

16.   See Peter Hernon, "Traces of Academic Library Leadership," in *Academic Librarians as Emotionally Intelligent Leaders*, ed. Peter Hernon, Joan Giesecke, and Camila A. Alire, 57–73 (Westport, CT: Libraries Unlimited, 2008).

17.   Ibid., 68.

18.   For a discussion of outcomes, see, for instance, Peter Hernon and Robert E. Dugan, *Outcomes Assessment in Higher Education: Views and Perspectives* (Westport, CT: Libraries Unlimited, 2004); and Peter Hernon, Robert E. Dugan, and Candy Schwartz, *Revisiting Outcomes Assessment in Higher Education* (Westport, CT: Libraries Unlimited, 2006).

19.   See, for instance, Fred E. Fielder, *A Theory of Leadership Effectiveness* (New York: McGraw-Hill, 1967); and Fred E. Fielder and J. E. Garcia, *New Approaches to Leadership: Cognitive Resources and Organizational Performance* (New York: Wiley, 1987).

20.   See Gerald V. Miller, "The Leadership Dimension Survey: A Download from Pfeiffer's Classic Activities for Developing Leaders," in *Pfeiffer's Classic Activities for Developing Leaders*, ed. Jack Gordon (New York: Wiley, 2003). Available at http://www.pfeiffer.com/WileyCDA/PfeifferTitle/productCd-0787973130.html (accessed May 14, 2010). For even another choice, see Victor Dulewicz and Malcolm Higgs, "Leadership at the Top: The Need for Emotional Intelligence in Organizations," *The International Journal of Organizational Analysis*, 11, no. 3 (2003): 193–210.

21.   Neem, "Reviving the Academic Library."

BIBLIOGRAPHY

ARTICLES

Albanese, Andrew. "Digitization Suit at Cornell: Alumnus Claims Newly Available Article Constitutes Libel." *Library Journal* 133, no. 4 (March 1, 2007): 17–18.

Arns, Jennifer. "Challenges in Governance: The Leadership Characteristics and Behaviors Valued by Public Library Trustees in Times of Conflict and Contention." *The Library Quarterly* 77, no. 3 (2007): 287–310.

Avolio, Bruce J., Rebecca J. Reichard, Sean T. Hannah, Fred O. Walumbwa, and Adrian Chan. "A Meta-Review of Leadership Impact Research: Experimental and Quasi-Experimental Studies." *The Leadership Quarterly* 20 (2009): 764–84.

Blumenstyk, Goldie. "Average Return on Endowment Investments Is Worst in Almost 40 Years." *The Chronicle of Higher Education* LVI, no. 21 (February 5, 2010): A22–23.

Burke, C. Shawn Dana E. Sims, Elizabeth H. Lazzara, and Eduardo Salas. "Trust in Leadership: A Multi-Level Review and Integration." *The Leadership Quarterly* 18 (2007): 606–32.

Burke, C. Shawn, Kevin C. Stagl, Cameron Klein, Gerald F. Goodwin, Eduardo Salas, and Stanley M. Halpin. "What Types of Leadership Behaviors Are Functional in Teams? A Meta-Analysis." *The Leadership Quarterly* 17, no. 3 (2006): 288–307.

Carlson, Scott. "Is It a Library? A Student Center? The Athenaeum Opens at Goucher College." *The Chronicle of Higher Education* LVI, no. 4 (September 18, 2009): A16–17.

Cohn, William L. "An Overview of ARL Directors, 1933–1973." *College & Research Libraries* 37, no. 2 (March 1976): 137–44.

Dulewicz, Victor, and Malcolm Higgs. "Leadership at the Top: The Need for Emotional Intelligence in Organizations." *The International Journal of Organizational Analysis* 11, no. 3 (2003): 193–210.

Fidel, Raya. "Are We There Yet? Mixed Methods Research in Library and Information Science." *Library & Information Science Research* 30 (2008): 265–72.

Friedrich, Tamara L., Christina L. Byrne, and Michael D. Mumford. "Methodological and Theoretical Considerations in Survey Research." *The Leadership Quarterly* 20, no. 2 (April 2009): 57–60.

Gergen, David, and Andy Zelleke. "A Question of Presidential Leadership." *Boston Globe* (June 12, 2008): A13.

Heifetz, Ron, Alexander Grashow, and Marty Linsky. "Leadership in a (Permanent) Crisis." *Harvard Business Review,* 87, no. 7 (July–August 2009): 62–69.

Hernon, Peter, and Ellen Altman. "Embracing Change for Continuous Improvement." *American Libraries* 41, no. 1 (January 2010): 52–55.

Hernon, Peter, and Cheryl Metoyer-Duran. "Problem Statements: An Exploratory Study of Their Function, Significance, and Form." *Library & Information Science Research* 15, no. 1 (Winter 1993): 71–92.

Hernon, Peter, Ronald R. Powell, and Arthur P. Young. "University Library Directors in the Association of Research Libraries: The Next Generation, Part One." *College & Research Libraries* 62, no. 2 (March 2001): 116–45.

Hernon, Peter, Ronald R. Powell, and Arthur P. Young. "University Library Directors in the Association of Research Libraries: The Next Generation, Part Two." *College & Research Libraries* 63, no. 1 (January 2002): 73–90.

Hernon, Peter, and Nancy Rossiter. "Emotional Intelligence: Which Traits Are Most Prized." *College & Research Libraries* 67, no. 3 (May 2006): 260–75.

Hernon, Peter, and Laura Saunders. "The Federal Depository Library Program in 2023: One Perspective on the Transition to the Future." *College & Research Libraries* 70, no. 3 (May 2009): 351–70.

Hernon, Peter, and Candy Schwartz. "Leadership: Developing a Research Agenda for Academic Libraries." *Library & Information Science Research* 30, no. 4 (December 2008): 243–49.

Hernon, Peter, and Candy Schwartz. "What Is a Problem Statement?" *Library & Information Science Research* 29, no. 3 (2007): 307–9.

Howard, Jennifer. "Libraries Innovate to Counter Cuts." *The Chronicle of Higher Education* LVI, no. 14 (November 27, 2009): A1, A8–9.

Ilgen, Daniel R., John R. Hollenbeck, Michael Johnson, and Dustin Jundt. "Teams in Organizations: From Input-Process-Output Models to IMOI Models." *Annual Review of Psychology* 56 (2005): 517–43.

Johnson, David R., and David G. Post. "Law and Borders: The Rise of Law in Cyberspace." *Stanford Law Review* 48 (1996): 136–402.

Kotter, John. "What Leaders Really Do." *Harvard Business Review* 68, no. 11 (May–June 1990): 103–11.

Kreitz, Patricia A. "Leadership and Emotional Intelligence: A Study of University Library Directors and Their Senior Management Teams." *College & Research Libraries* 70, no. 6 (November 2009): 531–54.

Lyons, Joseph B., and Tamera R. Schneider. "The Effects of Leadership Style on Stress Outcomes." *The Leadership Quarterly* 20 (2009): 737–48.

Madera, Juan M., and D. Brent Smith. "The Effects of Leader Negative Emotions on Evaluations of Leadership in a Crisis Situation: The Role of Anger and Sadness." *The Leadership Quarterly* 20, no. 2 (April 2009): 103–14.

Martino, Joseph P. "The Precision of Delphi Estimates." *Technological Forecasting* 1, no. 3 (1970): 293–99.

McAnally, Arthur M., and Robert B. Downs. "The Changing Role of Directors of University Libraries." *College & Research Libraries* 34, no. 2 (1973): 103–35.

McCauley, Cynthia D., Wilfred H. Drath, Charles J. Palus, Patricia M. G. O'Connor, and Becca A. Baker. "The Use of Constructive-Development Theory to Advance the Understanding of Leadership." *The Leadership Quarterly* 17, no. 6 (2006): 634–53.

McKee, Annie, Frances Johnston, and Richard Massimilian. "Mindfulness, Hope, and Compassion: A Leader's Road Map to Renewal." *Ivey Business Journal* 70, no. 5 (May/June 2006): 1–5.

Mercer, David. "Simpler Scenarios." *Management Decisions* 33, no. 4 (July 1995): 32–40.

Metoyer-Duran, Cheryl, and Peter Hernon. "Problem Statements in Research Proposals and Published Research: A Case Study of Researchers' Viewpoints." *Library & Information Science Research* 16, no. 2 (1994): 105–18.

Mullins, John "Are Public Libraries Led or Managed." *Library Review* 55, no. 4 (April 2006): 237–48.

Neal, James G. "The Entrepreneurial Imperative: Advancing from Incremental to Radical Change in the Academic Library." *portal: Libraries and the Academy* 1, no. 1 (2001): 1–13.

Perry, Ken W. "Grounded Theory and Social Process: A New Direction for Leadership Research." *The Leadership Quarterly* 9, no. 1 (1998): 85–105.

Pors, Niels Ole. "Managing Change in Danish Libraries." *Journal of Academic Librarianship* 29, no. 6 (November 2003): 411–15.

Powell, Ronald R., Lynda M. Baker, and Joseph J. Mika. "Library and Information Science Practitioners and Research." *Library & Information Science Research* 24, no. 1 (2002): 49–72.

Riggs, Donald E. "What's in Store for Academic Libraries' Leadership and Management Issues." *The Journal of Academic Librarianship* 23, no. 1 (January 1997): 3–8.

Roselle, Anne. "The Case Study Method: A Learning Tool for Practising Librarians and Information Specialists." *Library Review*, 45, no. 4 (1996): 30–38.

Schilling, Jan. "From Ineffectiveness to Destruction: A Qualitative Study on the Meaning of Negative Leadership." *Leadership* 5, no. 1 (2009): 102–28.

Schriesheim, Chester A., and Claudia C. Cogliser. "Construct Validation in Leadership Research: Explication and Illustration." *The Leadership Quarterly* 20 (2009): 725–36.

Special Issue on "Destructive Leadership." *The Leadership Quarterly* 18, no. 3 (2007): 171–280.

Special Issue on "Leadership in Higher Education: Facts, Fiction, and Futures." *Leadership* 5, no. 3 (August 2009): 291–394.

Stoffle, Carla J., Barbara Allen, David Morden, and Krisellen Maloney. "Continuing to Build the Future: Academic Libraries and Their Challenges." *portal: Libraries and the Academy* 3, no. 3 (2003): 363–80.

Trahan, Eric. "Applying Meta-Analysis to Library and Information Science Research." *The Library Quarterly* 63, no. 1 (1993): 73–91.

Warner, Linda Sue, and Keith Grint. "American Indian Ways of Leading and Knowing." *Leadership* 2, no. 4 (May 2006): 225–44.

Welch, Jack, and Suzy Welch. "Chief Executive Officer-in-Chief: The President Needs the Same Skills as a Top-notch CEO—Only Sharper." *Business Week*, February 4, 2008, 88.

Winston, Mark, and Haipeng Li. "Leadership Diversity: A Study of Urban Public Libraries." *Library Quarterly* 77, no. 1 (January 2007): 61–82.

Yukl, Gary. "Leading Organizational Learning: Reflections on Theory and Research." *The Leadership Quarterly* 20, no. 1 (2009): 49–53.

BOOKS

Anderson, A. J. *Problems in Library Management*. Littleton, CO: Libraries Unlimited, 1981.

Anfara, Vincent A., Jr., and Norman T. Mertz. *Theoretical Frameworks in Qualitative Research*. Thousand Oaks, CA: Sage Publications, 2006.

Bass, Bernard M. *Leadership and Performance beyond Expectations*. New York: Free Press, 1985.

Bass, Bernard M., and Ronald E. Riggio. *Transformational Leadership*. 2nd ed. Mahwah, NJ: Lawrence Erlbaum Associates, 2006.

Bennis, Warren. *On Becoming a Leader*. Reading, MA: Addison-Wesley Publishing, 1989; Cambridge, MA: Persues Book Group, 2005.

Bennis, Warren, and Joan Goldsmith. *Learning to Lead: A Workbook on Becoming a Leader*. 2nd ed. Reading, MA: Addison-Wesley, 1997.

Bennis, Warren, and Burt Nanus. *Leaders*. New York: Harper & Row, 1985.

Bolman, Lee, and Terrence Deal. *Reframing Organizations: Artistry, Choice, and Leadership*. 2nd ed. San Francisco: Jossey-Bass, 1997.

Boyatzis, Richard, and Annie McKee. *Resonant Leadership: Renewing Yourself and Connecting with Others through Mindfulness, Hope, and Compassion*. Boston: Harvard Business School Press, 2005.

Drath, Wilfred H., and Charles J. Palus. *Making Common Sense: Leadership as Meaning-making in a Community of Practice*. Greensboro, NC: Center for Creative Leadership, 1994.

Fielder, Fred E. *A Theory of Leadership Effectiveness*. New York: McGraw-Hill, 1967.

Fielder, Fred E., and J. E. Garcia. *New Approaches to Leadership: Cognitive Resources and Organizational Performance*. New York: Wiley, 1987.

Garcia, June, and Sandra Nelson. *2007 Public Library Service Responses*. Chicago: Public Library Association, 2007.

Giesecke, Joan. *Scenario Planning for Libraries*. Chicago: American Library Association, 1998.

Goleman, Daniel, Richard Boyatzis, and Annie McKee. *Primal Leadership: Learning to Lead with Emotional Intelligence*. Boston: Harvard Business School Press, 2002.

Goodwin, Doris Kearns. *Team of Rivals: The Political Genius of Abraham Lincoln*. New York: Simon & Schuster, 2005.

Goulding, Anne. *Public Libraries in the 21st Century: Defining Services and Debating the Future*. Surrey, UK: Ashgate Publishing, 2006.

Hackman, J. Richard. *Leading Teams: Setting the Stage for Great Performance*. Boston: Harvard Business School Press, 2002.

Heath, Chip, and Dan Heath. *Made to Stick: Why Some Ideas Survive and Others Die* (audio CD). New York Random House, 2007.

Heifetz, Ron. *Leadership without Easy Answers*. Cambridge, MA: Belknap Press of Harvard University Press, 1994.

Heifetz, Ron, Alexander Grashow, and Marty Linsky. *The Practice of Adaptive Leadership: Tools and Tactics for Changing Your Organization and the World*. Boston: Harvard Business Press, 2009.

Hernon, Peter. *Statistics: A Component of the Research Process*. Norwood, NJ: Ablex, 1994.

Hernon, Peter, Camila A. Alire, and Joan R. Giesecke. *Academic Librarians as Emotionally Intelligent Leaders*. Westport, CT: Libraries Unlimited, 2008.

Hernon, Peter, and Ellen Altman. *Assessing Service Quality: Meeting the Expectations of Library Users*. 2nd ed. Chicago: American Library Association, 2010.

Hernon, Peter, and Robert E. Dugan. *Outcomes Assessment in Higher Education: Views and Perspectives*. Westport, CT: Libraries Unlimited, 2004.

Hernon, Peter, Robert E. Dugan, and Candy Schwartz. *Revisiting Outcomes Assessment in Higher Education*. Westport, CT: Libraries Unlimited, 2006.

Hernon, Peter, Ronald R. Powell, and Arthur P. Young. *The Next Library Leadership: Attributes of Academic and Public Library Directors*. Westport, CT: Libraries Unlimited, 2003.

Hernon, Peter, and Nancy Rossiter. *Making a Difference: Leadership and Academic Libraries*. Westport, CT: Libraries Unlimited, 2007.

Kane, Mary, and William M. K. Trochim. *Concept Mapping for Planning and Evaluation*. Thousand Oaks, CA: Sage Publications, 2007.

Kellerman, Barbara. *Bad Leadership: What It Is, How It Happens, Why It Matters*. Boston: Harvard Business School Press, 2004.

Kellerman, Barbara. *Followership: How Followers Are Creating Change and Changing Leaders*. Boston: Harvard Business School Press, 2008.

Kent, Allen. *Use of Library Materials: The University of Pittsburgh Study*. New York: Dekker, 1979.

Klenke, Karin. *Qualitative Research in the Study of Leadership*. Bingley, UK: Emerald Group Publishing Ltd., 2008.

Kouzes, James M., and Barry Z. Posner. *The Leadership Challenge*. 3rd ed. San Francisco: Jossey-Bass, 2002.

Krathwohl, David R. *Social and Behavioral Science Research: A New Framework for Conceptualizing, Implementing, and Evaluating Research Studies*. San Francisco: Jossey-Bass, 1985.

Lindgren, Mats, and Hans Bandhold. *Scenario Planning: The Link between Future and Strategy*. New York: Palgrave/Macmillan, 2009.

Matthews, Joseph R. *The Customer-Focused Library: Reinventing the Public Library from the Outside-in*. Westport, CT: ABC-CLIO, 2009.

McClure, Charles R., and Paul T. Jaeger. *Public Libraries and Internet Service Roles: Measuring and Maximizing Internet Services*. Chicago: American Library Association, 2009.

Nelson, Sandra. *The New Planning for Results: A Streamlined Approach*. Chicago: American Library Association, 2001.

Northouse, Peter G. *Leadership: Theory and Practice*. Thousand Oaks, CA: Sage, 2007.

Ralston, Bill, and Ian Wilson. *Scenario Planning Handbook: A Practitioner's Guide to Developing and Using Strategies to Direct Strategy in Today's Uncertain Times*. Mason, OH: Thomson, 2006.

Schwartz, Peter. *The Art of the Long View*. New York: Doubleday, 1991.

Solove, Daniel J. *The Future of Reputation: Gossip, Rumor, and Privacy on the Internet*. New Haven, CT: Yale University Press, 2007.

Taylor, Steven, and Robert Bogdan. *Introduction to Qualitative Research Methods*. 2nd ed. New York: Wiley, 1984.

Weinberg, David. *Everything Is Miscellaneous: The Power of the New Digital Disorder*. New York: Times Books.

Wood, Elizabeth J., Rush Miller, and Amy Knapp. *Beyond Survival: Managing Academic Libraries in Transition*. Westport, CT: Libraries Unlimited, 2007.

BOOK CHAPTERS

Bennis, Warren, Daniel Goleman, and Patricia Ward Biederman. "Creating a Culture of Candor." In *Transparency: How Leaders Create a Culture of Candor*. San Francisco: Jossey-Bass, 2008.

Christensen, C. Roland. "Every Student Teaches and Every Teacher Learns: The Reciprocal Gift of Discussion Teaching." In *Education for Judgement: The Artistry of Discussion Leadership*, by C. Roland Christensen, David A. Garvin, and Ann Sweet. Boston: Harvard Business School Press, 1991.

Fitsimmons, Gary N. "Academic Library Directors in the Eyes of Hiring Administrators: A Comparison of the Attributes, Qualifications, and Competencies Desired by Chief Academic Officers with Those Recommended by Academic Library Directors." In *Advances in Library Administration and Organization*, vol. 26, edited by Edward D. Garten, Delmus E. Williams, James M. Nyce, and Janine Golden. Bingley, UK: Emerald Group Publishing Limited, 2008.

Mayer, John D., and Peter Salovey. "What Is Emotional Intelligence." In *Emotional Development and Emotional Intelligence: Educational Implications*, edited by Peter Salovey and Davie J. Sluyter. New York: Basic Books, 1997.

Niels, Ole Pors. "Dimensions of Leadership and Service Quality: The Human Aspect in Performance Measurement." In *Proceedings of the Fourth Northumbrian International Conference on Performance Measurement in Libraries and Information Services: Meaningful Measures for Emerging Realities*, edited by Joan Stein, Martha Kyrillidou, and Denise Davis. Washington, DC: Association of Research Libraries, 2002.

DISSERTATIONS

Gertzog, Alice. "An Investigation into the Relationship between the Structure of Leadership and the Social Structure of the Library Profession." PhD diss., Rutgers University, New Brunswick, 1989. Available from *Dissertations & Theses Full Text*, AAT 8923596.

Harer, John B. "Performance Measures of Quality for Academic Libraries Implementing Continuous Quality Improvement Programs: A Delphi Study." Ph D diss., Texas A&M University, 2001. Available from *Dissertations & Theses: Full Text*, AAT 3011718.

Venetis, Mary Jo. "Identification of Remote Leadership Patterns in Academic and Public Libraries." PhD diss., University of North Texas, 2008. Available from *Dissertations & Theses Full Text*, AAT. 3352149.

GOVERNMENT PUBLICATIONS

U.S. General Accounting Office [now Government Accountability Office]. Program Evaluation and Methodology Division. *Case Study Evaluations.* Transfer Paper 10.1.9. Washington, DC: General Accounting Office, 1990.

U.S. General Accounting Office [now Government Accountability Office]. Program Evaluation and Methodology Division. *Content Analysis: A Methodology for Structuring and Analyzing Written Material.* Transfer Paper 10.1.3. Washington, DC: General Accounting Office, 1989.

WEB RESOURCES

"ACRL/Harvard Leadership Institute for Academic Librarians." Available at http://www.ala.org/ala/mgrps/divs/acrl/events/leadershipinstitute.cfm (accessed September 23, 2009).

American Library Association, Association of College and Research Libraries. "Excellence in Academic Libraries Award." Chicago: Association of College and Research Libraries, 2009. Available at http://www.ala.org/ala/mgrps/divs/acrl/ awards/excellenceacademic.cfm (accessed November 23, 2009).

American Library Association, Association of College and Research Libraries. "Excellence in Academic Libraries Award: Guidelines." Chicago: Association of College and Research Libraries, 2009. Available at http://www.ala.org/ala/ mgrps/divs/acrl/awards/excellenceguidelines.cfm (accessed November 23, 2009).

American Library Association, Association of College and Research Libraries. "Task Force on Academic Library Outcomes Assessment Report." Chicago: Association of College and Research Libraries, 1998. Available at http://www.ala.org/ala/ mgrps/divs/acrl/publications/whitepapers/taskforceacademic.cfm (accessed November 23, 2009).

Awasthi, Shally, Jil Beardmore, Jocalyn Clark, Philip Hadridge, et al. *The Future of Academic Medicine: Five Scenarios to 2025.* New York: Milbank Memorial Fund, 2005. Available at http://www.milbank.org/reports/0507FiveFutures/0507Five Futures.pdf (accessed June 25, 2008).

Boyd, Danah. "Social Network Sites: Public, Private, or What?" *Knowledge Tree* (2007). Available at http://kt.flexiblelearning.net.au/tkt2007/?page_id=281 (accessed December 8, 2009).

"Brainy Quotes: Lao Tzu Quotes." Available at http://www.brainyquote.com/quotes/ authors/l/lao_tzu.html (accessed February 1, 2010).

"Brainy Quotes: Neil Armstrong." Available at http://www.brainyquote.com/quotes/ keywords/research.html (accessed January 11, 2010).

"Brainy Quotes: Warren Bennis." Available at http://www.brainyquote.com/quotes/ quotes/w/warrengbe385287.html (accessed December 12, 2009).

"Cesar's Way: Cesar's Tips." Available at http://www.cesarsway.com/articles/ Cesar%27s%20Tips/649?page=1&cat=2 (accessed May 14, 2009).

Council on Library and Information Resources. "Public Library Case Studies." Washington, DC: The Council. n.d. Available at http://www.clir.org/pubs/reports/case/case.html (accessed September 23, 2009).

Doyle, Jeff. "The Impact of the Economic Recession on Higher Education and Approaches to Budget Cuts for Residence Life Departments." n.d. Available at http://www.reslife.net/html/hottopic_0409b.html (accessed October 27, 2009).

"Dr. Carl Sagan Quotation (American Astronomer, Writer and Scientist 1934–1996)." n.d. Available at http://thinkexist.com/quotations/research (accessed January 11, 2010).

ebrary. *The Economic Downturn and Libraries: Survey Findings* (2009). Available at http://www.ebrary.com/corp/collateral/en/Survey/CIBER_survey_2009.pdf (accessed December 28, 2009).

Fudrow, John. "Extensible Librarian: Libraries, Assessment, and Technology." Pittsburgh, PA: University of Pittsburgh, December 25, 2009. Available at http://johnfudrow.wordpress.com/ (accessed December 28, 2009).

Georgia State University, University Library. "Training & Assessment Librarian." Available at http://www.library.gsu.edu/jobs/pages.asp?ldID=70&ID=2744&typeID=0 (accessed October 7, 2009).

"Google Books Settlement Agreement" (2009). Available at http://books.google.com/googlebooks/agreement/#3 (accessed November 19, 2009).

Harvard Business Publishing. "For Educators" (2009). Available at http://hbsp.harvard.edu/list/hbr-case-study (accessed February 2, 2010).

Harvard Business School. "Learning in Practice: Make Your Case for Leadership" (2010). Available at http://www.hbs.edu/learning/case.html (accessed February 1, 2010).

Impact Assessment. "Academic Leadership Case Studies" (2009). Available at http://www.insightassessment.com/cases.html (accessed January 6, 2010).

Johnson, Chip. "Oakland Mayor—Pompous, not Politic." *San Francisco Chronicle,* December 11, 2009. Available at http://www.sfgate.com/cgi-bin/article.cgi?f=/c/a/2009/12/11/BAJE1B279T.DTL (accessed December 11, 2009).

Law, Margaret. "The Systematic Review: A Potential Tool for Research-Grounded Library Management." In *Proceedings of the 33rd Canadian Association for Information Science Annual Conference, 2005,* 1. Available at http://cais-acsi.ca/proceedings/2005/law_2005.pdf (accessed January 11, 2009).

"Libraries of the Future." *Inside Higher Ed* (September 24, 2009). Available at http://www.insidehighered.com/layout/set/print/news/2009/09/24/libraries (accessed September 24, 2009).

Library Assessment Conference. "Assessment Plans: Four Case Studies." Seattle, WA, 2008. Available at http://www.lib.uchicago.edu/e/atatarka/aplans.html (accessed September 11, 2009).

Mietzner, Dana, and Guido Reger. "Advantages and Disadvantages of Scenario Approaches for Strategic Foresight." *International Journal of Technology Intelligence and Planning* 1, no. 2 (2005). Available at http://www.lampsacus.com/documents/StragegicForesight.pdf (accessed December 29, 2009).

Miller, Gerald V. "The Leadership Dimension Survey: A Download from Pfeiffer's Classic Activities for Developing Leaders." In *Pfeiffer's Classic Activities for Developing Leaders*, edited by Jack Gordon. New York: Wiley, 2003. Available at http://www.pfeiffer.com/WileyCDA/PfeifferTitle/productCd-0787973130.html (accessed May 14, 2010).

"Multifactor Leadership Questionnaire." Menlo Park, CA: Mind Garden, Inc. Available at http://www.mindgarden.com/products/mlq.htm (accessed December 11, 2009).

Neal, James G. "Raised by Wolves: The New Generation of Feral Professionals in the Academic Library." *Library Journal* (February 15, 2006). Available at http://www.libraryjournal.com/article/CA6304405.html (accessed February 24, 2009).

Neem, Johann. "Reviving the Academic Library." *Inside Higher Ed* (November 19, 2009). Available at http://ww.insidehighered.com/views/2009/11/19/neem (accessed November 19, 2009).

NetMBA (Business Knowledge Center). "Scenario Planning."(Internet Center for Management and Business Administration, Inc.) Available at http://www.netmba.com/strategy/scenario/ (accessed December 16, 2009).

Nitecki, Danuta A. "Preparing Librarians for Research-Based Management." In *Proceedings of Preparing Information Professionals for International Collaboration, the Asia-Pacific Conference on Library & Information Education and Practice (A-LIEP 2009), March 6–8, 2009, University of Tsukuba, Japan.* Available at http://a-liep.kc.tsukuba.ac.jp/proceedings/index.html (accessed January 1, 2010).

"Ohio Libraries under Siege." *Daily Kos* [blog]. Available at http://www.dailykos.com/story/2009/6/21/745304/-Ohio-libraries-under-siege (accessed October 31, 2009).

"Organizational Description Questionnaire." Menlo Park, CA: Mind Garden, Inc. Available at http://www.mindgarden.com/products/odq.htm (accessed December 11, 2009).

"Scenario Planning Resources." Available at http://www.well.com/~mb/scenario_planning/ (accessed December 16, 2009).

Seattle Public Library. "About the Library: Budget—2010 Proposed Budget." Seattle, WA: Seattle Public Library, 2009. Available at http://www.spl.org/default.asp?pageID=about_history (accessed October 31, 2009).

Suffolk University, Sawyer Library. "Mildred F. Sawyer Library: Long-Range Plan: Strategic Directions, July 1, 2005–June 30, 2010." Boston, MA: Sawyer Library. Available at http://www.suffolk.edu/files/SawLib/2005-2010-strat-plan.pdf (accessed September 23, 2009).

University of Alberta Libraries. "Assessment Librarian." Available at http://libraryassessment.info/?p=116 (accessed October 7, 2009).

University of Colorado at Boulder, University Libraries. "Job Opportunities: Electronic Collections & Assessment Librarian." http://ucblibraries.colorado.edu/about/jobdevelopment.htm (no longer available).

Urban Libraries Council. *Making Cities Stronger, Public Library Contributions to Local Economic Development*. Chicago: Urban Libraries Council, 2007. Available at http://urbanlibraries.org/associations/9851/files/making_cities_stronger.pdf (accessed November 19, 2009).

YouGov. *What Does Your NetRep Say about You? A Study of How Your Internet Reputation Can Influence Your Career Prospects.* Commissioned by Viadeo, Spring 2007. Available from http://www.viadeo.com/NetRep//NetRep%20by%20Viadeo%20-%20Spring%202007.pdf (accessed December 8, 2009).

OTHER

Hayes, Robert M. *Use of the Delphi Technique in Policy Formulation: A Case Study of the Public Sector/Private Sector Task Force.* Los Angeles: University of California, Graduate School of Library and Information Science, 1982.

Miller, Rush G. "Beyond Survival: How Can Libraries Maintain Relevance in the Digital Age?" Unpublished PowerPoint presentation at the ALAO Conference, October 30, 2009.

INDEX

ABOUT THE EDITOR AND CONTRIBUTORS

PETER HERNON is Professor, Graduate School of Library and Information Science, Simmons College, Boston, where he teaches courses on research methods, evaluation of library services, academic librarianship, leadership, and government information. He received his PhD from Indiana University, Bloomington, and has taught at Simmons College, the University of Arizona, and Victoria University of Wellington (New Zealand). Besides various activities in New Zealand, he has delivered keynote addresses in eight other countries: Canada, England, France, Finland, Greece, Portugal, Spain, and South Africa.

He is the coeditor of *Library & Information Science Research*, founding editor of *Government Information Quarterly*, and past editor-in-chief of *The Journal of Academic Librarianship*. Professor Hernon is the author of approximately 300 publications, more than 45 of which are books. He has received awards for his research and professional contributions, including being the 2008 recipient of the Association of College and Research Libraries' (ACRL) award for Academic/Research Librarian of the Year. The first edition of *Assessing Service Quality* was the 1998 winner of the Highsmith award for outstanding contribution to the literature of library and information science. Together with Robert E. Dugan and Danuta A. Nitecki, he is the 2010 recipient of the Greenwood Press award for outstanding contribution to the literature of library and information science for *Viewing Library Metrics from Different Perspectives* (ABC-CLIO, 2009).

MLIP PROFESSORS OF PRACTICE

JOAN GIESECKE, the Dean of Libraries, University of Nebraska–Lincoln (UNL) Libraries, joined UNL in 1987 and became dean in 1996. Prior to this, she was the Associate Dean for Collections and Services. She has held positions at George Mason University in Fairfax, Virginia, Prince George's County Memorial Library System, and the American Health Care Association. She received a doctorate in public administration from George Mason University, an MLS from the University of Maryland, a master's degree in management from Central Michigan University, and a BA in economics from SUNY at Buffalo. Her research interests include organizational decision making and management skills. She has developed a training program for managers and has presented a variety of papers on management and supervisory skills. She is a former editor of the journal *Library Administration and Management* and has published numerous articles on management issues. Her books include *Practical Help for New Supervisors*, *Scenario Planning for Libraries*, and *Practical Strategies for Library Managers*.

DANUTA A. NITECKI, Dean of Libraries at Drexel University and Professor, College of Information Science and Technology, is both a practitioner and an academic, and has been a manager or administrator of public services in academic research libraries since 1972, working at the Universities of Tennessee, Illinois, and Maryland, and Yale University before coming to Drexel. She also has taught research methods and evaluation online for professional development, and in classrooms at the master's and PhD levels in the United States and abroad. She has presented nationally and internationally, and authored over seventy publications, covering topics related to service quality, document delivery, impact of digital images on teaching and learning, and application of technologies to public services. Her current interests include assessment of public services, the challenges of preparing librarians to engage in research-driven management, and collaborations in support of teaching and learning. She received her PhD from the University of Maryland, College Park and holds master's degrees from Drexel University (in library and information science) and the University of Tennessee (in communications).

MAUREEN SULLIVAN is an independent organization development consultant whose practice focuses on the delivery of consulting and training services to libraries and other information organizations. She has more than twenty-nine years of experience as a consultant in organization development and effectiveness, strategic planning, leadership development, introducing and managing organizational change, organization and work redesign, establishment of staff development and learning programs for today's workplace, creating a work environment that supports diversity, revision of position classification and compensation systems, and the identification and development of competencies. Her experience includes twelve years as the human resources administrator in the libraries at the University of Maryland (1977–1980) and Yale University (1983–1991).

Sullivan is a past president (1998–1999) of the Association of College and Research Libraries (ACRL). During her term as President she helped establish the ACRL/Harvard Leadership Institute in partnership with the Harvard Graduate School of Education. She is now a member of the faculty for this annual program. She was president of the Library Administration and Management Association for the 1988–1989 term. In 1999 she received the Elizabeth Futas Catalyst for Change Award from the American Library Association. She is the 2010 ACRL Academic/Research Librarian of the Year.

PHD STUDENTS IN THE MLIP PROGRAM

ANNE MARIE CASEY, Director of Hunt Library at Embry-Riddle Aeronautical University, has an AMLS degree from the University of Michigan.

JON E. CAWTHORNE, the Interim Dean of Library and Information Access at San Diego State University, holds an MLS from the University of Maryland at College Park and a BA in English and radio communication from Evergreen State College.

CYNTHIA CHADWICK, the Organizational Development Coordinator for the Arapahoe Library District, Colorado, has a master's degree in divinity from the University of Chicago and was named a *Library Journal* "Mover and Shaker" in 2004.

KATHLEEN DE LONG, Associate University Librarian, University of Alberta Libraries, has an MLIS and another master's degree (in public management) from the University of Alberta.

RENÉE DI PILATO, a branch manager with the Alexandria (Virginia) Library, is an active member of the American Library Association and was selected for the Emerging Leaders class of 2008. She holds an MSLS from the Catholic University of America and an MPA from George Mason University.

PATRICIA A. KREITZ is Technical Information Services Director at the SLAC National Accelerator Laboratory at Stanford University. She has an MLS from UC Berkeley and an MA in medieval history from UC Davis, and is active in the Association of College and Research Libraries.

MONIQUE LE CONGE became Director of Library & Cultural Services for Richmond, California in October 2004. After earning a BS in design from UC Davis (1987) and an MLIS from UC Berkeley (1988), she worked in public libraries in California. In 2008 she was President of the California Library Association.

ADRIENE LIM, Associate University Librarian at Portland State University, provides leadership related to overall library planning and management, resource services, technologies, and digital initiatives. She has an MLIS and a BFA, both summa cum laude, from Wayne State University.

MARY PIORUN, the Associate Director for Community, Technology and Global Relations at University of Massachusetts Medical School, received her MSLS from the Catholic University of America in Washington, DC, and completed the MBA program at Bentley College. In May 2008 she received the W. Michael Hoffman Prize for Business Ethics from the Bentley College Center for Business Ethics.

RACHEL RUBIN, the Director of the Bexley (Ohio) Public Library, has also worked for both the Columbus Metropolitan Library and the Worthington Libraries in Ohio.

FELTON THOMAS JR., the Director of the Cleveland Public Library, was named a "Mover and Shaker" by *Library Journal* in 2002. He worked in Nevada libraries for more than twenty years before joining the Cleveland Public Library in January 2009.